UNDERSTANDING UNIVERSITY COMMITTEES

UNDERSTANDING UNIVERSITY COMMITTEES

How to Manage and Participate Constructively in Institutional Governance

David A. Farris

Foreword by Walt Gmelch

STERLING, VIRGINIA

Published by Stylus Publishing, LLC.
22883 Quicksilver Drive
Sterling, Virginia 20166-2019

Library of Congress Cataloging-in-Publication Data
The data for this title have been applied for.

13-digit ISBN: 978-1-62036-938-8 (cloth)
13-digit ISBN: 978-1-62036-939-5 (paperback)
13-digit ISBN: 978-1-62036-940-1 (library networkable e-edition)
13-digit ISBN: 978-1-62036-941-8 (consumer e-edition)

Printed in the United States of America

All first editions printed on acid-free paper
that meets the American National Standards Institute
Z39-48 Standard.

Bulk Purchases

Quantity discounts are available for use in workshops and
for staff development.

Call 1-800-232-0223

First Edition, 2020

For Megan, Eva, and Rose; you inspire me with your strength and curiosity.

CONTENTS

FOREWORD

As a former dean and department chair, now professor, I highly recommend *Understanding University Committees: How to Manage and Participate Constructively in Institutional Governance* to my colleagues. After 45 years in higher education (35 years in academic administration), I assumed I effectively practiced the craft of meetings and committee work. Now I realize this is not the case! An old saying attributed to John Gardner posits, "Education is to professors as water is to goldfish. They swim in it but never think to study it."

Reading David A. Farris's book gave me new insights and platforms for practice. It is the first book to examine committees as a unique phenomenon. He researched and illuminated the morass of meetings professors live by and enlightened us with new perspectives on what is frequently unnoticed and often left in the dark for us discover on our own. Astutely, the author also wisely consulted the business literature on teams and group dynamics to embellish his search for effective conditions for committees.

The book does not blindly promote management by committee. He intersperses humor so as not to take himself or the subject matter too seriously, citing Milton Berle's (n.d.) quip, "A committee is a group that keeps minutes but loses hours" (para. 1). The author successfully promotes enthusiasm for committees, provides helpful hints throughout the book for diagnosing problems, and provides a fresh perspective on how to use committees effectively.

Now, more than ever, universities need this fresh perspective. The role of faculty and campus government has changed dramatically over time. Many new and critical committees have emerged on campuses due to new trends, regulations, financial conditions, and most recently unforeseen challenges from the COVID-19 pandemic. Who would have predicted that in March 2020 faculty, with only days or a couple weeks' notice, would have to flip their class from face-to-face to online. Today, we find essential committees governed via Zoom. As we respond to this new normal, faculty must lead the way.

Scholars and practitioners alike speak about the leadership crisis in higher education, at multiple levels, including faculty governance. With the vast majority of academic decisions in universities made by faculty committees, leadership at the committee level is critical. Unfortunately, faculty and administrators assume their committee roles, absent of: (a) training on how to run an effective committee, (b) understanding of the ambiguity and complexity of committees, (c) knowing appropriate methods of team decision-making, and (d) awareness of the actual cost of committee work. While academics value their autonomy, committee work shifts the responsibility: from just yourself as an individual to being responsible for a group, from the solitary individual to the social participant, from an authority or expert who can proclaim to a colleague who must persuade, and from a scholar immersed in one's classroom and research agenda to a communications practitioner who must succeed in effective teamwork. The committee's ultimate challenge is to create a dynamic collective culture, not a collection of independent experts.

Faculty, serving in administrative roles as chairs and deans, tend to "manage by meeting." Half of the day in the life of a department chair is spent in formal meetings (the average length of each meeting is 50 minutes!), and nearly an additional quarter is spent in informal meetings. Thus, department chairs find themselves in meetings for nearly three quarters of their day (Gmelch & Miskin, 2011).For deans, the number of meetings exponentially rises, and I am afraid provosts live by meetings alone. Some universities proliferate so many committees that they have established a "committee on committees." Faculty volunteer for, or are assigned to, a collection of committees, and list them in their annual review as service. This pathology of listing misses the critical role faculty can play in governing campus policy and practices. As a dean I frequently found myself confounded and confused as to who governed and who appointed members to the dozens of faculty, department, college, university, and community committees. My professional library still shelves self-help books and videos such as *Death by Meetings* (Lencioni, 2004) and *Meetings, Bloody Meetings* (Robinson, 2012).

Committees, councils, and task forces are common in the academy, but teams are more than work groups. What is a team? How do teams differ from committees? Moreover, when should one expend extra time and energy to operate as a team? Too often, the choice between a working group and a team is neither recognized nor consciously made. Academics are accustomed to operate in academies where individual accountability counts most. A working group relies primarily on these individual contributions of its members for group performance (and possibly resulting in declining individual effort, a phenomenon referred to as *social loafing* and discussed further on p. 58 of this book). In this case, the sum of the members' individual efforts measures the outcome. This is why committees are more likely to perform as work groups, not teams, in colleges and universities. In contrast, a team strives for the synergistic achievement of its members working together. Ideally, teams require both individual and mutual accountability, a diversity of skills and perspectives, a set of well-understood common goals, and an approach of open discussion and consensual decision-making.

We tend to see committees as groups of faculty. The author jokingly suggested to a colleague that maybe committee inefficacy could be addressed by renaming them teams or task forces. Many may associate committees with teams, but I learned early in my consulting career that groups were not teams. Recently, when I was conducting team building training at one of the largest research universities in the country, someone from the provost's office flatly told me, "We don't use the term *teams* on this campus." As illustrated in that anecdote, neither the university environment nor the practices of faculty generally encourage a culture conducive to teamwork. Ironically, while we talk about the importance of collegiality, the realities of institutions of higher education interfere with collaborative effort and teamwork. Current faculty governance policies and practices build barriers to effective teamwork. Subcultures built on traditions of autonomy, independence, and individual rewards render the building of an academic committee collectivity difficult, if not impossible. Collective effort lacks a standard of value in the academy. External pressures add to the penchant for fragmentation. Lately, short-term gains seem more realistic than achieving long-term goals. Given the tension between faculty autonomy and committee collectivity, how can academies move toward a collaborative culture? From my perspective, four factors help build collaborative committees and teams: purposeful facilitative leadership; a commitment to foster teamwork; faculty and committee members who make *common good* the subject of collective dialogue, inquiry and decision-making, and assessment and reward provided to the team and not individuals. The author sheds light on these and countless other critical issues.

In summary, academic teams do not just happen. Committees are groups, but groups are not necessarily teams. To what extent can committees develop as teams? In chapter 10, the author boldly discourages organizations from forming committees whenever possible. Instead, committees (teams) should serve issues that are complex, cross-functional, and requiring persistent attention. Ironically, few challenges universities face today demand this level of commitment and attention. However, your skill in team building will make the difference between your committee functioning as a work group of autonomous individuals accidentally thrown together under a titular heading or functioning as an effective productive collectivity of team members able to meet the challenge of the charge and demonstrate commitment to community. Do you want to preside over a collection of colleagues or lead a committee collectivity? Developing your committee as a team presents more challenges and more rewards but requires more risks and obstacles. David A. Farris's book will help you on your journey.

Walt Gmelch
Dean Emeritus,
Professor of Leadership Studies,
University of San Francisco

ACKNOWLEDGMENTS

I would like to thank Jaime Lester for her persistent encouragement and assistance with this book; without her support this book would not have been possible. My friend and mentor Supriya Baily also provided guidance on critical sections of this book. My wife and daughters encouraged me to pursue this project and graciously tolerated my absences to research and write. I cannot express how much I appreciate the administrators and faculty who contributed their time, perspectives, and experiences to help bring this fascinating aspect of academia into focus. I am especially grateful to the editorial staff at Stylus Publishing for their patience and comments as we worked through drafts of this manuscript. Most important, I would like to thank everyone at George Mason University for being amazing friends and colleagues.

INTRODUCTION

I f you have worked for institutions of higher education (IHE) for any length
of time, chances are you have served on one or more committees. The utility
of committees is so ingrained into the culture of higher education that they
are indispensable. Try to imagine a college or university without committees.
Everyone I spoke to while writing this book testified to the importance of committees in executing their responsibilities, yet no one could recall a colleague,
mentor, or supervisor who provided them with guidance on how committees
should be conducted or described the behaviors that are conducive to effective
committees. Many people were amazed to realize that our conversation was the
first and only time they critically reflected on their committee experiences or
evaluated their behavior and the conduct of their colleagues. Given the importance of committees in facilitating collaboration, shared governance, and productivity in IHE, shouldn't we devote more attention to the management and
performance of committees?

You might recall a committee that was remarkable because it was an
enjoyable experience; however, your initial reaction to the prospect of a
committee is probably a combination of skepticism, resentment, and appre-
hension at the work and potential challenges that are typically associated
with group work. Don't worry; this sentiment seems to be shared by many
of our colleagues in IHE. Throughout my exploration of university committees, I was surprised to discover that there is practically no research on
why committees function the way that they do, and therefore there is very
little information on how to effectively construct, manage, and utilize this
ubiquitous organizational construct. It is possible that we can improve the
performance of committees through analysis, subtle changes in how we conduct ourselves, and committee management. Drawing on your own experiences, consider those committees in which you struggled to define your role;
you might have been confused about the committee's objectives, or you
may have been surprised by some of the group dynamics that dominated
the group and its work. You might also have questioned why one or two
individuals seem to do all the work, why some committees are cohesive and
efficient, why it's easier to serve on committees with your closest colleagues
than on a committee of strangers, and why some committees lead into larger

1

institutional initiatives that demand additional effort. Why are we motivated to serve on some committees while other committees provide clandestine opportunities to catch up on outstanding work? Gender, racial, and
ethnic diversity in committees can yield tremendous benefits to individuals
and our institutions. How can we create diverse and inclusive committees
through formal and informal leadership to maximize committee outcomes?
There are a variety of factors that shape our committee experiences and performance. Each committee is a medley of personalities, politics, and priorities that results in a fascinating social phenomenon if we view committees
through the lens of social science.

One of the challenges that I reiterate throughout this book is that each
of us should adopt an objective and critical evaluation of our individual performance and how it influences others or the committee at large. We often
misplace the locus of control in the hands of the chairperson even though
significant power can be exercised through informal leadership, our disposition, and leveraging social networks. Although we may not want to admit
it, our personalities and idiosyncrasies contribute to the committee's performance, and we must own our contribution. As individuals and members of
groups, we tend to identify external variables that impede our performance
(e.g., that guy is just obstinate, we couldn't agree, the timeline was unrealistic, the administration will never approve this, I wasn't provided with
the necessary information, etc.). Relatively speaking, we might find it more
difficult and uncomfortable to catalog our own behaviors that detract from
committee performance (e.g., distracted by personal or professional obligations, apathy, resentment, feeling unappreciated, or mistrust). All of these
factors and many more can manifest in committees and work divergently,
synergistically, negatively, or positively to influence committee climates and
outcomes.

In the introduction to *The Organization of Higher Education*, Michael
Bastedo (2012) called on the academic community to return to the study of
work. Bastedo summarized his challenge to scholars in the following statement: "Deep study of the organizational mechanisms underlying these basic
organizational issues has immense promise for educational theory and practice" (p. 14). There are numerous books and articles on leadership in higher
education, how to coordinate meetings, and how to manage small groups;
however, no resource is dedicated to understanding the organizational, cultural, and interpersonal dynamics specific to university committees.

As IHE advance toward more business-like models of operation, attention to organizational efficiency and productivity naturally follow (Douglass,
2015). Organizational governance in IHE is inherently complex because of
organizational structures, diverse activities, and political climates (Bess & Dee,

2008a, 2008b; Birnbaum, 1988; Schloss & Cragg, 2013). A common organizational response to coordinating multidisciplinary functions within IHE is the formation of university committees composed of a cross section of faculty and administrative personnel tasked to develop amenable solutions to a wide variety of issues. In addition to functioning as the most common method for practicing shared governance, collaboration, planning, hiring, promotion, tenure, and decision-making in our colleges and universities, committees also function as social learning systems, serve as professional development incubators, and are the hub of IHE social and professional networks.

Committees are not only ubiquitous throughout colleges and universities as a governance resource but also notorious for being inefficient. The efficacy of committees has long-reaching implications on the viability of IHE in that committees are a commonly used management technique by which organizational strategies and programs are developed and implemented. Committee composition, interpersonal dynamics, and committee member behavior are topics that warrant investigation if committees are to be used and managed effectively. One overlooked function of committees is the role they play in professional advancement. As one administrator I spoke with noted, "Have you ever seen anyone get ahead that didn't serve on committees?" This may be one of the most profound statements I have heard regarding the function and purpose of committees. Committees are not just laboratories for creating new ideas, implementing the vision of university leadership, and refining organizational procedures; committees are the proving ground for future leaders in IHE. Last, our performance in committees is an exhibition of our professionalism, integrity, and character. When we serve on committees, we function as ambassadors for our department, college, office, and colleagues. Our performance, like it or not, for better or for worse, is perceived by some as indicative of our respective work groups' values, work ethic, competence, and worth. Our peers judge our conduct, draw conclusions about our motives, assign value to our work, and assess our potential usefulness as a future collaborator and colleague.

This book balances empirical research and existing theory with practical examples and strategies that can be used to diagnose common impediments to committee success and devise strategies to improve performance. The reflections, musings, and conclusions shared by the faculty and administrators whom I interviewed illustrate the human, organization, and group dimensions of committees through the lens of veteran higher education professionals and faculty with diverse experiences. Over the course of 4 years (2015–2019), I interviewed five administrators and five faculty to complete my doctoral research on university administrative committees and gather material for this book. Their personal communications were invaluable. Drawing heavily on the theory of organizational citizenship behavior (Organ et al., 2006), this book examines committees from an inside-out perspective rather than the traditional outside-in problem-solving and analysis frameworks adopted by most leadership studies and managerial texts. The outside-in perspective encourages us to perceive committees as malleable structures that are manipulated by applying external forces, rules, or constraints. Instead, I suggest that we imagine committees as amorphous social functions of which we are the embedded host motivated by the ideals of collaboration and fellowship. We are, or should be, fully immersed in this experience and accountable for the committee's performance, but to do this, we must first understand some of the internal, external, and interpersonal dynamics that influence committees. This book is not intended to be a prescription for the conditions that impede committee performance but rather a diagnostic tool for identifying pain points and where to begin a dialogue around our individual performance and challenges that arise in committees. The following chapters explore the various individual, social, and organizational aspects that influence our propensity or hesitancy to engage in committee work. Portions of this book were previously published online in an article posted to *Inside Higher Ed* (Farris, 2017) and in print in the *Journal of Higher Education Policy and Management* (Farris, 2018). Other sections were adapted from my doctoral dissertation on organizational citizenship and university committees (Farris, 2016).

Chapter 1 dissects the idea of committees and the important function they play in IHE. There are distinct differences among meetings, task forces, teams, and committees; however, why they are different and why those differences matter require some attention. Committees serve many functions in IHE, some of which were mentioned previously, but members may not be capitalizing on their committee experiences. Committees are crucial to individual learning and advancement, but they are rarely perceived as such, and therefore many individuals may be missing the rewards of committee participation. This chapter draws heavily on existing research on group work, social learning systems, double-knit organizations, and teams.

Chapter 2 describes the ideal committee member profile constructed from empirical research on organizational citizenship behavior in committees. This chapter outlines behaviors that are conducive to committees and normative behaviors that are observed by most faculty and administrators. The purpose of this chapter is to identify advantageous discretionary behaviors that can be promoted through committee composition, leadership, management, and task design.

Chapter 3 reviews the various forms committees can assume, as well as institutional characteristics that contribute to or detract from committee work. Institutional structures and material support have tremendous influence on committee member engagement and morale. This chapter concludes with a brief overview of the effects of organizational politics and culture on committee engagement.

Chapter 4 investigates committee composition and how the formation of the committee promotes success or introduces obstacles to the group's performance. Are there noticeable differences between committees that appoint members and committees that solicit volunteers to participate? How are committees structured to succeed from conception?

Chapter 5 explores logistical issues that are managed by committee leadership, administrative support, and committee members who affect committee efficacy. This chapter draws on meeting management literature and conversations with administrators and faculty to outline best practices for making the most out of time spent in committees.

Beginning with chapter 6, we transition to how our individual performance influences committees. Chapter 6 discusses committee leadership characteristics and how leadership, both informal and formal, can create a cohesive, productive committee or contribute to dysfunction.

Chapter 7 explores those aspects of our professional life (which sometimes stray into personal matters) and personality traits that precede our performance in committees. This chapter also explores the work conditions that serve as antecedents to the various roles we assume in committees and concludes with a synopsis of the predominant motives for engaging in committee work.

Chapter 8 is dedicated to group dynamics and the interpersonal relationships that support or obstruct committee meetings. Committee climate, that is to say the social aspects of committees, has a dramatic impact on group cohesion, productivity, and other helpful behaviors that contribute positively to the committee and its work. An administrator I interviewed summarized this idea succinctly with this observation: "There is a difference between a meeting where there are doughnuts and one where there are not any doughnuts." Why do doughnuts appear at one meeting but not others?

In chapter 9 we shift to the organic elements of committees: committee evolution, workflow, and decision-making. There are distinct phases in committee evolution that are important to identify in order to establish reasonable expectations and employ appropriate strategies to shepherd the committee through its development. Recommendations on how committees can diagnose performance issues and how to restructure underperforming committees are also provided.

Last, for those of you who are curious about how the information for this book was gathered, chapter 10 provides information regarding the research methods used, and I offer some concluding thoughts on this subject and a call to continue research on committees.

It is my hope that the ideas, concepts, and research shared in this book spark questions about how we can adapt our performance to improve our committee experiences and ultimately the outcomes committees produce. How do we as members, leaders, and informal change agents leverage what we understand about individual motives, work conditions, professional ambitions, and personalities to navigate and potentially alter the eclectic group dynamic that exists when a diverse group of professionals and academics are thrown together and expected to function as a seasoned team? I expect that this book will help you gain some insight into the conditions that can promote enthusiasm for committees, help you diagnose obstacles and challenges that may arise in committees, and, most important, provide you with a new perspective on an important aspect of organizational behavior in IHE.

I

WHAT IS A COMMITTEE?

The word *committee* is derived from the Latin words *com*, or *with*, and *mittere*, which means to put or send. Together, the Latin word *committere* means to entrust or give custody. *Committere* is the precursor to the word *commit*, which entered the English vocabulary in the 15th century. Add *ee*, which simply denotes that a person or persons are responsible for the action of the formative word, and we have *committee*. The contemporary definition of *committee* according to Merriam-Webster (n.d.a.) is a group of people who are chosen to do a particular job or make a decision about something.

One of the challenges of studying committees is their amorphous and enigmatic nature that defies a concise theoretical definition. Is a committee a team, a task force, a work group, or something else? Relative to other small groups, the idea of committee work is disadvantaged by the definition of a committee, which lacks urgency or intention. By way of comparison, a *task force* is "a temporary grouping under one leader for the purpose of accomplishing a definite objective" (Merriam-Webster, n.d.b., para. 1). Researchers have gone to great pains to differentiate the various group structures that exist in organizations. Teams embody the idealistic attributes of shared purpose, mutual accountability, and exceptional performance; potential teams have all the right ingredients to be great but lack accountability and shared purpose; pseudoteams lack emphasis on shared performance, and individual potential is actually stifled by the group; and last, work groups focus on information exchange, and members support one another to accomplish their individual responsibilities (Katzenbach & Smith, 1993). Committees fall somewhere on the spectrum between team and work group, but where exactly depends on the composition of the committee, its leadership, and its task.

In many respects committees function like work groups, which have seven distinct characteristics: (a) there are two or more members, (b) they conduct tasks on behalf of a larger organization, (c) members have shared

7

goals or objectives, (d) members engage socially or virtually, (e) work tasks are interdependent, (f) the group acts semiautonomously and is self-regulating, and (g) the group's work is influenced and constrained by the larger organization (Kozlowski & Bell, 2003). At the most basic level, committees constitute a group, that is, "a collection or set of individuals who interact with and depend on each other" (Zander, 1982, p. 1). While discussing this issue with a colleague, I joked that the solution to committee inefficacy is to simply rename them teams or task forces, and we should realize the disciplined performance that is associated with these labels.

Many individuals perceive committees as teams, or as Kevin Rockmann, a scholar and professor of organizational behavior with George Mason University's School of Business stated, he does not "differentiate between a committee and team"; instead, he imagines committees as a variation of teams and expects the committee to emulate the characteristics and processes outlined in team research. Unfortunately, many committees do not subscribe to the disciplines and structures found in traditional teams. One of the purposes of this book is to encourage readers to be intentional and strategic regarding their participation in and management of committees. For some, this may require a paradigm shift in how committees are conceptualized or reexamination of committees from an objective and critical perspective.

Committees are convened to address nearly every issue imaginable in IHE. Some examples of committee work cited by the individuals I spoke with include tenure and promotion, graduate program management, syllabus review, institutional space use and scheduling, faculty development, environmental stewardship, student retention and engagement, strategic planning, university event management, budgets, campus planning, and even a committee on committees, just to name a few. Committees are formed when "institutional needs arise that cannot be addressed via existing structures (because they are considered inadequate for a particular set of circumstances); new governance structures must be developed" (Quarless & Barrett, 2017, p. 117). Although the authors are referring to administrative task forces, committees, especially ad hoc committees, serve essentially the same function. Put another way, "the opposing desiderata of broad-scale involvement and decision-making efficacy can theoretically be resolved through the creation of a single body" (Schuster et al., 1994, p. 183), which the authors argued is a committee. To be clear, no topic is too important or too benign to preclude the creation of a committee if one is desired or needed. While the charge of the committee may be explicit, the organizational role of committees extends beyond the implicit purpose of shared governance to include important organizational and individual functions that enhance the capacity of individuals and the institution to learn, adapt, mature, and perform.

The ancillary value of committees is often overlooked and underappreciated. Committees provide unique opportunities to blend expertise, knowledge, personalities, ideas, and resources in ways that greatly benefit individual growth and institutional knowledge.

Last, and perhaps most important, committees serve as a public stage where reputations are made or tarnished. First impressions are established within a fraction of a second (Bar et al., 2006). In cohesive committees, members become trusted colleagues and even friends. Through committee work, individuals establish themselves as reliable, punctual, collegial, informed, and congenial. However, committees also serve as the institutional thresher by teasing out those who are difficult to work with, obstinate, shortsighted, or self-centered. It does not take long for a person to establish a reputation, good or bad, among their peers in committees. This reputation will precede them in future endeavors, and word tends to travel fast in IHE. What is more, our performance in committees is not merely a reflection of our professionalism, integrity, and character. We are also serving as ambassadors for our department, office, and colleagues. Our performance, like it or not, for better or for worse, is perceived by some as indicative of our respective departments' values, work ethic, competence, and worth. Houston Miller, a professor of chemistry at George Washington University, pointed out that members of promotion and tenure committees often evaluate faculty performance and service in committees to determine if "this person is really going to be somebody who will be a good citizen" because "basically you're signing up to be a family member with this person forever." What better place to prove our value to the institution than our performance in committees among a diverse audience of peers and colleagues?

Instrument for Shared Governance

Similar to the concept of academic freedom, the term *shared governance* is used so liberally in academia that it is generally misunderstood. In 1966, the American Association of University Professors issued the *Statement on Government of Colleges and Universities*. In addition to recommending specific responsibilities for members of academe, it proclaimed that "a college or university in which all the components are aware of their interdependence, of the usefulness of communication among themselves, and of the force of joint action will enjoy increased capacity to solve educational problems" (p. 376). This statement does not define the mechanics of shared governance, but it does succinctly capture the philosophical value of shared governance and why committees are integral to the operation of IHE. As Kim

Eby, associate provost for faculty affairs and development at George Mason University acknowledged, "I have not done anything at this institution without the contribution and collaborations of faculty members from across this campus, period." This statement illustrates the interdependence inherent to most organizational processes and the utility of committees in bringing disparate stakeholders together. In many cases, committees serve as the only cross-departmental solution capable of orchestrating the work of IHE.

The idea of shared governance arose from the diametric relationship between university administration and faculty and disputes over how institutional functions should be managed and by whom. Indeed, there is research that indicates that "faculty members and administrators continue to work in individual silos" (Kezar, 2003, p. xi) and "see and understand governance differently" (p. xii). One faculty member I spoke with suggested that "there's always a divide between administration and faculty" in IHE that is inevitably reflected in committees. Sharon Fries-Britt, a professor of higher education at the University of Maryland, who has extensive experience as an administrator and a faculty member, conceded that the "academic side works so differently," not better or worse than the administrative functions but remarkably different in many ways, particularly in regard to management, expectations, and productivity. The governance challenges within IHE are only becoming more complex as demands from external stakeholders for accountability and participatory roles increase. Historically, institutional governance has been shared between two parties: the administration and the faculty. Today, colleges and universities must also consider the desires, expectations, and demands of, for example, alumni, parents, staff, students, advisory boards, and politicians (Bejou & Bejou, 2016). While a difference of perspective is challenging enough when two parties employed by the same organization have a shared referential experience, the opinions of external agents who are new to higher education (e.g., parents, public officials, students, and employers) are particularly problematic because they are rarely familiar with the organizational history, culture, restraints, norms, legal issues, and complexity inherent to IHE. This diversity of opinion is a double-edged sword; the challenges of reconciling conflicting perspectives introduce a modicum of frustration for some but can also lead to more innovative solutions, or as Houston stated, "There are problems, and you need to have diversity of opinions" to solve them. A diversity of viewpoints is needed to solve the challenges facing IHE today, and gender, racial, and ethnic diversity of committee composition is also needed to reflect the needs and desires of increasingly diverse institutions. Strategies for creating diverse and inclusive committees is a core theme throughout this book and is addressed in chapters 3, 4, 6, and 7.

One faculty member I spoke to described shared governance as "democratized decision-making." Many scholars have noted that administrators and faculty have different interpretations of shared governance (Bowen & Tobin, 2015). Institutional governance is far too complex an issue to discuss in detail here, but suffice it to say that administrators and faculty tend to disagree on which constituency should or does maintain primary authority for the governance of the institution. "Shared" implies that all individuals engaged in the process of governance have equal authority, expertise, agency, and voice in decision-making. In practice, shared governance is a modified version of participative decision-making (Cotton et al., 1988) whereby members of an organization are granted opportunities to be involved in decision-making processes that affect their work. In IHE these opportunities exist via committees and other governance structures, but it does not mean that all voices are equal, that participation is mandatory or encouraged, or that all committee members engage appropriately in decision-making opportunities.

As committee members, we must be cognizant of the inherent conflict and bias that are products of our professional experiences and perceived roles within our respective organizations. A savvy administrator will remain sensitive to faculty sentiments and resentment toward the growing role of the administrative class in IHE; faculty will appreciate the managerial and administrative expertise that many administrators bring to academia. Perhaps a better way to conceptualize the shared governance power dynamics in committees is to think of our respective expertise and decision-making authorities not as shared with but rather borrowed from the group; we might be more deliberate about how our positions and authorities are used and more careful to preserve their value.

Despite these differing perspectives, committees are by design a melting pot in which administrator and faculty opinions, ambitions, expertise, and experience are blended. Committees serve as the principal forum to present and debate ideas, respond to emerging issues, drive organizational innovation, address operational deficiencies, and establish strategies in ways that consider the variety of demands, opinions, and objectives represented by institutional academic and administrative leaders. In committees, all members have a leadership role by virtue of the fact that they are at the table and have opportunities to engage. In the ideal scenario, a committee will yield a product that satisfies the needs of the institution and committee members' agendas. One of the objectives of this book is to provide guidance on how to create committees that are conducive to fair, equitable, and engaging participative decision-making experiences to yield the best results from our committee efforts.

Committees are an essential component of institutional governance; however, they are not the only cog in the machinery of IHE. Scholars have argued that a lack of defined decision-making processes contributes to the inefficiency of committees (Tierney, 2001). It is important to situate our committee experiences in the larger context of the organization and recognize that the process of shared governance constitutes much more than the discussions held in committee. This holistic perspective encourages us to perceive our role in committees as discrete, yet important, components of a system that is more complex than meets the eye. A graphic that frames the role of university committees within the landscape of institutional governance can illuminate some of the challenges that committees might encounter. Figure 1.1, adapted with permission from Santa Clara University's (2016a) Shared Governance Flowchart, provides a visual interpretation of where committees might fit within organizational governance structures.

Providing some distance between the hours spent in punctuated committee meetings and the constant evolution of the organization allows us to differentiate which actions are within our control and those institutional governance processes that must be tactfully negotiated. Understanding the role of committees, particularly in respect to other authorities and governance procedures, provides perspectives that help define the function of committees and set realistic expectations regarding committee outcomes. Documenting governance procedures, using a graphic similar to the one in Figure 1.1, can be a useful exercise for institutional leaders to illustrate and convey the institution's governance process for current and future leaders or decision-makers.

Organizational Social Learning System

Much research has been conducted on the career paths of administrators and faculty. Many studies recognize that committee work is obligatory; however, extant literature tends to place importance on service (i.e., how many and which committees does one serve on) rather than the potentially transformative experience committee work offers. Committees serve a much more important role in IHE than the obvious shared governance function discussed previously. As a committee member, you have likely recognized the social and professional development benefits of committee service, but these benefits tend to be an afterthought or overlooked entirely. I suggest that we approach committees with three objectives in mind: one, provide our best performance in service to the committee; two, leverage committees

Figure 1.1. Shared governance process.

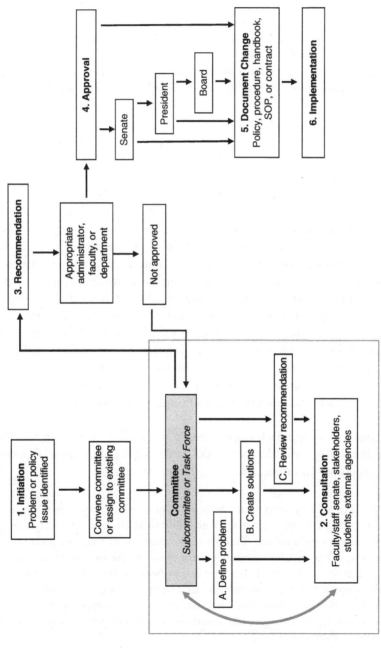

Note. Adapted with permission from *Shared Governance Resources*, by Santa Clara University, 2016a (www.scu.edu/governance/resources-/).

to expand our social and professional networks; and three, recognize the invaluable learning experience committees provide to glean information and knowledge about how our respective institutions function. Houston recognized that in committees

> there's a networking that does take place, which leads to conversations that are valuable. So, if you go through life thinking, 'I'm not sure I want to do this; I really can't see the immediate advantage to me right now,' that's not very helpful. But I think that it is a good investment in making those connections, [for future opportunities and professional development].

Networking, defined as "the exchange of information or services among individuals, groups, or institutions; specifically: the cultivation of productive relationships for employment or business" (Merriam-Webster, n.d.b., para. 1), is often cited as one of the most beneficial ways to advance one's career in IHE (Baltodano et al., 2012; Gander et al., 2014). In existing literature, the idea of networking is often restricted to opportunities available through professional organizations and conferences rather than connections within one's own institution. The candid nature of conversations and diversity of experience in committees provide access to vertical dimensions of the institution that might not be accessible through department contacts and external professional networks. Furthermore, committees provide prime opportunities to gain horizontal knowledge about relevant efforts in other areas of the organization, operational synergies, and opportunities to collaborate on current and future work. Houston pointed out that committees provide opportunities to "get to know people" and "that's kind of an important thing" to individual and department success.

One way to approach committees is to imagine them as institutional social learning systems. Wenger (2000) explained the value of social learning to members of subcommunities (i.e., the committees):

> We have an experience that opens our eyes to a new way of looking at the world. This experience does not fully fit in the current practice of our home communities. We now see limitations we were not aware of before. We come back to our peers, try to communicate our experience, attempt to explain what we have discovered, so they too can expand their horizon. In the process, we are trying to change how our community defines competence (and we are actually deepening our own experience). We are using our experience to pull our community's competence along. (p. 227)

Wenger went on to suggest that organizations can sow the rewards of social learning by

- acknowledging informal learning and providing opportunities and structures to support this process,
- emphasizing service to the organization through participation and community engagement, and
- proactively and strategically arranging disciplines that compose the learning system environment to provide "coordination among practices to create complex knowledge beyond the purview of any [one] practice" (p. 244).

Researchers have noted that sharing information and ideas among members of an organization promotes individual learning and development (Argote et al., 2003; Eddy & Vanderlinden, 2006) and can foster innovative thinking (Drach-Zahavy & Somech, 2001). The diverse pool of administrators and faculty that constitutes most committees affords broad access to a breadth of experience and knowledge that is not available in other work contexts.

Richard McDermott (1999) integrated the idea of small teams as communities of practice within an individual's day-to-day community (i.e., department or office). An individual representing a specific discipline who is tied to other members of the organization through committees becomes a bridge linking areas of expertise that forms a physical and organizational connection between these functions (Van Der Vegt & Bunderson, 2005). Wenger et al. (2011) stressed the importance of diverse groups coming together because members can "use each other's experiences of practice as a learning resource and they join forces in making sense of and addressing challenges they face individually and collectively" (p. 9). Robert Smith (2006), the author of *Where You Stand Is Where You Sit*, noted, "Professionals can broaden their views through contact with colleagues from a wide variety of disciplines within the institution" (p. 20). Smith implied that a holistic perspective and understanding of organizational operations empower faculty and administrators to better serve the institution.

The connection that occurs among individual holders of institutional, technical, and historical knowledge in a committee is best explained by the theory of double-knit organizations. Figure 1.2 shows another way of conceptualizing a professional network that results from professional relationships established through committees; it represents a simple network in which one person has access to eight different fields of expertise by way of their relationship with other members of the organization through collaborative groups (i.e., their department and the committees in which they engage). Figure 1.2 illustrates the linkage and conduit for sharing expertise within a committee using double-knit organizational theory to explain the knowledge relationship between committee members.

Figure 1.2. Committees illustrated as double-knit organizations.

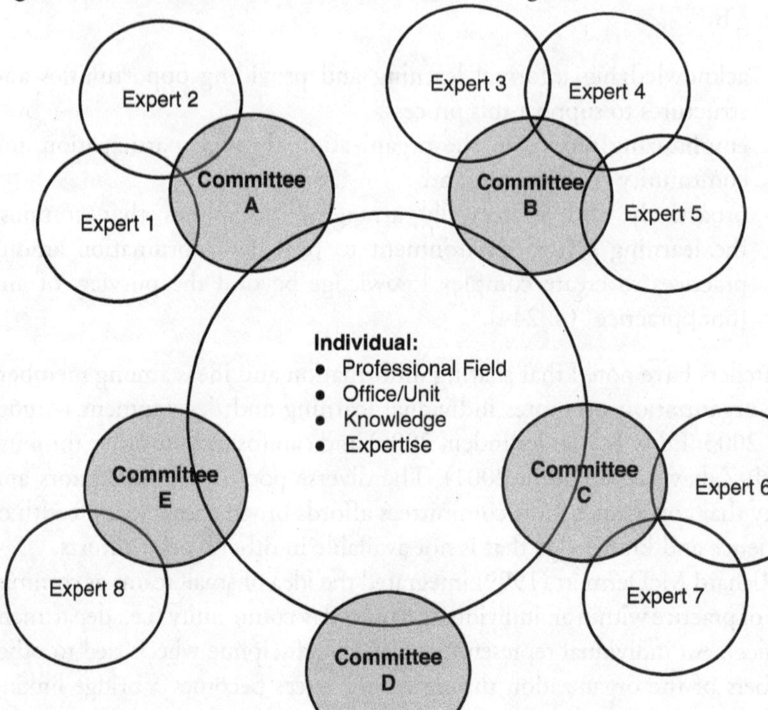

Recognition of superorganizational and informal organizational networks and their impact on organizational performance was first proposed by Barnard (1938). In addition to the educational and professional development benefits of committees, the social networking aspect of committees provides ancillary benefits to the organization. For example, research shows that administrators' work satisfaction is positively correlated with assessments of teamwork and collaboration in the university. When administrators have positive relationships with other members of the organization, they report higher levels of job satisfaction and are less likely to leave (Volkwein & Parmley, 2000). All these benefits sound wonderful, but they are contingent on arranging the right committee composition, developing a healthy committee atmosphere, and promoting a positive committee culture, all of which collectively serve to promote higher levels of cohesion among committee members. A cohesive committee environment is critical to promoting social learning because intragroup learning tends to occur more frequently when individuals perceive their environment as psychologically safe (Edmondson, 1999). Identifying the conditions that support psychological safety and how to orchestrate an environment conducive to individual learning is the subject of the following chapters.

Professional Development Incubator

"Have you ever seen anyone get ahead in higher education that didn't serve on committees?" This is a comment made by Nick Swayne, an associate dean who oversees several academic programs at James Madison University, during an interview about committee work for my doctoral research. This may be one of the most profound statements I have heard regarding committees. Committees are not just laboratories for creating new ideas, implementing the vision of university leadership, and refining organizational procedures; they are the proving ground for future organizational leaders. Kim also perceived the value of committees as development opportunities. She said, "When a committee is done well, it's 100% professional development, about how the institution works. I have a better understanding of my institution and how to make a difference in my institution." Furthermore, committees provide opportunities to develop leadership skills that are necessary to advance through the ranks of higher education. As one scholar noted, committee opportunities can be "structured in such a way as to promote leadership development by building in program objectives that support acquisition of leadership skills for all the committee members" (Bisbee, 2007, p. 85).

Committees provide one of the few opportunities and arguably the best environment in which faculty and administrators can learn collegiality, negotiation, tact, and collaboration. In a survey of community college administrators, 88% of respondents claimed that their participation in committees, task forces, and commissions was important to their professional development (Vanderlinden, 2005). In committees, a person can demonstrate their aptitude and capacity for problem-solving, collaboration, and leadership. Perhaps some perceive service on university committees as one approach in a broad professional development strategy; I suggest that committees constitute the hub of professional development experiences in IHE and are the key to learning and advancement.

Committee service is a critical component of administrator and faculty career pathways that presents opportunities for university professionals to advance within their respective institutions (Rosser, 2000). Furthermore, contemporary research regarding professional development in IHE recognizes that committees are prime opportunities to practice leadership skills (Eddy & Vanderlinden, 2006). Engagement in committees, through leadership and participation, telegraphs commitment to the institution and facilitates the transition to future employment opportunities (Fugate & Amey, 2000). Houston emphasized the importance of engagement in the faculty tenure process: "It's important for people to have a sense that you're a good citizen and you're doing things both within and outside the institution." Service through university committees is perhaps the primary way of illustrating capacity for engagement and value, which often leads to future leadership opportunities, promotions, or invitations to participate in institutional projects that can support professional development aspirations.

Twombly (1990) also explained the importance of development in the context of career paths within IHE: "Learning that occurs in a lower-level position on the ladder prepares individuals to assume the next higher position in a sequence" (p. 9). I would go so far as to suggest that if one is not successful in committees, one will likely be unsuccessful in the field of higher education leadership (in both academic and administrative functions). If we accept that committees serve as career stepping-stones in administrative and faculty pathways, how should institutions align committee opportunities with an individual's relative experience and status to maximize this professional development mechanism? If we imagine typical career growth as a progression from tactical functions to operational programs then later to strategic-level decision-making within an organization, we must also consider how we can create conditions for committee members to observe, learn, and practice the necessary skills to be successful at each phase of their professional development. As individuals mature in their committee roles and establish a reputation as a collegial and proficient committee member, they are likely to be asked to serve on or be appointed to committees with increasing levels of responsibility. Figure 1.3 depicts the relationship between faculty and staff career paths and the significance of the topics and decisions addressed in committee.

Figure 1.3. The evolution of committee participation.

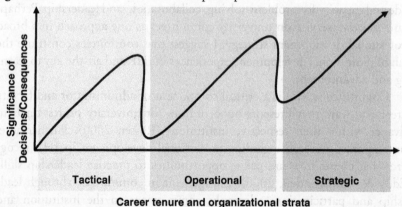

Entry-level faculty, administrators, and staff are typically engaged at a tactical level; that is, they are carrying out the instructions of their supervisors, conducting routine tasks, and working on the front line of the organization. Tactical tasks can typically be negotiated within an office, department, or college or with minimal involvement of external stakeholders. University faculty and personnel get their first experience serving on a committee by engaging with their peers, providing feedback to their supervisors, modifying daily routines, and helping develop policies and guidelines for work tasks assigned to them. Examples of academic and administrative tactical operations might include curriculum development, doctoral program administration, admissions, scholarships and awards, college honors program, college and departmental strategic planning, hiring decisions, standard operating procedures, and residence life programming. Tactical activities tend to be localized with limited impact on the larger organization outside of an individual's immediate office, department, or college. This is not to suggest that tactical tasks are not significant. When aggregated, individual tasks can make a tremendous impact; however, the implications tend to be isolated to the specific points of contact between the individual and those with whom they interact (e.g., dean and faculty, principal investigator and graduate assistant, parking attendant and visitor, resident hall adviser and student, human resource officer and faculty, admissions officer and student).

At the operational level, faculty and administrators have responsibilities for ensuring that their work is carried out in a manner that complements or is coordinated with other departments and functions. At the operational level, interoffice, department, and college synchronization are required, which necessitates committee work. Examples of operational-level functions include faculty senate subcommittees, development and administration of interdisciplinary and core curriculum programs, implementation of campus-wide administrative procedures, modification of the university's academic calendar, installation of enterprise-wide information technology applications, incident response team operations, and coordination of commencement and graduation ceremonies. Operational activities have the potential to erode or create barriers between functions if and when department interests intersect or conflict. At the operational level, committees become critical to anticipating how decisions promote or interfere with the work of others. For example, decisions to upgrade a travel authorization and reimbursement process have implications that affect all faculty and staff. Similarly, mandating a core curriculum will have lasting impacts on all colleges. At the operational level, effective individuals will comprehend and assimilate the needs, priorities, and perspectives of other colleges,

departments, and units. Faculty, administrators, and staff who are successful at the operational level will have the requisite social skills to balance
conflicting priorities and adjust activities to maximize the performance of
institutional and external stakeholders.

Seasoned committee members who establish a reputation as reliable and
conscientious are likely to find themselves appointed to strategic committees
at the highest levels of the institution. Administrators and faculty who have
weathered the tactical and operational levels of organizational management
and governance are likely to find themselves in committees dedicated to strategic initiatives that demand a heightened sensitivity to organizational politics, culture, and history. At the strategic level, administrators and faculty
potentially wield tremendous influence over the direction of the organization; their decisions can have significant impacts on financial, reputational,
and operational aspects of the organization's performance. Individuals at
this level should be trustworthy, collaborate well with others, exercise a
high degree of leadership, and be able to navigate organizational politics.
Strategic committees are typically staffed by senior members of the organization who have the requisite maturity, professional experience, institutional
knowledge, and disposition necessary to operate effectively in this environment. Administrators and faculty assimilating into a new organization may
find this level of organizational governance frustrating given their lack of
institutional knowledge. At the strategic level, committee members must be
able think abstractly and anticipate how their colleagues and the organization will respond to change using knowledge gained or gathered from their
tactical and operational experiences. Examples of strategic-level committees
include institutional strategic and campus planning, budget and finance,
undergraduate education, academic standards, and diversity.

Decisions regarding who should serve on which committees and questions about individual competencies and professional maturity can be
considered relative to the committee's charge and authority. An individual's performance in a committee may be a pivotal moment in their career.
Alignment of individual skills with an appropriate degree of responsibility
can position individuals and committees for success. In some cases, it may
be necessary to examine the organizational role of the committee (i.e., tactical, operational, or strategic) to assist in the process of defining committee
objectives, composition, and individual roles. For example, a strategic planning committee may recognize that subcommittees are necessary to address
tactical or operational issues. Conversely, an operational committee may
come to the conclusion that an institutional strategy is needed, which may
require the assistance of a standing committee or new meeting of senior
leadership.

So, what is a committee? It's a mechanism for shared governance, an instrument for individual and group learning, and a proving ground for future leaders in IHE. Committees can serve as training opportunities for rising administrators and faculty to learn about university activities and governance while simultaneously providing a forum for them to develop and exhibit leadership and group work skills. Committees, with the right composition and forethought, serve as apprenticeship programs that provide coaching, mentorship, and institutional knowledge. The functions of committees and tangential opportunities committees provide are contingent on creating the right conditions for these phenomena to occur. Before we begin dissecting the various dimensions of a committee, consider your own committee experiences and the following questions:

- What types of committee issues intrigue you?
- How have committees contributed to your professional development?
- Are there opportunities for you or your staff to increase your knowledge and influence by participating in university committees?

For this exercise of exploring committees to be successful, you will need to provide the subject of analysis: your committee experiences. With some thought you will likely reach some of the same conclusions that are presented in the following pages and add your own wisdom on committees in the process.

2

THE IDEAL STATE

Patricia Gumport (2012) provided three compelling reasons to study organizational behavior in IHE. One of them is to examine existing research to "model—and thus simplify—complex behavior, providing analytical leverage for postulating general theories intended to apply across academic settings" (p. 22). Defining the ideal committee member can help identify desired characteristics and various social and task elements that can be orchestrated to produce high-performing committees. The ideal state is a cohesive, productive, and effective body that produces quality outputs and sound decisions, in a timely manner, while simultaneously providing a stimulating and professionally worthwhile experience for committee members. By understanding the various pressure points within committees, we can potentially decipher and manipulate our environments to yield behaviors that are conducive to committee meetings. Ultimately we want to answer a question that Sharon raised during our interview: "What does it mean to be in committee meetings, and what does it mean to engage in these meetings?"

Specific behaviors are one variable in the formula of ideal committee conditions, and they are a legitimate litmus test of the internal and external antecedents and moderators that influence committee work. Leadership, group dynamics, personalities, and organizational characteristics coalesce to form a unique profile for each committee that works in somewhat predictable ways to influence individual behaviors. Empirical research (Farris, 2016, 2018) coupled with our individual experiences provide us with a blueprint for what the exemplary committee looks like. One of the principal findings from my initial research on committees was a succinct catalog of behaviors that constitute normative committee behavior (i.e., what people tend to do) and exemplary behavior (i.e., what we hope every committee member does). Think back on your own committee

Portions of this chapter are derived in part from an article published in the *Journal of Higher Education Policy and Management* (Farris, 2018), copyright the Society, available online at www.tandfonline.com/doi/full/10.1080/1360080X.2018.1462438.

experiences, and you will likely deduce many of the same behaviors that are discussed in this chapter. You can likely identify those individuals with whom you would gladly work again and catalog three to five behaviors or attitudes that they exhibited that endeared you to them as capable and reliable colleagues. What characteristics did those individuals display that left a favorable impression? Conversely, you can also identify, perhaps more easily, those behaviors and attitudes that were off-putting, obstructive, and detrimental to the committee. What were those behaviors, and how did they affect the committee's work?

Administrators and faculty indicated three principal behaviors that are indicative of vested committee members: first, active engagement that exceeds typical committee member effort; second, making a conscious effort to compromise with colleagues; and third, offering voluntary assistance to help others and/or the committee. The list of behaviors that constitute organizational citizenship behaviors in university committees is extensive and includes but is not limited to the following:

- Being actively engaged in committee conversations
- Showing deference and respect to committee leadership
- Coming to meetings on time and prepared
- Taking on small projects that benefit the committee
- Expressing positive body language
- Actively working to improve cohesion in the group
- Compromising with others and tolerating setbacks and mildly disruptive behaviors
- Intervening to defend a colleague from attack
- Talking to members outside of committees to advance committee work
- Maintaining and promoting a positive attitude
- Addressing disruptive behaviors when they occur or offline with the offending member

Collectively, these behaviors epitomize the ideal committee member. These behaviors are variations of organizational citizenship behaviors that were identified in the late 1980s and continue to be defined in various work contexts by scholars around the world. Organizational citizenship behaviors are discretionary behaviors that are not documented as a condition of employment; tend to be spontaneous; are offered without expectation of reward or recognition; and, when aggregated, constitute a pattern of behavior that contributes to organizational efficacy and productivity (Bateman & Organ, 1983). Individuals who exhibit organizational citizenship behaviors serve to shore up gaps in organizational performance by identifying opportunities to serve the organization in a capacity not prescribed by their employer.

Numerous studies demonstrate a connection between organizational citizenship behaviors and increased group performance (e.g., Ehrhart et al., 2006; LePine et al., 2008; N. Podsakoff et al., 2009; P. Podsakoff et al., 1997). Research shows that organizational citizenship behaviors increase coordination of activities among team members and work groups (N. Podsakoff et al., 2009; C. Smith et al., 1983), facilitate productive interpersonal relationships (LePine et al., 2008; Nielsen et al., 2009; Organ et al., 2006; P. Podsakoff et al., 1997), generate higher quality group outputs (Braun et al., 2012), and are positively correlated with group performance (Nielsen et al., 2012). Organizations in which organizational citizenship behaviors are prevalent realize improved performance through increased levels of social capital and camaraderie among group members (Barrick & Mount, 1991; Bolino et al., 2002; Borman et al., 2001; LePine et al., 2008; Nielsen et al., 2009; Organ et al., 2006).

Daniel Katz (1964), a prominent scholar of organizational behavior, suggested, "An organization which depends solely upon its blueprints of prescribed behavior is a very fragile social system" (p. 132). It is practically impossible to dictate how committee members must behave given the variability of committee topics, personalities, and conditions that influence committee work. Beyond the obvious positive contributions organizational citizenship behaviors offer to committees, organizational citizenship behaviors also defend against and even counteract negative behaviors and counterproductive committee environments. Kidwell et al. (1997) found that organizational citizenship behaviors foster cohesive group environments that are "favorable to social exchanges among group members which in turn . . . increase the chances of quality work relationships developing and encouraging norms or expectations concerning behaviors that would reinforce such relationships" (p. 788). Individuals who exhibit organizational citizenship behaviors in groups increase committee efficacy and productivity (P. Podsakoff & MacKenzie, 1997). Furthermore, individual exhibitions of citizenship behaviors tend to promote expressions of similar positive behaviors among other group members (Bolino et al., 2010). Conscientious groups that endeavor to collaborate tend produce a higher quality product in greater quantity than comparable groups without the benefits of organizational citizenship behaviors (P. Podsakoff et al., 1997). These examples illustrate the potential benefits of organizational citizenship behaviors within committees, specifically regarding the formation of cohesive groups and promotion of productive behaviors that are conducive to collaboration.

Ehrhart and Naumann (2004) suggested that the study of organizational citizenship behaviors in groups yields information that helps leadership

focus on certain group members that may be particularly influential in the development of group organizational citizenship behavior norms, such as high status or prototypical members. They can attempt to create conditions that make the development of OCB norms more likely. (p. 972)

Scholars also challenge the academic community to investigate group dynamics to maximize productivity. "Researchers and practitioners need to identify efforts that work towards increasing commitment of team members, thereby increasing organizational citizenship behavior in the organization" (Foote & Tang, 2008, p. 933). Despite the abundance of research on organizational citizenship behaviors, scholars admit that practical recommendations for encouraging these qualities to improve organizational performance are conspicuously absent (LePine et al., 2008).

Guzzo and Dickson (1996) noted that very little research considers context as an element in team performance. A concise but comprehensive description of behaviors that constitute organizational citizenship behaviors is necessary if we desire to redeem organizational benefits associated with these behaviors. I examined a wide variety of organizational citizenship behaviors during my initial research on this topic and discovered that organizational citizenship behaviors tend to manifest in three distinct and predominant forms in committees: active engagement, compromise, and helping behaviors. These behaviors as they appear in the context of university committees are recounted by administrators and faculty and discussed in greater detail in the following sections.

Active Engagement

Derek de Solla Price (1963) suggested that the square root of the number of individuals in a group contributes 50% of the work (e.g., in a group of 16, 4 will contribute 50% of the total effort). While Price's Law is specific to publications in a given field, anecdotal evidence and my conversations with faculty and administrators confirm this rule to also be true in most committees. Without exception, the administrators and faculty with whom I spoke confirmed that merely attending committee meetings and representing one's own interests do not constitute engagement. Instead, we agreed that active engagement requires an inordinate level of effort (relative to other committee members) that is characterized by preparing for committee meetings, reading materials in advance, researching committee topics, actively listening, consistently contributing to discussions, voluntarily taking on assignments, completing assigned work, and expending effort outside of committee meetings to further the work of the committee. Examples of active engagement include efforts that go "beyond the limits of the meeting" (Nick), "being a good team player . . . really seeing it through" (Adam), "being prepared" (Marleen), "contributing to ideas . . . verbalizing and writing stuff that feeds back [to the committee]" (Adam), "doing homework assignments" (Brent), and "doing the work behind the scenes" (Sarah). Actively engaged committee members exhibit verbal and nonverbal cues that indicate that they are engaged in the committee by

leaning in, and they are interested, and they are thinking, and they are contributing, and they are not just saying yes or no to everything. They are like,
"Okay I get what you're saying. We can accomplish that, but what about
if we did it a little bit differently?" So, making those contributions that are
meaningful and actually moving toward accomplishing a goal. (Nick)

Kevin qualified his expectations for engagement in the following way: "You
have to be prepared, you have to have done your homework, you have to be up
to speed on whatever the issue is and be ready to be led." Active engagement
in committees is novel to the degree that Nick remarked, "You rarely see people going way above the norm, do you?" Marleen McCabe, a human resources
officer and Title IX coordinator, confirmed that impactful levels of effort can be
rare. She stated that "we kind of count on a handful of people who are always
willing" to carry the committee's work forward. Similarly, when one administrator was asked if he observed anyone willing to volunteer to take on work in a
committee, he remarked incredulously and with a laugh, "Um . . . I haven't been
on committees with those folks a lot to be perfectly honest with you!"

By way of comparison, the collection of behaviors frequently observed in
committees reflect marginal effort or disinterest. When asked to characterize the
average committee member, administrators and faculty confess that many people
exhibit what constitutes normative committee behavior; that is, showing up, often
unprepared, distracted by other work or personal devices; appearing or acting
disengaged; not responding to calls to take on voluntary work; and not completing assigned tasks on time. The following quotes illustrate normative committee
behaviors: "People who don't really do anything and may not even come" (Sarah),
"show up most of the time and leave and not take notes" (Nick), "not investing
anything beyond their attendance" (Marleen), and "sitting there in the corner on
their iPad, you know . . . web surfing or doing email the whole time" (Brent).
Passive attendance and being unprepared are traits exhibited by many committee members. For example, when Brent Ericson, an assistant dean of students,
was asked what constitutes normative behavior in committees, he responded, "I
think the normative behavior is to be there, to show up, at the meetings . . . but I
think it's to show up, be present, contribute, say a couple of intelligent things per
meeting." Sarah Cheverton, an administrative and instructional faculty member,
described typical behavior and effort much more succinctly: "I think a lot of
folks, their contribution to the committee starts when the meeting starts and ends
when the meeting ends." Marleen expanded the list of behaviors that characterize
normative performance in committees; she included individuals who do not read
materials ahead of time, arrive late, are distracted by media, or present an attitude
that indicates that they consider the meeting a waste of time.

The boundary between active engagement and normative behavior
becomes clear when contrasting statements regarding what is considered

TABLE 2.1

Normative Committee Behavior Versus Active Engagement

Normative Committee Behavior	*Active Engagement*
Attends meetings	Comes prepared to committee meetings
Makes minimal contribution	Consistently contributes to the conversation
Does not volunteer for additional work or tasks	Collaborates with others
Comes unprepared for committee meetings	Takes on tasks or volunteers for assignments
Is distracted by personal device or other work	Actively listens
Seems disinterested or disengaged	Displays positive body language
Does not respond to requests for information	Completes assigned tasks on time
Considers the committee's work only when present at committee meeting	Continues dialogue outside of the committee

active engagement with observations of typical committee member behavior. Table 2.1 contrasts the dimensions of active engagement with normative committee behavior as described by administrators and faculty.

It is obvious which family of behaviors is preferred in committees. In practice, committee members, including ourselves, oscillate between normative behaviors and active engagement depending on work conditions, mood, committee dynamics, and myriad other factors that influence individual performance in the workplace, some of which are discussed later. I do not intend for this list to be a disparagement of most committee members. Every person is going to experience conditions that encourage normative committee behaviors. Furthermore, a committee that is composed entirely of actively engaged members could be as dysfunctional as a committee of disengaged members. In summary, we should be cognizant of our performance and aware of those around us. When time and effort allow, we should aspire to create an environment that encourages active engagement by modeling these behaviors to yield the most from our committee experiences.

Compromise

Compromise in committees is characterized by showing deference to other committee members, exercising restraint, acknowledging limits to personal expertise, making concessions for the good of the group, and behaving in a manner that considers others' perspectives. Marleen explained compromise as it is typically exhibited in committees:

> Be reasonable and hear that there's more than one way of looking [at an issue] and that there are many different interests, especially in a college environment that we need to modulate at times, depending on what the task is of the committee.

Sarah also accepted that personal and professional interests can and often do conflict with the positions of other committee members, which necessitates compromise to advance the group's objectives. Sarah argued that effective participation in committees requires balancing individual objectives against the needs of the group. She maintained that effective committees establish a collaborative climate that recognizes that all members of the group are reliant on the committee's collective effort to meet their respective professional and departmental goals. Adam Crowe, a former public safety professional at Virginia Commonwealth University, characterized individuals who compromise as those who "work hard, they don't complain, they're not a person that is driven by the desire or seeking of self-recognition or authority." Sharon also provided a remarkable example of compromise in a committee. Her department was awarded a tenure line that she gave to a different division within her unit, because she had witnessed their challenges and recognized that they needed the position more than her department. She explained that she made this decision, without any expectation of reciprocity, based on the needs of the organization and who would benefit the most from the resource. She went on to explain that she made a similar decision to share funding from her unit to support student fellowships within her college. Sharon offers a perfect example of someone who embodies the spirit of collegiality and compromise.

For committees to be successful, Marleen found that "there's more negotiation, and you need to come across as somebody who is willing to negotiate without really compromising too much." Adept committee members recognize that it is necessary to regulate behavior in committees based on individual and group objectives. In some circumstances, committee members find that committee work intersects with issues of individual integrity, ethics, and opinion. In matters of integrity and ethics, it might be difficult for some, especially junior or minority committee members, to find or exercise their voice. In matters of opinion, it's a balancing act between individual and group objectives. One administrator explained this predicament in more elaborate terms:

> I think you are often in positions at work where you may not agree with what your assigned goals will be. You might philosophically disagree with what you have been told to try to advance. It is work, and it's committee work, and work within an organization.

This statement indicates that compromise in committees is a premediated and calculated action that often, but not always, puts the needs of others, the organization, or the committee's work ahead of one's own interests. Compromise is effective when committee members can agree to disagree and then move forward to develop a mutually agreeable solution.

Individuals who compromise in committees share Sarah's mentality of

> it's not just about you, it's not just about this particular group, it's we're doing this because we need to make sure that conditions are right for this group of people to do what they need to do, and that's what we're going to focus on.

Compromise in many cases takes a concerted effort to reach agreement and may involve working behind the scenes to unpack obstacles to the committee's work and to lay a foundation for success in future committee meetings. Compromise in committees is a discretionary effort that is offered to effect unity among the committee and encourage progress. Administrators and faculty indicate that they compromise with their colleagues in committees to promote or preserve a climate of collegiality, collaboration, and cohesion.

Helping Behaviors

Helping behaviors support productivity within the committee because individuals are "willing to step up and participate or maybe even take on more . . . responsibility" (Brent) and are "more than willing to step to the plate when asked" (Marleen). *Stepping* up, a term used frequently by interviewees to describe the conscious effort of helping a fellow committee member, implies that helping behaviors are both discretionary and constitute extraordinary effort. Administrators and faculty also say they occasionally intervene as peacemakers to resolve conflict and disagreement. For example, Nick has intervened in committee conflicts to mitigate the impact of disagreement on committee progress:

> You can sit there and watch it, but it's ugly and it doesn't help move things forward. So, you say, Wait a minute. I think that if everybody takes a breath we can make more progress. . . . Even if it's a personal matter, it affects the performance of the committee.

Steve Bell, an English professor with a military background, claimed he also intervenes when he perceives a colleague being unfairly burdened with a legitimate counterperspective in a group setting. The most common form of helping behavior is providing direct support to other members of the committee by voluntarily taking on additional work. For example, Nick said,

> I have colleagues that I know have strengths and weaknesses, and if they sign on to do something that I know they are motivated to do, but they may have some weakness, and I know that I can supplement them if we work well together, I would be happy to help and have done that.

Similarly, Adam claimed that he occasionally helps colleagues when he gets the sense that they are "overwhelmed with coordinating certain functions, and they happen to be things I can help with, so it's like, hey let's do this together." Another way helping behaviors manifest in committees is providing unsolicited information to assist colleagues with their responsibilities or committee roles. Marleen summarized her efforts to engage in this type of assistance and go the additional step of providing material support if necessary: "If there are resources that I am aware of, I have no problem reaching out and saying, 'Hey were you aware of this?' or 'Do you need help with this?'"

Likewise, Nick explained that providing historical context for issues raised in committees helps new committee members acclimate to the group and become more productive members. In the absence of this unsolicited orientation, he said, "People on a committee don't understand the history, why we are where we are, and who the other players are." In addition to improving group dynamics, helping behaviors also serve as informal feedback loops that ostensibly improve organizational performance by encouraging productive behaviors and civic-oriented attitudes.

Many administrators and faculty asserted that they routinely engage in conversations with colleagues outside of committees to help them navigate political pressures and interpersonal dynamics within committees. Sarah, who is very conscientious, took it upon herself to inform her colleagues when she identified an issue that they may have overlooked in a committee: "It's important to talk to them outside [of the committee] to prepare them for something or maybe you've seen something happen at the committee that you think they really should have paid attention to and they aren't."

Collectively, these organizational citizenship behaviors (active engagement, compromise, and helping behaviors) serve to facilitate committee work and simultaneously promote cohesion, unity, and camaraderie among committee members. At a fundamental level, these behaviors lubricate the interpersonal relationships and group dynamics that are critical to creating positive committee environments; however, these behaviors do take effort. One of the administrators I spoke to summarized how difficult it can be to be a contributing member to a committee: "I think you have to work hard to be a contributor, work harder than I used to think you had to" and "a good committee member has to figure out a way to bring things to the conversation that may need to be brought up that possibly are digressions . . . yet still contribute to what the product is." Another administrator provided an alternative and honest assessment of the level of effort active engagement requires:

> It's sort of like, in some cases, you know, that this is going to be grueling, mind-numbing work, right? Why am I going to do it? But there are lots of committees out there that are an opportunity to learn and prosper and demonstrate your capacity to perform, and some people rise to the occasion and some people don't.

During a conversation about issues of gender, race, and ethnicity in committees, one of my mentors is a female faculty colleague, remarked that gender norms predispose women to be agreeable, compromise, and offer help. In other words, women are somewhat conditioned to exhibit organizational citizenship behaviors, whereas men are not. This is just one example of the intersectionality of identity and performance in university committees, the foundational theme behind the origin of this book. A more detailed conversation regarding gender, race, and ethnicity in committees is provided in future chapters.

My initial research revealed that our performance in a committee lies along a spectrum of effort that is influenced by group dynamics, leadership, workload, and the committee's work. Each member determines the level of effort they contribute based on several factors that precede, moderate, or otherwise influence expressions of organizational citizenship behaviors in committees. Active engagement, compromise, and helping behaviors constitute a band of distinct behaviors on a spectrum of effort that exceed obligatory participation. Figure 2.1 illustrates the spectrum of behaviors typically observed or practiced in committees and examples of the salient conditions that encourage or discourage the expression of organizational citizenship behaviors discussed previously.

The rest of this book is dedicated to exploring the organizational, group, and individual characteristics that promote beneficial organizational citizenship behaviors and which aspects we can explore, manipulate, manage, or at least grapple with that can lead to better committee meetings. I use a building-block approach, outlined in Figure 2.2, to examine the various elements that contribute to or detract from committee performance. Figure 2.2 implies hierarchy, precedent, and interdependence. Actually, the influence of each of these dimensions is unique to each committee. These dimensions can be complementary or contradictory, they can affect committees in mutually exclusive or interdependent ways, and they can be both critical and irrelevant to the committee's success and change over the life of a committee.

When these elements align in the proper orientation, committees are positioned to be successful, committee members are likely to exercise organizational

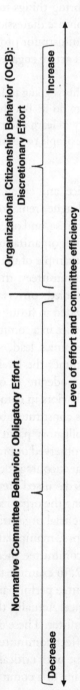

Figure 2.1. Spectrum of behavior in committees.

Figure 2.2. Committee structure.

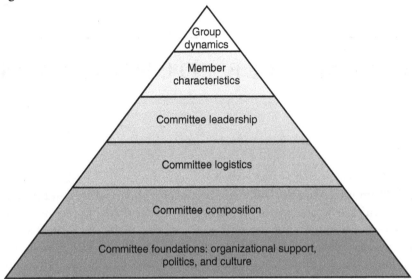

citizenship behaviors, and committees will likely function as high-performing teams. It is no mistake that this graphic resembles Maslow's (1968) hierarchy of needs, which is crowned by self-actualization. Everyone has the capacity to engage in organizational citizenship behaviors. The deciding factor is a mix of organizational, work, and social conditions that manifest in committees. As functioning groups, committees require a similar recipe of support, environment, and reflection to become self-aware and reach their full potential. Each of the elements are discussed in greater detail in chapters 3 through 8. Compartmentalization is a rudimentary form of data analysis that can be used to isolate variables in complex social phenomena. By dissecting committees into discrete components, we can identify individual units of analysis that can help us diagnose challenges to committee success and find opportunities to improve member engagement, productivity, and satisfaction. Before we move to the next chapter, reflect on your committee experience and consider the following questions:

- What distinguishes a good committee from a bad committee, and are there specific behaviors that you can associate with each?
- Have you observed or engaged in the organizational citizenship behaviors outlined in this chapter?
- When you were actively engaged or compromised or aided a colleague, what was your motivation?
- Are there other behaviors or attitudes not captured in this chapter that contribute positively or negatively to committee work?

3

COMMITTEE FOUNDATIONS

Committees are not only ubiquitous throughout colleges and universities as a strategy for facilitating planning, shared governance, and administration but also notorious for being inefficient or ineffective. Our inattention to committee design, application, and management allows committees to occasionally run amok in IHE. Investing time and effort into committee composition, critically thinking about the committee's objectives, and fabricating an administrative structure to support committee efforts can result in more efficient and productive committees. This chapter explores the various types of committees commonly found in IHE and how organizations can support committee efficacy and productivity.

Committee Typologies

In 1975, Walter Hobbs explored the construct of committees and found two common modalities: advisory and decision-making, the former being highly structured with formal procedures, the latter a more organic structure with less definition. Both modalities serve valuable functions, and many committees adopt a hybrid form that is marked by quasiformal roles and relaxed procedures. Some committees transition between advisory and decision-making depending on the task at hand. For example, a committee that convenes to evaluate the institution's learning management system (LMS) may be asked to extend its original charge to include reviewing viable alternatives, selecting a new solution, managing the LMS integration, and facilitating the institution's transition to the selected LMS. Similarly, a group of faculty might be convened to explore development of a PhD program for a college or school and later transition into leadership or advisory roles once the program is established. Regardless of their purpose and function, committees assume one of four distinct committee types: joint big decision committees, standing committees, subcommittees, and ad hoc committees. The characteristics that differentiate these committee typologies are worth noting. Table 3.1 provides a brief synopsis of each type of committee and some distinguishing features of each.

Joint Big Decision Committees

Perhaps less common than the other forms of committees but one that is indispensable to IHE are joint big decision committees (Keller, 1983; Schuster et al., 1994) or JBDC. JBDC are convened to address issues that affect a significant portion of or the entire institution and cannot be addressed by an existing committee or governance structure. These committees consist of a wide cross section of faculty, staff, students, and even external agents such as consultants, vendors, alumni, and the community. JBDC are temporary committees charged to find solutions to very complex problems that have multiple stakeholders. JBDC convene for as long as necessary then disband once a decision or outcome is reached. One of the challenges to JBDC is the diversity of the committee's membership and respective agendas, which can lead to conflict and impede efficacy and productivity (Yamada, 1991). Examples of issues that are addressed by JBDC include changes to institutional budget models, long-term strategic planning, and organizational restructuring.

Standing Committees

Standing committees conduct functions that are integral to institutional and departmental governance, compliance, and management. Standing committees tend to focus on strategic endeavors and are composed of senior-level administrators and faculty appointed to the committee by way of a formal charter or departmental bylaws that prescribe the committee's charge, rules, and deliverables. Institutional and departmental websites often document standing committees formally recognized by the organization and may include a list of individual members (by name or position), as well as the committee's charter, agendas, meeting minutes, and reports. Some institutions even maintain a standing committee on committees; that is, a body responsible for routinely and holistically evaluating the charge and composition of all standing committees to identify overlap, duplicative effort, and opportunities for organizational efficiency. Examples of functions that are typically governed by standing committees include accreditation, admissions, diversity and inclusion, international programs, curriculum planning and review, promotion and tenure, campus planning, institutional safety, institutional compliance, and research compliance.

TABLE 3.1
Committee Typologies

Type	Leadership	Charge	Duration	Membership	Output	Decisions
JBDC (significant decisions)	Appointed by an executive	Address issue that does not align with existing committee	Temporary and for as long as necessary	Wide cross section of the institution	Recommend action or put forth a solution	University-wide and/or strategic
Standing committee (advise and decide)	Defined in a committee charter or department bylaws	Prescribed in the committee charter	Routine	Defined in the committee charter	Reports, proposals, and policies	Strategic-level actions affecting multiple functions
Subcommittee (advisory)	Appointed by the standing committee	Assigned by the standing committee	Regulated by the standing committee	Limited and appointed by the standing committee	Reports, policies, procedures, manuals, and proposals	Operational-level actions focused on emerging issues
Ad hoc committee (advisory)	Chair appointed by issue owner	Defined by the immediate need or problem	Temporary and often time constrained	Appointed or recruited by the committee chair	Proposals and procedures	Tactical-level actions based on firsthand knowledge of the issues

Subcommittees

Subcommittees are convened to address specific issues that are related to or support the goals of its parent standing committee. Subcommittees are convened when a standing committee desires to take up an issue that cannot be effectively debated, researched, or addressed in place of or in addition to the standing committee's routine duties. Subcommittees may be permanent or temporary. A subcommittee is given explicit instructions from the standing committee regarding assignments, timelines, considerations, and deliverables. Subcommittees typically provide updates to a standing committee on a routine basis by way of briefings, reports, or proposals. Examples of topics assigned to subcommittees might include student research programs, employee benefits, student retention, student learning and development, faculty compensation, international partnerships, animal care and use, alumni giving, and faculty development.

Ad Hoc Committees

When a department, college, or function cannot effectively resolve an issue or formulate a solution to a problem independently, a typical reaction is to convene an ad hoc committee. Ad hoc committees are temporary bodies convened at the discretion of one or more individuals or departments that appoint themselves or one of their colleagues to serve as the committee chair. Members are generally solicited by the chair to serve on the committee. Traditionally, ad hoc committees do not subscribe to formal rules of engagement; instead, they are self-directed, and the committee or the committee chair determines when to disband. Ad hoc committees are the most agile and efficient (if designed properly) and can telegraph the institution's commitment to solving emerging problems and acute challenges to university operations (Hartley & Wilhelm Shah, 2006). Examples of issues that might precipitate ad hoc committees include large institutional events, public relations issues, student concerns, campus construction projects, temporary strategic partnerships, and departmental moves or reorganizations.

These four forms of committees appear throughout IHE; however, committee functions, applications, and procedures vary across academe. Sharon spent a portion of her career in administration before becoming a professor in the College of Education at the University of Maryland. She noted, and other faculty agree, that "the role that committees played and how they function are dramatically different" between administrative and academic sides of the institution. For example, she remembered administrative committees using committee meetings as work sessions but rarely observed this practice in academic committees. Other differences between faculty and administrative committees according to the individuals I spoke with include the following: Faculty tend to be more outspoken, to be less tolerant of committee meetings that run over time, to question the justification for a new committee, and to emphasize the role of the committee chair to control the committee's objectives and outcomes. Conversely, administrators seem to observe positional authority, tolerate inconveniences of poorly managed committees, suggest committees more frequently as solutions to organizational challenges and problems without the scrutiny faculty tend to exhibit, and spread the responsibility for committee results around the table. The ideal committee lies somewhere within the spectrum of faculty and administrative committee preferences. These differences illuminate many of the topics that are addressed later in this book; namely, the role of institutional culture, committee composition, leadership, and group dynamics.

Despite these differences, institutional culture, committee composition, and committee objectives shape the form and function of committees and extend to both academic and administrative committees. The distinctions and definitions provided in the following sections are intended to provide a lexicon of committee types based on common characteristics found in committees throughout IHE. Ultimately committee performance is a product of the larger organization, which plays a significant role in determining the committee's success.

Before we go on, it is important to recognize that many decisions can be made without a committee. Instead, some issues are better decided by a single individual or small group of key stakeholders who meet once or twice to work through an acute problem. Fred Allen (n.d.), the famous American comedian, observed that "a committee is a group of the unprepared, appointed by the unwilling, to do the unnecessary." Allen is correct that committees can unnecessarily complicate an issue. Administrators and faculty whom I spoke to shared stories of subjects being brought to committee for a variety of illegitimate reasons. As one faculty member stated, if a solution is "the best thing to do and it's obvious and self-evident," don't convene a committee—you are just going to "waste faculty members' time." In some instances, we subject ourselves to the wrong process for all the right reasons. Careful consideration should be given to which topics rise to the level of committee and which can be decided with a less byzantine process.

Organizational Support

Research has shown that workplace environment has a significant impact on group performance, potentially more so than the individual or collective abilities of group members (Mohrman et al., 1995). Organizations that desire to support the work of university committees, in all forms, will adapt governance structures and hierarchies that are conducive to committee work, provide appropriate resources, acknowledge the important work of committees, and foster a culture that supports collaboration. Organizations and the individuals responsible for establishing university committees can create conditions that contribute to the committee's success by remaining cognizant of the various institutional domains that influence committee performance. Kevin pointed out, "When organizations don't do their homework, let's just throw this to committee; it's sort of garbage in, garbage out."

Perceived organizational support has two dimensions within the workplace: task context and social context (Dierdorff et al., 2012). Task context is the technological processes of the organization (e.g., resources, information, time, and bureaucracy). Social context is the social-political environment of the workplace as it relates to or affects task performance. Organizational support can take many forms, but for the sake of brevity we will discuss only three task context issues that resonated with the individuals I spoke to while writing this book: organizational structure, institutional goals, material support, and committee training. A brief conversation on the social context elements of organizational support, which I contend are derivatives of organizational climate and group dynamics, are discussed later in chapters 6, 7, and 8.

Organizational Structure

One person I spoke to remarked that in higher education "there are a variety of governance structures that are very different from a typical organization." Organizational structures encroach on committee work in two surreptitious ways: Governance structures and hierarchies, external to the committee, either (a) facilitate committee work by providing committees with autonomy and authority necessary to effectively execute the charge of the committee or (b) obstruct the committee's work, which can discourage participation.

When members perceive organizational hierarchies that potentially jeopardize committee work, committee members can become frustrated and discouraged from participation. Members who perceive a lack of autonomy or decision-making authority within committees tend to withhold their effort for a more worthwhile endeavor; namely, their day-to-day responsibilities. One administrator explained the effect on their desire to engage in committees when the institution disregards the time and effort they and their colleagues invest in committees:

> So all this energy goes into this [committee] and then nothing happens, or you feel there was some kind of lip service . . . the next time, it's like why bother. . . . If you want your people to be really involved in something, then make it real. Don't do this crap.

Institutions that fail to execute a committee's recommendation or disregard the committee's efforts force committee members to ask themselves, "Why bother with this exercise if it's all for naught?" In other instances, the work of the committee may be marginalized to make room for other institutional priorities; this has the same effect as dismissing the committee's work. One faculty that I spoke with said that some committees "get short shrift" because the larger governance group doesn't make time for committee reports. Another faculty member lamented the plight of the institution's faculty senate: "They spent so much time and then nothing ever holds any water with the administration anyway. It's almost like we don't have a voice." As a result, committee members questioned the value of their efforts and began to disengage.

Alternatively, committee work can receive too much attention! When committee actions are subject to external approval processes or complicated bureaucratic procedures, the committee can be forced into stasis until the larger organization processes the committee's recommendation. Mechanistic approval processes and complicated chains of command create roadblocks that impair group momentum and productivity. Adam provided an example of a convoluted approval process that became a source of frustration for the members of his committee:

> Here's what we want to do. We need to take it up the chain. Great. They take it up the chain, they got it approved, got back down. Great; let's move forward. It went back up the chain. Disapproved. Went back down. Went all the way up to the cabinet level; finally, got a blessing. Came back down. It was crazy!

Committee inertia is a powerful deterrent to participation. Both inattention and overattention can lead to paralysis in the committee. When members sense that a committee is stalled by inactivity that results from internal and external barriers to progress, engagement declines precipitously. Even in committees that do maintain forward momentum, bureaucratic hurdles that obstruct committee work tend to discourage full participation.

It would be inappropriate to suggest that committees should not be answerable to university, college, or department leadership, but they should be granted a level of authority and autonomy that is commensurate with their charge. Without appropriate authority the committee risks alienating its members. For example, Nick stated, "The lack or the inability to actually pull the trigger is, to me, mind blowing. I want out of that committee as fast as possible!" Instead, leadership should be cognizant of potential obstructions and modify the committee's charge accordingly or be transparent about the nature of the committee's work. Organizations can support committees by providing committees with clear parameters regarding their authority, defining approval processes, establishing realistic timelines, stipulating reporting procedures, and providing clear conduits to university leadership and governance structures to support the committee's efforts.

To facilitate the work of the committee, it is important to position committees within the organization in ways that contribute to the committee's success. Consideration for which college or department calls the committee, who leads the committee (and who they report to), extant cultural and relational conflicts, and expectations regarding approval processes should be clearly understood. Committees should be informed of their role in the larger organization and have some familiarity with how the committee's activities integrate with or complement organizational governance processes. Questions that can clarify issues around organizational structure include the following: Who must approve committee recommendations, who can overrule the committee's recommendations, and are there other departments or units that are not represented on the committee that have authority or influence? Committees might consider using a force field analysis (Lewin, 1947) to map and evaluate the various internal and external factors expected to support or resist the committee's work and direct efforts accordingly. Mapping the committee's position in the large organizational landscape can reveal gaps in committee composition and work strategies. See Figure 1.1 for a hypothetical governance and institutional decision-making process to help facilitate this exercise.

Institutional Goals

Most of the administrators and faculty I interviewed stressed the importance of aligning the charge of the committee with short-term and/or long-term organizational objectives and goals as documented in departmental or institutional strategic plans. As one administrator commented, "If you are unclear about why the organization is doing something, you're not going to be as helpful." The linkage between the committee's work and institutional vision not only provides legitimacy to the committee but also helps define the boundaries of the committee's charge. Committees that are affiliated with the institution's overarching strategic plan are more likely to solicit engagement because there is an inherent sense of agency and importance associated with the task. Committee work that provides a sense of empowerment, based on a pronouncement from the administration or the perceived utility and impact of the committee's work, is also a strong motivator for committee members to engage in organizational citizenship behaviors. Sarah admitted that early in her career she was more likely to exceed performance expectations when she felt empowered by the work she was assigned. When she was first appointed to a high-level committee as a new administrator, Sarah confessed it was "an ego stroke," but she was also "much more motivated to contribute." Empowerment can result from appointment to a high-level committee, as in Sarah's case, or be conveyed as an organizational priority that gives committee members the sense that the welfare of the organization is entrusted to their care. Recall the origin of the word *committee*: to entrust or give custody. Committee chairs should allocate time when the committee convenes, and periodically thereafter, to discuss the committee's charge in relation to the institution's strategic plan to ensure continued alignment and relevance. Committees should expect to modify their charge and composition over time to remain consistent with social, economic, political, and cultural organizational evolutions. Committees that fail to recognize changes in the organization's trajectory or shifts in external forces (e.g., regulations, best practices, stakeholder expectations, etc.) jeopardize the products of the committee members' hard work.

Material Support

Organizations that are intent on making committee work productive will allocate resources needed to carry out the assigned charge. Material support might be confused with funding needed to implement the committee's recommendation; money is important, and arguably the scarcest resource, but there are other, more subtle forms of material support that influence committee performance. If meetings are held in person, the institution should provide adequate and well-provisioned meeting spaces. Researchers have discovered a variety of environmental stressors, including work space comfort and functionality, that influence performance (Vischer, 2005). I was surprised by how many people associated the value of a committee with the condition of the meeting spaces. One administrator I spoke to recalled a committee that was convened in a wood-paneled room with fluorescent lights and no windows. He admitted it was difficult to be engaged and excited about the committee's work when the room resembled his friend's basement from the 1960s. Meeting and classroom space is often a scarce commodity at most institutions. If possible, meeting spaces should be differentiated from classrooms in the institution's space utilization procedures and appropriated for meeting and administrative functions only to ensure availability.

Many IHE are making significant investments in classroom technologies and hardware to create areas that are conducive to learning. Should we not also examine how our work environment is structured to promote collaboration and engagement? Configurable room layouts and comfortable chairs with sufficient electrical outlets, Wi-Fi, audiovisual equipment, projectors, speaker phones, Ethernet jacks (that are active), and whiteboards are resources that may be necessary to facilitate meetings. The availability of video-teleconferencing applications and enterprise conference call services is valuable to engage members who are unable to attend in person. Virtual technologies can help overcome issues of availability and ensure that members remain connected to the committee's work. Together, technology, meeting space design, location, and condition all contribute to the committee's performance by creating an environment that is comfortable, functional, and sufficiently equipped to facilitate group work and meetings (Vischer, 2007).

Virtual meeting technology (e.g., Lifesize, Poly, Spark, Easymeeting) has improved significantly in recent years; however, some institutions have been slow to migrate away from face-to-face meetings. Many institutions have enterprise licenses for video-teleconference applications (e.g., join.me, Webex), which can be used to conduct virtual committee meetings but require both the organizer and the user to have the necessary applications and familiarity with the system. Virtual meetings require different rules of engagement and decorum to be effective, and some individuals may not be comfortable working in a virtual environment.

Last, money is a key indicator of how important a committee's charge is to the institution. How often have you served on a committee that was assigned the task of implementing an unfunded mandate? For example, a committee charged with creating a strategy for improving security at large public venues may perceive its task as futile unless appropriate funding is set aside at the outset. Engagement is likely to be much higher if members recognize that their efforts are backed by financial support. In some cases, particularly following a crisis, committees are promised funding, but it is unusual for committees to be given a blank check. Each institution will adopt its own process, and it is not uncommon to assign a committee to explore the viability and cost of new solutions before allocating funding; however, expectations should be explicitly clear. For example, a new committee assigned to explore enterprise travel request and reimbursement procedures may be instructed as follows:

This committee is being convened to explore the viability of a new travel authorization and reimbursement system. The committee will research and compare different commercially available travel applications to determine if the institution's current travel system should be replaced with a new solution that provides greater utility while complying with institutional travel policies. Cost, implementation, integration with existing university systems, and information technology security must be evaluated. The committee will recommend a course of action to the vice president for consideration. The administration will take the committee's recommendation under advisement and determine if a new solution is required.

Setting clear expectations about the committee's work can avoid frustration later in the process. Notice that this statement leaves the door open for future funding and suggests that the decision will be based, in part, on the quality of the committee's work.

Committee Training

Ronald Berk (2012) pointed out in his article "Meetings in Academe: It's Time for an 'Extreme Meeting Makeover!'" that "meetings can be major time wasters, accomplishing very little, often deteriorating into just another social event," and this is due in large part because "most administrators, faculty, and clinicians are simply not trained in meeting management" (p. 50). Indeed, one faculty member I spoke with commented,

> Administrators have not been trained to be administrators. Whether it is
> a regular faculty member or a faculty member who has become an admin-
> istrator, neither one has really gotten training on how to lead that team or
> form a committee, or how to define the committee or project, or how to
> bring things to closure.

Training, mentorships, and apprenticeships that encourage professional development among university and committee leadership can have positive impacts on the efficacy of committees (Kezar & Eckel, 2004). Training can not only mitigate some of the frustration typically associated with committees and meetings but also facilitate committee experiences as professional development opportunities. As Kim stated in her interview, "We probably need to help people understand how to run a good committee. It's not a secret, there is a whole literature on some of these things." Research shows that training programs can improve team member performance (Goldstein & Ford, 2002). Why are we not equipping administrators and faculty with knowledge and skills needed to effectively manage committees and routine meetings? Kloppenborg and Petrick (1999) not only recommended that individuals who manage meetings receive training but also suggested that meeting managers employ traditional quality improvement strategies to encourage intellectual, moral, emotional, social, ethical, and political virtues over a series of five meetings to improve meeting productivity! This is an ambitious goal, and I think most committee members will be satisfied with starting on time, staying on task, and sticking to the committee's objectives. Although a committee does not fit the precise definition of a team, training can help committee members, especially new staff and faculty, understand the organizational expectations and idiosyncrasies of committee work.

At my current institution, everyone who is expected to serve on a position search committee is required to attend formal training. This training is designed to educate search committee members on applicant review and hiring procedures, legal issues, antidiscrimination and bias tactics, and search committee member responsibilities. Ethics, institutional review board, procurement, and travel training are other common examples of mandated trainings in IHE that are required to protect the institution's reputation and resources. Should we not also respect the time and effort of the institution's human capital? A short course, online or in person, is relatively easy to design and implement to orient new faculty and staff to their respective committee responsibilities.

Some institutions provide resources for faculty and staff on the principles of shared governance, an outline of the institution's governance structure, and an overview or list of existing committees.[1] A committee training program can provide information on university governance structures, ethical decision-making, committee charters, institutional goals, meeting management fundamentals, and committee resources (e.g., meeting spaces, document management, and video-teleconference technology). A sample committee training curriculum might include the following topics:

- Philosophy of shared governance
- Overview of the institution's governance structure
- Roles and responsibilities of the staff senate and faculty senate
- Committee member selection (recruitment versus appointment)
- Alignment of committee objectives and goals with institutional or department strategic plans
- Development of committee charters
- Committee meeting logistics
  - Procedures for reserving meeting space on campus
  - Expectations regarding meeting schedules and announcements
  - Teleconference and videoconference resources

- o Meeting length
- o Document management applications
- o Meeting minutes
- o Assignment of action items
- • Principles of committee leadership
- • Overview of decision-making techniques
- • Strategies for soliciting healthy conflict and debate
- • Expected elements and format for committee proposals
- • Budget request procedures

Providing training may be a burden too great for one department to bear; instead, committee chairs might be expected to attend training or participate in routine committee chair meetings, which can function as a pseudo community of practice. This "committee of best practice" could serve additional functions as a coordinating body, an advisory board for new or transitioning committees, and an arbiter of committee disagreements. This committee of committees, if you will, might also recommend ways that the organization can support committee work through policy, structure, culture, and technology. In the absence of committee training, institutions should establish guidance on what it means to serve on a committee and expectations of committee members and make this information available to university administrators and faculty during orientation, through departmental meetings, and online.

Institutional Culture

Each college and university possesses its own unique blend of organizational culture and politics that influence committees in a variety of ways. Tierney (2008) made an interesting point regarding culture and decision-making in IHE; he argued that organizational culture dictates which governance model is preferred and legitimate, which naturally extends to how committees function in institutional governance processes. Participation in university committees is predicated on perceptions of what organizations expect in terms of contribution to committees, organizational objectives, and organizational tolerance for discretionary behavior (i.e., organizational citizenship behaviors). Scholars continue to struggle to develop a concise definition of *organizational culture*. The best definition that I have found suggests that we conceptualize it as the "personality" of an organization (Gayle et al., 2003). Consider for a moment your institution's personality; is your institution pleasant or obnoxious, humble or arrogant, thoughtful or reactionary, collaborative or independent, agreeable or mean, mature or naïve, sophisticated or rudimentary, disciplined or undisciplined?

Organizational culture influences behavioral norms through nuanced cues conveyed by the atmosphere of the institution (Ehrhart & Naumann, 2004). The latent effect of collegiality on committees establishes expectations for how individuals should engage with their colleagues. Collegiality is often pitted against the encroaching influence of traditional hierarchical governance models that are being introduced in IHE by the growing professional administrative class. The emphasis on organizational hierarchies or appreciation for the collegium are reflected in how committees are formed, members interact, and decisions are reached. Houston observed that IHE are more democratic than other organizations, and, as such, faculty and staff possess (real or perceived) agency to affect change. He said, "There is sort of this sense that [higher education] is different than other organizations; where the sense of democracy is stronger. If you're some company you're not going to walk into some board meeting and hijack it, right?" As a result, administrators and faculty take liberties to exercise this right by voicing their opinions, protesting decisions, and acting in other ways that might not be tolerated in traditional hierarchical organizations. Collegiality is a natural response in an environment that demands higher levels of tolerance for dissenting opinions, conflicting goals, and diverse perspectives.

In most institutions, collegiality is an implicit expectation, or, as one administrator observed, "Being friendly, being engaging, being willing to at least give lip service to collaboration is important in higher education." Most administrators and faculty with whom I spoke noted not only that divergent viewpoints are common in university committees but also an unwritten rule that each person's opinion should be given equal credence. This sounds ideal, but one administrator remarked with irritation, "If you are not an academic, you have no clue how patient you have to be, how everybody needs to make their point." There is a fine line between constructive debate and debilitating oration. Collegiality is often touted as an organizational strength; however, this pervasive cultural influence may be antithetical to committee work. Some of the interviewees I spoke with claimed that efforts to maintain a collegial atmosphere actually discourage debate and encourage too much compromise, which lead to mediocre results. A veteran administrator went so far as to suggest that some people adopt an alternative role identity to conform to committee expectations and to avoid confrontation and protect their true opinions and position. They stated, "I do not view most people's behaviors as authentic; well, this is a terrible generalization. I think that people are careful about being their authentic selves . . . in these committee meetings." Yet another administrator with whom I spoke succinctly summarized the conundrum of collegiality in the context of committees: "So we all get along here . . . but we don't get along here." These reflections suggest that collegial climates can pose a danger to committee work in that it can obfuscate the true relationships between members, their relative positions on issues, and honest discourse.

In contrast, and more alarming, is that some scholars have argued that IHE are beginning to reflect the rise of incivility in our society, which is eroding the sense of community and collegiality long associated with IHE (Cipriano, 2011). Indeed, multiple administrators and faculty whom I spoke to broached the issue of bullying in IHE. Bullying can take many insidious forms that are perhaps masked by attention to the nobler concept of collegiality. One faculty member remarked that sometimes "we forget we are human." Our lack of civility and compassion means some members are showing up to committee meetings with bad attitudes, nefarious intentions, and poor behavior. In other cases, institutional cultures discourage bullying and promote civility. For example, Steve "never bad-mouths other faculty members" not only because it is not in his nature but also because there is an "unspoken code" that this type of behavior, among others, is not acceptable at Liberty University. Liberty University might be a unique case given that the institution is dedicated to a set of religious ideals that are integrated into the curriculum and governance. Other institutions may lack an explicit and documented set of cultural principles around engagement and collaboration.

Accountability is another theme that arose in my conversations with administrators and faculty. Kevin provided one of the most profound statements on IHE; he astutely observed that many functions and supervisors in IHE tend to "reward effort, not performance." For example, some faculty are recognized for their service on committees in promotion and tenure review, but there is no mechanism to evaluate their performance in committees or their contribution or lack thereof. Sharon commented that the administration or departmental leadership sometimes fail to "hold faculty accountable for some of the outcomes" of committees. Both Kevin and Sharon suggested that institutions should be more deliberate about setting objectives and holding committees responsible. This is not to suggest that there is no accountability in committees but to suggest that the lack of accountability in some committees might be a product of IHE culture and a function of committee leadership. The lack of accountability, especially in committees where formal lines of authority are absent, presents significant challenges for administrators and faculty alike. Conversely, Sharon noted that for standing committees, such as promotion and tenure committees, work is often regimented, and the committee is very effective.

Although we tend to experience organizational culture on a micro level, macro cultural issues can pervade our motivation and surreptitiously undermine our best efforts. Ruiz-Palomino and Martínez-Cañas (2014) found a significant relationship between ethical culture (using a composite instrument that measured the ethics of leadership, supervisors, peers, and policies) and an individual's propensity to engage in organizational citizenship behaviors. This research suggests that a person's perception of the organization's culture and the ethics of their colleagues and supervisors encourages or discourages organizational citizenship behaviors. High assessments of ethical company culture tend to encourage citizenship behaviors. Negative assessments of company culture, not surprisingly, discourage citizenship behaviors. It's not only ethical culture that influences behaviors to engage or disengage from civic duties but also superficial attitudes regarding the organization's image and reputation. Faculty and administrators who see the organization in a positive light are more likely to engage in organizational citizenship behaviors than are persons who have a negative opinion of the organization (Dukerich et al., 2002). Institutional accomplishments and scandals, particularly those that gain the attention of the media, are likely to influence internal perceptions of the organization, with potential impacts on committee engagement. Committee engagement is, to some degree, a function and measure of morale.

Last and most important, we need to consider the structures, processes, and cultural aspects that promote or discourage gender, racial, and ethnic diversity and inclusion. Acker (1990) recognized that organizations are gendered and tend to conform to masculine ontologies that are evident in divisions of power, conceptions of gender roles, organizational symbols, social structures (i.e., communication and behavioral norms), social identities, and the underlying logic that governs decision-making throughout the organization. Commonly enforced ideas of hierarchy, bureaucracies, rules of engagement, roles and their associated value, and the concept of work/job were formed in organizations, including IHE, that are historically male (Marshall, 1993) and White (Delgado & Stefancic, 2012). Lester and Sallee (2017) demonstrated that even the structure of academic work is discriminatory in that it is based on White male constructs of what it means to "work" and fails to account for inherent pressures and expectations associated with female gender roles. For example, traditional work routines do not provide flexibility to carry out family responsibilities that have historically been seen as a woman's role. Rigid work hours, expectations of after-hours availability, limited paid leave (including maternity and paternity leave), and prioritization of work over family tend to discriminate against women (Wolf-Wendel & Ward, 2006) and a growing number of men who have family responsibilities.

It's only recently that organizations are beginning to reimagine work–life balance and how work is interpreted differently by the various individuals and groups that constitute the workforce.

IHE have also not adequately addressed barriers to success and inclusion for underrepresented faculty and administrators. In addition to facing discrimination during the hiring process, underrepresented faculty report a disproportionate burden to serve institutions through doing committee work, mentoring students, and arranging events but do not receive the recognition, advancement, and research opportunities that typically accompany these efforts (Gregory, 2001; Griffin, 2012; Griffin et al., 2014). Explicit and clandestine bullying, harassment, and discrimination experienced by unrepresented faculty and administrators in IHE constitute a toxic environment that precludes equal treatment, unjustly disqualifies individuals from job and career growth opportunities, places inordinate pressure to conform and perform to organizational expectations, and oppresses expressions of voice, experience, and individuality that offer unique contributions to colleges and universities (see Zambrana, 2018). Minority women face particularly difficult circumstances, as they are often the subject of gender and racial/ethnic discrimination, commonly referred to as interactive discrimination (Irvine, 1978) or double-blind discrimination (Warner, 1995).

Stanley (2006a) noted that racism, sexism, xenophobia, and homophobia cut "across many areas of the academy such as teaching, research, service, and overall experiences with the campus community" (p. 705). Taken in their totality, these experiences and conditions create a hostile environment where women and underrepresented populations are routinely oppressed or dismissed or struggle to be heard. The latent processes, attitudes, and organizational constructs that disadvantage underrepresented populations have become so ubiquitous and accepted throughout Western society, including in higher education, as to make some forms of discrimination practically invisible (Ladson-Billings, 1998). Institutional cultures that systematically or inadvertently discriminate against members of the community are forms of institutional sexism and racism.

Institutional technologies, procedures, and biases manifest holistically and locally to affect, among other things, institutional cultural and group dynamics. Institutions must acknowledge that organizational processes and norms built on Western Eurocentric ideologies privilege White faculty and administrators and systematically discriminate against people of color (Delgado & Stefancic, 2012). A short catalog of some of the obstacles produced by mainstream culture and hegemonic thinking that discriminate against women and underrepresented faculty and administrators (women and men) includes discounted intellectual competency and commitment (hooks & West, 1991; Nelms, 2002), a lack of mentors in leadership and comparable positions (Stanley & Lincoln, 2005), a small or nonexistent peer group critical for support and sense of community (Martinez, 1999), becoming a target of inter- and intragroup conflict seeking someone to blame (Gant, 2011), inadequate compensation (Barr, 1990), poor job access (Barr, 1990), perceptions of being a product of affirmative action practices rather than individual excellence (i.e., tokenism) (L. Watson, 2001), and pressure to conform to the dominant White European culture (Sadao, 2003).

One of the first places to begin the shift from masculine White to gender-neutral inclusive organizations is by focusing on who occupies positions of power and authority. Ragins (1995), a scholar of organizational behavior, noted, "Organizational culture is shaped and supported by the power holders of the organization. These individuals influence the values assumptions and ideologies of the organization's culture" (p. 97). The demography of authority in IHE has significant ramifications on which behaviors and traits are celebrated and rewarded and which are marginalized and underappreciated. In colleges and universities, where males (specifically White males) tend to hold leadership positions (J. Jackson, 2002), female and minority (racial and ethnic) committee members are disadvantaged by the cultural norms propagated by the university's predominantly White male leadership.

Research has found that women tend to rise to positions of authority in organizations that embrace ideals associated with feminine values (e.g., humane orientation, sharing of power, interpersonal relationships, and multiple lines of communication) (Bajdo & Dickson, 2001). The rise of women to positions of power can shape organizational culture, thereby creating a potential self-sustaining cycle of empowerment, opportunity, and advancement. Similarly, scholars have noted that the selection and promotion of underrepresented faculty and administrators to visible positions of leadership (Altbach et al., 2011; Gasman et al., 2015), coupled with a strategic diversity plan (Wolfe & Dilworth, 2015), encourage equity and inclusion. Committees serve as an ideal forum to exercise organizational diversity and inclusion strategies.

Jerlando Jackson (2006) argued that efforts to improve institutional diversity and inclusion and to combat inequities must occur at all levels of the organization: the student body, professoriate, and administration. Diversity and inclusivity within one strata of the organization drive change among the others, with diversity in leadership coupled with proactive diversity and inclusion strategies having the greatest impact. By appointing women and underrepresented faculty and administrators in tactical, operational, and strategic committees, it is easy to infer how committees might be leveraged to mitigate some of these inequities across all strata of the organization. Committees are microcosmic organizations that can illuminate the inequities in IHE and can serve as a venue for exploring solutions to these cultural and social problems. Committees are the primary and most visible instrument of institutional governance; as such, committees provide opportunities to orchestrate diversity in leadership, offer engagement and opportunity for underrepresented communities, expose issues of discrimination and bias through dialogue, and over time transform institutions into inclusive and diverse organizations by promoting these ideals in committee proceedings. Rooting out expressions of racism and sexism is both an individual and an organizational obligation. For this revolution to occur, we must appoint women and underrepresented faculty and administrators to lead important committees, choreograph committees to be diverse, encourage genuine consideration of the perspectives and experiences expressed by disadvantaged members of our community, and rectify institutional policies and procedures that are antithetical to the ideals of inclusion and diversity.

Political Considerations

Organizational politics are an abstruse force that influences how faculty and staff conduct themselves in committees. More than one person I spoke with recognized that committees are sometimes convened to make a display of shared governance. As one faculty member remarked, "Politics are very much blended into a lot of [institutional] processes." Occasionally, informal performance expectations are implied by the political nature of topics taken up by committees and/or the expectations of senior administrators external to the committee. Political pressure is capable of coercing effort from committee members who are conscious of the administration's desired outcomes. Research has shown that higher perceptions of task significance equate to higher levels of engagement and effort (Farh et al., 1990; Piccolo & Colquitt, 2006; Purvanova et al., 2006). When institutional or departmental leadership is vested in the committee, committee members are likely to perceive the committee's work as highly significant and tend to be more engaged.

Depending on the composition of the committee, members may be serving as proxies for someone else's agenda. In these instances, members are serving not as free agents but as representatives of a coalition or individual who desires a specific outcome from the committee's work. In some instances, the entire committee may be cognizant of its leadership's desired outcome and recognize that resistance or objection will be perceived as negative. When the outcome of a committee is a foregone conclusion, members are likely

COMMITTEE FOUNDATIONS   *53*

to question the value of their time, expertise, and effort. This sentiment can also result when a committee is convened to validate a solution or course of action that has already been decided on but requires affirmation that only a committee can provide; in other words, a rubber stamp of approval. For example, one faculty member pointed out that department leadership will

> bring everybody together in a committee, but it's not really a committee. It's just a committee in the sense that the dean wants to feel better about everyone being included, but everybody knows that at the end of the day, it's the dean's decision.

Another faculty member recalls high-level committees where "the administration, at whatever level, has the committee because they just need buy-in and I certainly have found myself feeling like that's exactly what just happened to me. You say, 'Oh, I'll never fall for that one again.'" In other cases, the administration will convene a committee "to figure out what they already figured out, if that makes any sense," exclaimed yet another faculty member. Reluctance to contribute under these conditions is consistent with research that found an individual's sense of autonomy is positively correlated with their propensity for civic engagement (Dierdorff et al., 2012).

Committee members often interpret political pressure as a dictate for the committee's work. One administrator reflected on their experience working on a committee that was heavily influenced by organizational politics and remarked, "When you are on a committee that is highly political . . . there are certain results that need to happen. . . . It is very important to massage and maneuver that, and it's a very frustrating committee." Many of the administrators with whom I spoke acknowledged that they become reluctant to expend more than the minimal effort required to keep up appearances of collegiality and collaboration when they perceive a committee as a political charade. When the outcome of a committee is a foregone conclusion, some even make excuses to not be involved in the committee at all. For instance, when Marleen realized a committee was no more than a pretense for supporting someone's premeditated agenda, she felt that it was "totally demoralizing, because what you're asking is intelligent people to give their input and they know it's not going to really make any difference." One administrator I spoke with admitted that he will disengage from the committee by claiming he is overcommitted and cannot afford to participate when he discerns an ulterior motive for convening a committee. Committees convened to give an issue "lip service" (Sarah) is a "deceptive approach" (Adam) that has a profoundly negative impact on participants' willingness to engage in the committee. The other way that organizational politics can disrupt committees is the tacit expectation that certain individuals will be present to provide their blessing or give consent regardless of the value they do or do not contribute to the committee. If the right institutional gatekeepers are not included in the process, the committee runs the risk of engaging in a futile exercise.

When the work of the committee is a foregone conclusion, the group functions as a so-called kangaroo committee; the committee is merely going through the motions to satisfy the appearance of due process, shared governance, or collegiality to appease the desires of the organization's leadership. When committees are forced to abdicate their autonomy to the will of a higher authority, committee members typically become apathetic and less likely to fully engage in the committee. Reluctance to engage in a rubber stamp committee may be compounded by another cultural aspect unique to higher education. Traditionally, higher education culture is resistant to hierarchical governance structures (Birnbaum, 1988), which might explain some of the resistance or resentment expressed by committee members who feel compelled to toe the company line.

As a member of the committee, especially the chair, organizational pressures exerted on committees should be explicitly or tacitly acknowledged, and the committee's work, composition, and discussions should be adjusted accordingly. For example, a committee convened to resolve issues of declining international student enrollment should be advised by the committee chair of the administration's ambitions and recommended strategies so as to not run afoul of senior leadership's intentions and expectations. Recognizing the external latent forces that shape committee dynamics is essential to understanding each member's perspective and perceived deviant behavior. In an ideal environment, committees are completely protected from political pressure to explore, debate, and reach the best possible outcome (Ancona & Caldwell, 1992), but unfortunately it's practically impossible for committee members to disassociate their committee work from the larger sociopolitical institutional issues.

Administrators and faculty also explain that their behavior in committees is governed by the ambiguous boundaries of what the institution furtively communicates via political pressure as priorities and tolerance for organizational change. Nick eloquently qualified the power of organizational culture and individual effort; he asked, "What are at the limits, not necessarily what's possible but what's possible within the norms of the organization which is sometimes a really narrow band and sometimes it's broad?" Organizational politics (e.g., alliances, grudges, negotiations, power dynamics, disputes, animosity, friendships, romances, insider information, and individual ambitions) create a lens through which we interpret the actions of others and make sense of the undercurrents in social settings. Committee members try to interpret the political currents of their institution and act accordingly in committees. As one administrator asked, "If I contribute to this in an honest way, is it going to be a good thing or a bad thing?" In other words, members are often evaluating their engagement in committees against potential repercussions or rewards based on their assessment of the institution's fluid political climate. It may be difficult to identify the latent political influences on individual committee members; however, shared work experiences can expose these relationships and lead to a mutual appreciation of our colleagues' respective constraints and opportunities concerning a specific issue.

When committee issues are perceived to have potential political consequences, members often avoid actively engaging in or taking a high-profile role in committees because they are unable to anticipate the outcome or consequences of their involvement. For instance, one administrator explained the conundrum between aspiring to make a positive organizational change and preservation of one's reputation: "So having what we've got even though people are annoyed with it is better than making a decision and sticking your neck out. . . . If you make a decision and change it, now we don't just hate the product, we're blaming you." This statement implies that behavior in committees is judged by other committee members using an unwritten code of conduct that mirrors the political environment of the institution.

Baer and Frese (2003) conducted a study that examined innovative and psychological safety in organizations. They found that psychologically safe environments encourage employee voice and engagement in organizational functions, thereby improving organizational performance. Committee members are more likely to speak up when they perceive their position as safe and the organization as receptive to feedback. Institutional politics and culture play a significant role in how administrators and faculty assess the institution's tolerance for constructive criticism and change and engage in institutional governance. When political pressure is exerted on committees, voice, active engagement, and discretionary behaviors that deviate from cultural norms are discouraged. Furthermore, when organizational politics intersect with the work of the committee, most of the individuals I spoke with indicated that they become more cautious, assume a less assertive role, and only do what is necessary to meet performance expectations, which typically mirror normative committee behaviors. In short, committees working under political pressure (i.e., duress) tend to lack creative or enthusiastic engagement.

The cultural and political dimensions of IHE discussed previously dictate who thrives in an organization, which behaviors and accomplishments are celebrated, and who is disadvantaged, and they have a significant impact on the establishment of normative behaviors that inevitably manifest in committees. The process of unraveling the complexities of identity, injustice, and inclusion in the context of committees takes time, effort, and intentionality that many faculty and administrators fail to identify and/or address. Maintaining focus on these issues is necessary to both create an inclusive committee environment and effect substantive permanent change in organizational gender and identity culture. Diversity and inclusion are a theme that will reappear throughout this book. The benefits of creating diverse committees are reviewed in chapter 4, and a discussion on leading diverse committees is provided in chapter 6.

Developing a catalog of organizational influences on committees is a challenging task but a worthwhile exercise. Sharon reflected on her time at the University of Maryland and recognized that "the longer I've been here, I feel like I have a better sense of some of the cultural stuff that gets missed by people who don't understand why what just happened is important, because it has historical context." Only time and experience can yield an appreciation of institutional culture and politics. Furthermore, the list of cultural and political influences, the corresponding impact on committee proceedings, and how individuals grapple with cultural issues are unique to each institution. Instead, it may be helpful to analyze your institution and committee experiences to identify the most salient cultural elements that permeate committee meetings and bring them up for discussion when appropriate. To help with this exercise, consider the following questions:

- How would you describe your institution's personality to an outsider?
- How is your organization's culture reflected in committees?
- What organizational norms or behaviors are promoted or discouraged by your institutional culture?
- Which communities and populations are respected, which are marginalized, and who champions or validates the views and voices of underrepresented faculty and administrators?
- What aspects of committee work does the organization appreciate or encourage (e.g., ethics, transparency, accuracy, efficiency, diligence, synergy, innovation, collaboration, profit)?

Note

1. University of Mary Washington, Seminole State College, University of Wisconsin–Madison, University of Louisiana–Monroe, and Radford University.

4

COMMITTEE COMPOSITION

Chapter 4 explores committee composition and how the formation of the committee is a precursor for success or harbinger of obstacles to come. How large should the committee be? Should you find someone with the right level of experience and authority or the individual who is the most sociable and ambitious? Are there noticeable differences between committees that appoint members and those that solicit volunteers? How can we encourage and leverage gender, racial, and ethnic diversity in committees to yield more equitable campus cultures and better committee outcomes? How are committees structured to succeed from conception? This chapter opens with a discussion on group size because it is a restrictive factor in all subsequent decisions regarding composition. Committee members should be appointed or solicited depending on the committee's task; however, special attention should be given to the formal and informal roles members are expected to fill. We will review how committee members' titles and positions can complicate committee dynamics and end with a brief discussion about how to recognize engaged, associated, or indifferent committee members.

Committee Size

Robert Copeland (n.d.) said, "To get something done, a committee should consist of no more than three people, two of whom are absent." If productivity and efficacy are important to committees, then size matters. Research has determined that a group's capabilities and expertise increase with group size, but individual effort decreases with size (Staats et al., 2012). One of the earliest studies that revealed the inverse relationship between group size and individual effort was performed by Maximillian Ringelmann, who studied group effort by measuring the amount of effort a team exerts on a rope (Moede, 1927). Ringelmann discovered that for each additional person added to a group, the collective pulling force on the rope increased, but there was a corresponding decline in individual effort. He suggested as groups become larger, more opportunities exist to shirk responsibilities because the effect is less apparent to the group's collective effort. This phenomenon is commonly referred to as *social loafing*. In short, "individuals in larger groups perform worse" (Mueller, 2012, p. 119). Social loafing or shirking can be observed in many committees. Kevin pointed out that it's not unusual to "have seven people on a committee, but there are really only two people contributing." What is more concerning is that social loafing can be contagious. When members of a committee perceive that others are engaged in social loafing, they become less inclined to engage with the group (Whiteoak, 2007).

According to the authors of *Decide and Deliver: 5 Steps to Breakthrough Performance in Your Organization* (Blenko et al., 2010), the optimal size of a group is seven members; each additional member decreases the efficacy of decision-making by 10%. Many studies argue that five people constitute the optimal group size (Hackman & Vidmar, 1970). Steiner (1972) observed that productivity loss begins to occur when groups exceed five people. Yet another study found that groups of three to eight are optimal for fostering group trust and productivity; however, these benefits begin to decline precipitously with nine or more members (Wheelan, 2009). The larger the group, the more difficult it can be to create an environment that yields positive group norms such as trust, cohesion, and helping behaviors. As one administrator remarked, when committees reach "15 to 20 people, death . . . . Forget it . . . you have just ground the whole thing to a halt." Put simply, committees should not exceed five to seven members. Good luck!

University administrators and faculty agree that many issues that warrant a committee require more than seven members to be adequately addressed. When a committee exceeds seven members, or whatever number is deemed essential, consider convening a subcommittee to parcel out committee work to preserve efficiency and productivity. Subcommittees serve a variety of purposes that advance the objectives of the committee and serve the institution, namely, by

- reducing the number of individuals engaged in general discussions thereby improving efficiency,
- allowing the committee to take up additional issues without detracting from the committee's core purpose,
- permitting the committee to branch out and engage other subject matter experts who are not permanent members of the committee,

- providing dedicated time to address topics in detail that are not able to be addressed in the larger committee, and
- offering leadership opportunities to committee members.

If a committee cannot accommodate all interested parties, meeting minutes or briefs can be distributed to those who cannot (or should not) physically attend committee meetings. Often, people are appointed to committees because they need to be made aware of, approve, or consult on the committee's work. If this is the case, email updates or committee reports should suffice. These ancillary members do not need to be present to fulfill their review, approval, and consulting roles. As one faculty member lamented, many of the meetings that he attended were "fluff" and the assignment could have been "done over email or some other forum." If you do elect to send committee updates or briefings in lieu of larger membership or standing meetings, correspondence must be concise. Steve admitted that many university faculty have the same tolerance as students for long emails. Don't be the one to receive a "TLDR" (too long didn't read) response to your efforts to keep a committee apprised of progress and action items.

Expertise

High-functioning committees are strategically organized. Each member should have a designated role that can be explained by the function, expertise, or perspective they provide. Furthermore, each member should have the requisite authority and resources to fulfill their respective role. As Marleen stated, "I guess it would be nice if people who are asked to be in a committee would have a clear understanding of what skill set is needed and what role they are expected to play." Sharon invests a significant amount of time socializing committee objectives with prospective committee members to ensure that she has the right committee composition. Whenever possible she will visit with potential committee members to gauge their interest in the committee's work, identify areas where they can serve as thought leaders or manage committee tasks, and begin the process of creating a personal connection that is vital to building a cohesive committee environment. It is incumbent on the chair to object to a committee appointment if these prerequisites are not met.

Establishing clear objectives is the foundational step in identifying the right individuals to serve on a committee. Identifying specific questions that must be addressed by the committee will help the committee organizer identify which individuals are required to staff the committee and simultaneously define their respective roles. Break down the committee's charge into specific questions to tease out the various issues that need attention and corresponding knowledge, skills, and abilities needed to answer the charge. Figure 4.1 provides a graphical representation of this process based on a committee I was recently appointed to cochair.

Engaging in a systematic and thoughtful process can mitigate some of the headaches associated with poorly conceptualized committees. Ultimately, we need to identify the essential individuals who are necessary to complete the committee's work. Task interdependence refers to the degree of mutual dependency among members to complete a given task (Wageman & Baker, 1997). Understanding interdependencies within the committee (coupled with strong procedures and clear responsibilities) is critical to establishing conditions that promote efficacy, performance, and individual satisfaction (LePine et al., 2008). It is important to not only determine which expertise is necessary but also consider where expertise is recruited. For example, academic issues should be addressed by committees with a faculty majority. As one faculty member pointed out, "Far better for a committee of faculty members to be deciding what's good and what's bad [for the faculty] than people who are up in the administration." Similarly, administrative issues may need a committee that is staffed predominantly by administrators. Balancing administration and faculty interests and representation in committees is a fine and sensitive line that can be delineated only with experience and understanding of institutional cultural norms.

The work conditions and expectations of adjunct and nontenure-track faculty have moved to the center of conversations around the future of higher education. In many institutions, nontenure-track faculty constitute over 60% of academic positions (Kezar & Sam, 2010). Given the substantial role and mass of nontenure-track faculty in IHE, it stands to reason that this population should have opportunities to participate in institutional governance and committees (American Association of University Professors, 2013; Baldwin & Chronister, 2001; W. Jones et al., 2017). Depending on the committee's charge, it may be necessary to appoint one or more nontenure-track faculty to the committee. I contend that there are likely very few if any institutional or departmental academic decisions that do not affect 60% of the academic workforce; therefore, we should assume that nontenure-track representation is needed on nearly every academic committee and should be strongly considered for all administrative committees. This practice will demand resolution of questions regarding contingent faculty work schedules (Hoeller, 2014), institutional support (Fulton, 2000),

Figure 4.1. Hypothetical committee composition process.

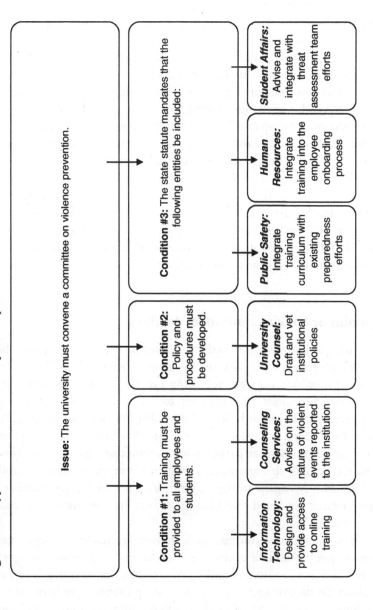

Issue: The university must convene a committee on violence prevention.

Condition #1: Training must be provided to all employees and students.

Condition #2: Policy and procedures must be developed.

Condition #3: The state statute mandates that the following entities be included:

Information Technology: Design and provide access to online training

Counseling Services: Advise on the nature of violent events reported to the institution

University Counsel: Draft and vet institutional policies

Public Safety: Integrate training curriculum with existing preparedness efforts

Human Resources: Integrate training into the employee onboarding process

Student Affairs: Advise and integrate with threat assessment team efforts

job security (Monnier, 2017), and service expectations (J. Morrison, 2008), which will—you guessed it—necessitate a committee!

We often assume that the required knowledge, expertise, and perspectives are commensurate with the positions on the committee; however, this is not always the case. It may be necessary to bring in additional faculty, staff, subject matter experts, or consultants to help push the committee to negotiate challenging issues. Outsiders can provide objective and alternative perspectives to advance issues that are ensnared or obfuscated by conflict, interpersonal dynamics, and organizational politics. To this point, research shows that having a guest in attendance at group meetings reduces in-group conflict and yields more time spent on tasks (Arrow & McGrath, 1993). Training programs are another external resource that serve as team-building experiences, help establish expectations within committees, orient members to an issue, and build a common foundation of knowledge for the committee's work. Webinars, online training, reports, books, articles, news feeds, discussion boards, communities of practice, peer reviews, and auditors are just a few examples of resources that can be integrated into committee work to provide a robust committee learning and decision-making experience.

Appoint or Solicit Committee Members

Now that we know what expertise and roles are required to support the committee's objectives and goals, we must find individuals willing to staff the committee, which begs the following question: Do we appoint or solicit committee members? Appointment to a committee is often precipitated by committee charter or bylaws of the college or department. Appointment leaves little room for negotiating one's involvement. Whether the member agrees or not, committee participation becomes an expectation of their position. It is possible that appointed members resent this involuntary obligation and reluctantly engage in the committee's work. A faculty member whom I interviewed confessed that many positions on committees are "staffed by arm-twisting."

Nomination committees are common in academic departments. A nomination committee is composed of faculty responsible for appointing their colleagues to various standing committees that are integral to the operation of the department (e.g., promotion and tenure, graduate admissions, teaching evaluation, syllabus review, and personnel planning). Although this process is seemingly efficient, it does have some drawbacks. As one faculty member stated, "It's very rare that you get a high-functioning committee via this process. At best, you'll get a good chair, one other person who is moti-vated, and everybody else is checked out." Appointments can also lead to challenges in productivity. A faculty member I interviewed was appointed to a committee and remembers the "annual report that one does (which is an absolutely painful process) that gets written under duress every year" as one of the more laborious responsibilities of serving on a committee they had no real interest in supporting. This statement accurately captures the reluctance that can result from an undesired committee appointment. I am not condemning nomination committees; I am merely suggesting that this process introduces challenges to committee composition that should be con-sidered. In some cases, members appointed by the nomination committee elect one of their peers to serve as the committee chair. This strategy gives the committee members a modicum of agency and a little more flexibility in how a nominated committee is structured. Perhaps appointed chairs can be granted autonomy to transfer members between committees or recommend colleagues who might be suited to the committee's task. Nomination com-mittees might also consider (and many already do) accepting recommenda-tions or applications from faculty to serve on specific committees that align with their respective professional interests and goals. These recommenda-tions, which are observed by some institutions, can promote higher levels of service and engagement among faculty committees.

Conversely, soliciting members provides opportunities to pick and choose members with the capacity for committee work, who are interested in the committee's task, and presumably who want to be part of the com-mittee. When Kevin was working on a PhD formation committee, he found that the group was extremely productive "because we picked [members]. . . . Here are the people we want, and we talked to everybody. Is this a good fit for you? Yes, it's a good fit. Yes, I am passionate about this. Yes, I am willing to work, yep absolutely." In this case Kevin was able to identify and recruit committee members who had sufficient time and were vested in the commit-tee's outcome. Houston offered a more simple and candid litmus test of who constitutes a good committee member: "Who can be helpful in a situation like this?" and "You're not a jerk, right?"

Last, although rare, the ranks of the committee may be filled by vol-unteers who request to be on the committee. An open call to administra-tors and faculty to staff a committee is not likely to yield the desired result; instead, volunteers should be recruited from specific disciplines associated with the committee's task. For example, a committee that is directed to develop and implement international travel policies and procedures might solicit faculty who have extensive travel experience to serve on the commit-tee and administrators responsible for institutional travel processes. When a committee is expected to integrate diverse perspectives to produce a resource for the entire campus community that will require significant work, a cadre of volunteer committee members might be most appropriate. For example, committees convened to address a campus sustainability initiative, ethics in teaching, or student free speech or to advise a university service (e.g., parking or dining services) may be best staffed by soliciting volunteers who are self-motivated and have professional or personal interest in the committee's work. Volunteers tend to have greater enthusiasm for the committee's work given their intrinsic motivation. Steve, a professor of English at Liberty University, has a personal and professional interest in literature (naturally); as a result, he regularly volunteers to serve on the institution's library committee responsible for book requisitions. With the right intentions, volunteers can be the most valuable members in terms of contribution and engagement; however, some individuals elbow their way on to committees to advance their own goals and attempt to influence others. Voluntary involvement does not ensure the right composition, nor does it insure the group against opportunists looking to bolster their résumé, promote their own agenda, or obstruct the committee's progress.

Membership is critical to the success of the committee because despite our best efforts to structure committees to be successful, in spite of organizational edicts and committee charters and to the frustration of management, the human factor plays a more dominant role in determining the success of a committee than all our administrative efforts combined (Birnbaum, 2000). It is imperative that we think about not only who *must* be on the committee but also who *should* be on the committee and choreograph membership based on the desired skills and dispositions that promote a cohesive and productive committee climate. Committee composition is not only a critical factor in predicting levels of engagement within the committee but also a measure of the committee's legitimacy and importance of the committee's work (Hartley & Wilhelm Shah, 2006). Committees staffed by senior, well-respected, or notoriously busy individuals suggest that the issue is worth the time and attention of people in high demand. It may be necessary to find one or two well-respected colleagues to chair or serve on the committee to drive interest and participation.

Gender, Racial, and Ethnic Diversity

Assimilating diverse perspectives, objectives, and needs is precisely why committees are formed. To the extent possible, committee membership should reflect institutional demographics: student body, faculty, and staff.

Constructing a committee that represents the institution's demography is complicated by the fact that the gender, racial, ethnic, and socioeconomic profiles of these groups (students, faculty, and staff) are often drastically different. The theory of representative democracy posits that leadership groups reflecting the demography of their constituency will make decisions that conform to the needs and aspirations of the communities they serve (Meier & Nigro, 1976). When assembling a committee, consider the functions and populations that the committee's work will affect and appoint members who can speak to the concerns and desires of those communities.

In chapter 3 we discussed the potential influence of organizational culture on the participation of women and underrepresented faculty and administrators in committees. In addition to the moral incentive to rectify injustices in IHE, there is also a convincing business case for creating diverse committees. The potential benefits of effective diversified work groups have been documented for some time and include, but are not limited to, the following:

- Generation of creative and innovative solutions (Joshi & Roh, 2009)
- Greater organizational flexibility and adaptability (Slater et al., 2008)
- Increased individual and group learning (Edmondson et al., 2007)
- Reduced intergroup conflict and stronger interpersonal relationships (Davidson & James, 2006)
- Increased employee engagement (Stevens et al., 2008)
- Information sharing and assimilation (Dahlin et al., 2005)
- Higher job satisfaction (Jehn et al., 1999; Van Der Vegt & Bunderson, 2005)
- Higher levels of task commitment (Jehn et al., 1999; Van Der Vegt & Bunderson, 2005)

My original research on committees confirmed that high levels of job satisfaction and organizational commitment are associated with expressions of organizational citizenship behaviors in committees (i.e., active engagement, compromise, and helping behaviors) (Farris, 2016). Even if we set aside the positive impact of diversity on participation, the remaining benefits justify diverse committees. Adversarial ideas not only challenge the status quo but also provide fertile ground for constructive conflict and expose committee members to a diverse pool of views that can contribute individual growth through learning and awareness. The process of assimilating and refining diverse perspectives can also lead to novel solutions that might not result from a committee with homogeneous membership. Although there are many benefits to be realized by forming diverse groups, research shows that diversity, if not managed thoughtfully, can detract from group performance (Jehn et al., 1999; Riordan & Shore, 1997; T. Simons et al., 1999). Recommendations on how to effectively manage diverse and inclusive committees are provided in chapter 6.

One of the challenges to creating a diverse committee is the representation of female and minority faculty and administrators in higher education management and leadership positions. Table 4.1, adapted from *The Almanac of Higher Education* (2019) and the *Digest of Education Statistics 2018* (T. Snyder, 2018), provides a summary of university faculty and administrators in academia by gender and race.

Although women constitute less than 50% of faculty positions, female faculty tend to perform more service work than their male counterparts (O'Meara et al., 2017). A study published in 2017 (Guarino & Borden, 2017) found that female faculty dedicate 30 more minutes of service activity per week than men, which equates to nearly one and a half additional service activities per year. Underrepresented faculty also report contributing more service time to organizational functions and governance than their White colleagues (Gregory, 2001; Griffin, 2012; Griffin et al., 2014; Nelms, 2002). Consideration of committee and service obligations should be factored in all committee appointee decisions; however, special attention should be given to the inequitable pressure on women and underrepresented faculty and administrators to serve the organization and adapt expectations accordingly. Given the scarcity of minority faculty and administrators in higher education (especially female minorities), it is likely that the same people are being asked to serve on multiple committees to provide representative diversity. The challenge of finding diverse representation becomes more difficult when convening strategic committees involving the highest levels of the organization, as the proportion of diverse faculty decreases in upper strata of faculty and administrative roles (Stanley, 2006b). Asking the same already overworked marginalized faculty and administrators to serve on multiple committees effectively transfers the burden of creating a diverse culture to those who are already disadvantaged by the system, thereby sustaining the cycle of inequity and adversity that needs repair (Harley, 2008).

Creation of diverse committees provides opportunities for members to explore their capacity for group work, organizational citizenship behaviors, and nontraditional gender roles that can contribute positively to the group's efforts. Performative theory suggests that individuals can be confined to prescribed roles through social interactions that reinforce explicit and implicit social organizational norms (Butler, 1988). Resistance to hegemonic Western organizational traditions and social discourse and a commitment to exploring new gender, racial, and ethnic identities can

TABLE 4.1

Faculty and Administrators in Higher Education by Gender and Race

Sector	Native American/Alaskan (%)	Asian (%)	Black or African American (%)	Hispanic or Latino (%)	Hawaiian or Pacific Islander (%)	White (%)	Two or more races (%)
Four-year public	0.6	4.0	10.9	6.2	0.2	77.2	1.0
Four-year private nonprofit	0.3	4.5	9.1	5.7	0.2	79.1	1.1
Four-year private for-profit	0.3	4.4	10.4	8.5	0.4	74.3	1.7
All institutions	0.5	4.0	10.6	6.3	0.2	77.4	1.1

Note. Adapted from *The Almanac of Higher Education 2019–20,* 2019, The Chronicle of Higher Education; and *Digest of Education Statistics 2018,* by T. Snyder, 2018, National Center for Educational Statistics; all institutions includes 4-year private, public, for-profit, nonprofit, and community colleges.

expand gender norms and ways of working in organizations and shift organizations to a more gender-neutral and inclusive climate where men, women, and underrepresented faculty and administrators can thrive. An example of how gender diversity and performative theory can positively affect committees is best illustrated by a personal experience. In most committees at my institution, I am often a minority among my female colleagues. We enjoy a vibrant and inclusive climate where ideas seem more profuse and discourse more considerate (but candid) than in predominantly male committees. I discovered that I adopt a different demeanor in diverse committees; I talk less and listen more, I am less domineering, I tend to be less defensive, I am more deliberate about the words I choose to use, I feel inclined to be more transparent, I am more considerate of others' perspectives, and I tend to be more cheerful and carefree. In diverse committees, I exhibit feminine and gender-neutral roles (see the section Gender, Race, and Ethnicity in chapter 7) that I recognize as more conducive to committee functions than the forceful recommendations and stolid positions I occasionally offer in committees.

I discovered my preference for gender-diverse committees is based on Helgesen's (1995) research on female groups and leadership that evolved into her "web of inclusion" theory. Helgesen observed that whereas most males tend to adopt and promote hierarchical structures in groups (which implies authority), females tend to orchestrate flat organizations in which leadership is embedded at the center of the group (which implies equality), there are multiple informal and formal connections among group members, communication is encouraged to flow freely, decisions are made collectively, and morale tends to be very high because members feel unified, accountable, and valued. Helgesen discovered that this feminine model enhances participation in organizational governance, is a pathway to unique solutions for complex problems, promotes learning (individual and organizational), creates an inclusive climate, empowers individuals, and facilitates communication. It is easy to see how a committee that adopts this structure and culture can yield many of the benefits of diversity listed earlier. We should be eager to join a committee that possesses these characteristics, and I argue that the notion of a committee originated with these ideals in mind. When composing a committee, consider stacking the committee with female faculty and individuals who embrace diversity to create an inclusive committee climate and a more equitable workplace.

Appointment of underrepresented and female faculty and administrators to committees does not resolve issues of discrimination and bias. Many of the faculty and administrators I have spoken to remarked that they are often the only person of color or female on committees; as such, they feel that there is an implied expectation that they will represent all issues pertaining to the needs, perspectives, and desires of underrepresented or female faculty and administrators, which is simply not possible or fair. The low proportion of underrepresented faculty and administrators on committees places them in a position of "high visibility and exaggeration of differences between themselves and the dominant group members" (Niemann, 2016, p. 453). In the tenuous position of being the only one or one of a few members who look different from the majority, attention focuses away from the minority member's expertise, experience, and aptitude to superficial assessments of the individual's perceived differentness (i.e., tokenism). This categorization by the dominant group as different produces feelings of isolation, the sense that one must work hard to prove oneself, polarization of roles and ideas based on perceived differences, and pressure to conform to stereotypes shared by the dominant group (Kanter, 1977). Tokenism erodes the committee's perceptions of underrepresented faculty and administrator credibility, leadership, and contributions for no other reason than underrepresented faculty constitute a smaller proportion of faculty and administrative positions. One way to combat tokenism is to appoint equal proportions of women, underrepresented faculty and staff, and men on committees to provide parity and a sense of equity. If the desired number of underrepresented faculty or administrators cannot be solicited to serve on a committee, consider limiting the participation of the dominant group to create a more equitable committee composition.

Individual Roles

In addition to the expertise and perspective each committee contributes to the group, each member also serves a functional group role. A group of researchers conducted a meta-analysis of research on team roles and found 13 unique classifications and corresponding characteristics (Driskell et al., 2017). This research includes popular group models put forth by Bales (1950) and Belbin (1993, 2010), who pioneered identity roles in effective work groups and teams. A synopsis of Driskell et al.'s (2017) roles and respective contributions is outlined in Table 4.2. I have taken the liberty of changing the role titles assigned by Driskell et al. and modifying the definitions slightly to include findings from my research and definitions provided by Bales and Belbin.

It is important to note that individual roles are not static; instead, roles are dynamic. Committee members can assume one or more discrete roles within a committee. The roles that committee members fill are influenced by group composition, committee task, work conditions, attitudes, and interpersonal dynamics. Recall your most recent committee experience;

TABLE 4.2
Group Roles and Functions

Positive Role	Contribution
Leader	Coordinates, facilitates, directs, and controls committee activities and meetings
Motivator	Provides support for the leader and team, encourages others, and exercises informal leadership to keep the committee moving
Social butterfly	Facilitates social interactions by having a good attitude, strives to build community, supports group efforts, and has an endearing disposition
Coordinator	Serves as the informal leader by supporting group functions, including work tasks and communication, and helps with committee coordination
Team member	Exercises followership, actively participates in committee meetings, takes on committee work, and works well with others
Administrator	Conducts research, takes notes, maintains records, assists with meeting preparation, and contributes to committee work processes
Evaluator	Objectively assesses the group's work, provides a counterperspective when necessary, and critiques the committee's work for quality and applicability
Problem solver	Provides or solicits information, assimilates information, analyzes ideas, and critically evaluates options in a manner that respects the committee's input
Finisher	Maintains attention to deadlines and deliverables and works to complete tasks in accordance with established procedures and agreed-on objectives
Negative Role	Contribution
Dominator	Attempts to usurp the committee's efforts for their own purposes and can be aggressive, offensive, or inconsiderate in their attempts to take control
Obstructionist	Objects to the direction of the committee, is resistant to change, and is generally disagreeable
Attention hog	Uses meetings to draw attention to themselves or their agenda or otherwise dominates the conversation without meaning, full input, or productivity
Malcontent	Does not contribute to the committee, complains, and detracts from the committee's efforts to build a cohesive environment

Note. Adapted from "Team Roles: A Review and Integration," by T. Driskell, J. Driskell, C. Burke, and E. Salas, 2017, *Small Group Research, 48*(4), 482–511.

can you identify behaviors that were especially beneficial to the committee and the corresponding functions outlined previously? Which role do you typically assume in a committee? To the extent possible, committee membership should be choreographed to ensure diversity of skills and dispositions to maximize synergistic and complementary work styles. It may be advantageous to discuss the various roles individuals will occupy early in the life cycle of the committee. Determining which members will serve in advisory, research, writing, and liaison roles is a critical step in helping the committee form a team identity.

Last, every group needs a deviant member to provide a counterperspective and keep the committee from falling into decision-making traps. Some chairs may be inclined to appoint individuals whom they know and like, but a circle of friends may be more interested in maintaining harmony than serious debate, and the results could be mediocre. Kim is intentional about appointing a devil's advocate. She does so because she doesn't "want to head into groupthink." She appoints someone on whom she knows she can rely to raise the counterperspective at opportune times. She also noted, with laughter, that individuals who fulfill this role rarely need encouragement to speak up! Deviant members can help avoid pitfalls like groupthink, complacency, and unrealistic ambitions by constructively challenging the committee's assumptions and recommendations. A distinction must be made between a deviant member, whose duty is to fill a beneficial role, and a member with deviant behaviors that impede committee progress. An adroit committee chair will protect the deviant member and cast their comments in ways that illustrate the positive contribution of their counterperspective. Without this protection, the deviant member is likely to be ignored by the committee, or their colleagues may grow to resent their participation. In the absence of a counterperspective, the committee chair may need to solicit dissenting opinions to test the mettle of the committee's recommendations.

The ideal committee will function like a well-practiced team: Each person knows their position and responsibilities, each person recognizes one another's strengths and weaknesses, and the group has experience working together. Assembling a committee should feel a little like picking teams; you should know which skills, expertise, and roles each member brings to the team and how they will benefit the committee. Simply having the right mixture of expertise is not a guarantee for success. A group of researchers devised a speed dating process for strangers expected to work together on teams and found that groups based on strong interpersonal relationships were more effective and productive than teams designed around individual professional attributes (Curseu et al., 2010). Depending on the committee, you may need to decide between the most knowledgeable committee candidate and the

most personable one—it makes a difference. When selecting committee can-
didates, it is important to resist appointing your friends and others who look
and think like you; diversity of thought, experience, and perspective is necessary to produce optimal committee outcomes (Hofstede, 2001).

Research also shows that group performance is positively correlated to
average competency levels (Bell, 2007; Mathieu et al., 2015). Incidentally,
research has also demonstrated that the more educated a person is or special-
ized a person's technical knowledge is, the more difficult it is for them to
collaborate (Gratton & Erickson, 2007). It's difficult to acknowledge that
educational achievement is an impediment to collaboration in colleges and
universities! This is not to suggest that personality outweighs the benefits
of competence, but a balance must be struck between these two attributes.
In short, members should be vetted to ensure that they have the requisite
experience and knowledge, as well as a personality and disposition that is
conducive to group work. The goal is to convene a committee of smart (but
not too smart), personable individuals with the requisite expertise.

Group Stratification

In university committees, position stratification appears to have a negative
influence on participation and engagement. The administrators and faculty
whom I interviewed suggested that interaction and debate in committees
tends to decrease when there is disparity among committee member titles,
seniority, and power (real or perceived). Adam hypothesized, and others
agreed, that "the degree to which the separation in the organization is present [in a committee] probably is inversely proportional to good collaborative effort. The greater the disparity among the people in the room, the less
collaboration there is." My conversations indicate that junior members of
the committee who perceive a committee as highly stratified are less likely
to engage in committees unless their motives are instrumental; that is, they
desire to make a positive impression on their colleagues for personal gain.
Another administrator claimed that in higher education, "we are all in a little
bit of a caste system" that determines whose opinions are valued and whose
input can be discounted based on position or title.

Hierarchy is often conveyed implicitly rather than explicitly. One
administrator who perceives their institution as very hierarchical explained
the perceptible shift in their thinking when they discover that a senior member of the administration is present: "Suddenly there's this like shift in my
mind of, oh, I need to be more respectful of this cat sitting over here because
he's the associate assistant of whatever." Sarah affirmed this sentiment. She

regulates her engagement based on the individuals in the room and the power they are perceived to possess. Her engagement depends on who is present, what their lines of authority are, and their relative authority over other committee members. She suggested that committee members reserve participation in committees that have more senior members for "fear of negative fallout" because of their affiliations or social connections. In other cases, the expectation of deference for positional authority is explicit. As one faculty member recalled, they bristled when a colleague pulled rank, which set the stage for disagreement and resentment, and thought, "Really? I'm supposed to now bow down to you just because you're a full professor?" Senior administrators and faculty tend to maintain the dominant voice and create unconstructive tension among junior members of the committee. The effect of hierarchy becomes most apparent when a senior and junior member of the same department or unit are present in the same committee. Junior faculty and administrators tend to defer to their seniors out of respect and to avoid a public disagreement. Furthermore, perceived levels of engagement by senior members of the committee broadcast the relative importance of the committee's work to other members. One administrator recalled how a dean's participation influenced the perceived value of the committee's work: "He's sort of a negative guy, and he didn't really do a whole lot. I mean he came to a couple of meetings and he said some things, but he didn't really do anything outside of the group." Subsequently, interest and engagement in the committee waned, and the resultant product was mediocre.

Alternatively, committees that are composed of members with similar titles and/or comparable authority and responsibilities tend to foster engagement and camaraderie. Nick observed that committees "have more heated debates when [committees] become more homogenized," and because "they are all part of the same team, they feel like they have equal footing." When individuals feel free to speak their mind without fear of retribution or ridicule, group performance and learning behaviors increase significantly (Edmondson, 1999). To encourage individuals to be fully engaged and contributing committee members, a psychologically safe environment should be fostered. Creating a sense of equity among committee members begins with attention to the positional power, expertise, and experience of committee members. Convening a group of positionally equivalent members will not necessarily create a psychologically safe environment, but it certainly encourages a sense of parity and self-confidence.

Parity of position, authority, and expertise among committee members establishes a sense of equality that empowers individuals to act on behalf of their department or self-concordant goals because they feel a sense of equity among other members of the committee. The ideal committee, according to those whom I spoke with, consists of members from the same strata of the organization. Table 4.3 illustrates the idea of the potential challenges of composing a committee with members from different layers within the organization.

Unfortunately, the positions listed in Table 4.1 can be replaced with gender, race, age, ethnicity, and any number of other individual characteristics with the same dislocating results. Research finds that people tend to associate and develop faster bonds with those whom they perceive to be most like themselves (Riordan & Shore, 1997; T. Simons et al., 1999; Tajfel & Turner, 1986). As committee leaders and members, we have opportunities to interact with individuals with whom we might not routinely engage professionally or personally. As outlined in chapter 1, committees are a social learning system, and to the extent that we can, we should leverage committee meetings to break down discriminatory barriers that members of our communities continue to experience. I personally have come to know more about the hardships faced by my colleagues through the network I have formed from my committee work to include learning about instances of racism, discrimination, gender bias, and other socially and organizationally destructive incidents, which has endeared me to my colleagues and encouraged me to take a more active role in combating inequality in all its forms. Committees can serve as a forum to build bridges and promote cultural ideals of inclusivity, diversity, and respect.

TABLE 4.3
Position Stratification Within Committees

Position	Department or Office A	Department or Office B	Department or Office C	Department or Office D
Dean or vice president				
Chair or executive director	✕			
Full professor or director				
Associate professor or assistant director				✕
Adjunct faculty or manager				

Committee Member Typologies

Even if we engineer the right size committee with members who possess the relevant expertise and complementary roles (both formal and informal), our success is not guaranteed. My conversations with administrators and faculty revealed that there are three types of committee members: engaged, associated, and indifferent. On a car parked outside one of George Mason University's research centers, I noticed a bumper sticker that proclaimed "Get involved! The world is run by people that show up." Nowhere is this truer than in IHE and within committees specifically, but we need more from committee members than just showing up. I am hesitant to imply that indifferent members are totally disengaged because not all are, but some members express a general apathy toward the committee's work and goals. Table 4.4 provides an outline of committee member typologies and some of the common characteristics of each.

If we examine a full committee, we are likely to find an assortment of members who are engaged, associated, or indifferent. Table 4.4 should not be misconstrued to imply that an individual aligns perfectly with one typology; instead, a person's performance in committees is driven by different factors that appear across all three typologies listed. A person's performance may change meeting to meeting or fall somewhere in between engaged and associated or associated and indifferent. A hypothetical portrait of a typical committee using the typologies outlined might look something like Figure 4.2. The large circles represent the committee, and the smaller circles illustrate the degree to which an individual's efforts and motivations align with the committee given the various antecedents and moderators of committee work discussed in subsequent chapters.

Figure 4.2. Typical committee typology configuration.

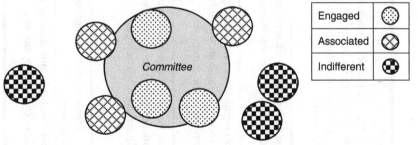

TABLE 4.4

Committee Member Typology

Engaged	Associated	Indifferent
• The engaged member demonstrates positive committee behaviors (active engagement, compromise, and helping behaviors).	• The associated member's sporadic engagement does not detract from the discussion, but this member does not actively engage unless called on or the issue affects other work expectations.	• The indifferent member is not engaged in the committee's work, is distracted or absent, and rarely completes tasks or comes prepared to meetings.
• The committee's work is of high professional or personal interest.	• The committee's work has tangential ramifications on professional or personal interests.	• The committee's work is not relevant to personal or professional goals.
• This member maintains strong working or social relationships with other members of the committee.	• This member is familiar with other members of the committee.	• This member does not have a connection to other members of the committee or has prior negative experiences.
• This member accommodates committee work and prioritizes committee deliverables when necessary.	• This member has some capacity for additional committee work and occasionally delivers what is needed on time.	• This member is overworked or has a high workload or is apathetic to the demands of the committee. They rarely or never engage in committee work.
• This member possesses high job satisfaction.	• This member is content with work conditions.	• This member possesses low job satisfaction.
• This member is motivated by prosocial, task, or challenging motives.	• This member is motivated by compliance with organizational norms and expectations.	• This member might be motivated for instrumental reasons or potential for recognition.

This graphic is consistent with the common observation that only a few people execute the work of the committee while the remaining members tend to exhibit normative committee behaviors. The next time you are on a committee, consider sorting the committee's membership into these three categories and include yourself. This exercise will reveal who is reliable, who needs encouragement, who needs motivation, who should be replaced, and who should be engaged using alternative methods (e.g., briefings, updates, or asked to make a single discrete contribution). You might also find that you are indifferent to the committee's work. In that case, consider replacing yourself or discussing your circumstances with the committee chair to determine how you or your department can be best represented.

Before we transition to a discussion on committee logistics and meeting management, consider the following questions:

- How are committees formed at your institution, and what is the average size?
- Does composition or size influence committee performance, and if so how?
- What types of committees are you appointed to, and how is your appointment justified?
- What committee role or roles (see Table 4.2) do you typically assume, and why?
- Do you tend to find the same individuals serving on committees, and if so why?
- Are power dynamics in committees evident, and how does this influence the committee's work?

5

COMMITTEE PLANNING
AND MANAGEMENT

This chapter explores how to manage committees for success. Steiner (1972) developed a theory for productivity loss that is still widely referenced today. He argued that individual productivity declines as a result of coordination challenges and motivation that results from complications inherent in group work. Individual effort in teams is primarily moderated by the additional effort required to work with others (Shiflett, 1979). In other words, working in groups creates resistance against individual effort. Imagine a wire strung between a series of lights (our committee members); if the conduit for workflow has a high resistance (think Ohm's Law), greater energy is required to force the work through the conduit. If we create a process that supports conducting effort, the work will pass with less resistance through the committee. Establishing clear goals and objectives, defining rules of engagement, determining how work will be shared, tracking action items, and maintaining attention to deliverables contribute to the efficacy of group work (Hackman, 1987).

Goals and Objectives

The most common complaint regarding committees is poor conceptualization of the problem or ambiguous committee objectives. One faculty member I spoke with recalled an experience where the chair opened the initial meeting with "All right, what should we do?" and the immediate reaction from the committee was "We're in for it!" Sarah expressed the desire for clear guidance this way: "The most effective committee would be one that everybody understands why they are there and what their job is." Brent recalled committees during which he "just kind of sat there" because he did not understand what the committee was trying to accomplish, and as result

78

he was "less engaged in that particular group." Adam has had similar experiences: "There have been some committees where I am like, 'Why am I in the room on this?'" Sarah recalled a committee that was established to talk about "windows" (presumably the computer application), but the point she wanted to convey is "the biggest problem in meetings is that we have topics, but we have no idea what we are really trying to achieve." Ambiguous committee objectives, unclear expectations, and confusion regarding individual roles obfuscate individual and group effort (Dill & Helm, 1988).

Clarity of purpose and objectives is essential to building effective committees. Whether it is a charge from the organization or established by the committee chair, committees must "understand the mission of the committee and have a vision for what needs to get done" (Nick) to be successful. McGrath (1984) outlined four primary functions of work groups: create a solution, choose an option, negotiate a course, and execute a responsibility. If committee members are unclear about their responsibilities as they relate to any one or more of these four functions, there is potential for frustration and dysfunction. When committee members are confused about the committee's goals and their individual responsibilities, members tend to contribute minimal effort or disengage.

Whenever possible, committee members should be granted an opportunity to participate in establishing the committee's goals. Individuals and groups tend to perform better when they are responsible for setting their own goals (Kerr & Tindale, 2004; Mathieu & Rapp, 2009). During the first meeting of the committee and periodically thereafter, the chair should lead the committee through an exercise to solicit feedback on the committee's work and objectives. "When group and individual goals conflict, dysfunctions can result" (Guzzo & Dickson, 1996, p. 315). Committees that degenerate into unproductive debates due to conflicting and unbending convictions about the direction of the institution or committee not only obstruct immediate group objectives but also can influence intragroup efforts that negatively affect the larger organization (Kramer, 1991).

Perhaps overused, but still effective, is the concept of SMART goals; that is, *specific, measurable, achievable, relevant*, and *time-bound* goals (Doran, 1981). If that's not challenging enough, consider creating even SMARTER goals by adding *evaluate* and *review* to the list of aspirational committee performance criteria. By way of example, a committee assigned to develop a violence prevention program may develop the following sample goal:

> In 12 months, develop a policy, procedures, resources, and a training program for faculty, staff, and students to reduce student-to-student acts of violence (i.e., stalking, abuse, assault, harassment, intimidation), create a

method for tracking outreach and training efforts, reduce acts of violence reported to university police and student affairs by 20% in 24 months and 10% every year for 3 years thereafter, and provide a written report to the university committee on student affairs in 12 months and annually thereafter that includes actions taken, proposed actions, outcomes, resources required, and recommendations for improvement.

In some cases, committee work is constrained by existing institutional policies, regulations, programs, or available resources. In other instances, the committee's work is expected to mirror best practices at other IHE or business strategies found in other industries. Examples of external factors that might dictate committee objectives and goals are accrediting agency standards, human resources and payroll policies, institutional plans or manuals, FERPA restrictions, federal regulations, employment contracts, vendor agreements, and codes of conduct. Whenever possible, committee leadership should make these resources available to the committee as reference documents to erect boundaries around the committee's efforts and provide justification for the committee's work. Over time, committees may stray away from their assigned or mutually agreed-on goals and objectives. Kim uses a simple tactic to keep the committee focused: She puts the committee's values and charge at the top of each meeting agenda to remind committee members of the goal and mutually agreed-on rules of engagement that govern committee discussions.

Committee Charters

A committee charter can alleviate some of the confusion about committee purpose, scope, and composition. Charters provide a solid anchor point for committee leadership to guide the committee's efforts and are backstops to prevent groups from spiraling off on tangential issues. Furthermore, charters serve as formal delegations of authority that are explicitly supported by the institution by way of presidential appointment or overarching governing body tasked with managing standing committees. A cursory review of 10 committee charters[1] revealed the following common elements:

- *Introduction* provides context for the committee's work and situates the committee's function in the larger organization. This section may also be referred to as the *preamble*.
- *Charge* outlines the committee's responsibilities, typically in detail, to include specific objectives, deliverables, and responsibilities. In many

charters, *purpose*, *mission*, and *mandate* are commonly used in place of *charge*.

- *Composition* dictates the individuals, typically by position, who serve on the committee. This section may also stipulate which members are voting or nonvoting members, perpetual or term (to include length of term), and appointed or recruited. Committee leadership is documented here if not stipulated in a separate section of the charter. Provisions for adding additional members or changing committee membership are often described in this section.
- *Responsibilities* lists institutional procedures, policies, statutes, and applicable regulations (federal, state, or local) that must be observed when executing the committee's charge.
- *Meeting management* describes the procedures that are used to manage committee meetings, to include determining meeting frequency, allowing alternates, and establishing quorum. This section may also include procedures for delegating authority. In rare cases, this section outlines provisions for removing members who are excessively absent.
- *Reports, records, and minutes* prescribes the methods that must be used to document committee meetings, to include how committee meeting minutes are stored, distributed, or made available to noncommittee members.

When deemed necessary, charters will dictate how disputes are resolved and by whom. While charters are invaluable in helping steer the committee's work, mission creep does occur, and occasional modifications to the charter are necessary to allow the committee to adapt to emerging issues. Committees that lack a charter are apt to find problems that distract the group from their original purpose. Committees that drift off course are likely to convene in perpetuity, as they take up various issues brought to committee by members in the interest of filling the agenda or leveraging the committee as an advisory board. As Kevin pointed out,

> Standing committees are there because somebody at some point decided that the committee needs to exist for all time to deal with a variety of things. What you see is a committee that basically comes up with work to justify the nature of the committee.

Set Expectations

Administrators and faculty feel that it is critical to establish expectations regarding how committees will conduct business and set expectations

regarding committee participation. Setting ground rules early in the committee's life cycle has a positive and lasting impact on committee climate. Rules
of engagement further define committee members' roles by establishing a
clear concept of the work that will be required. Brent stressed the importance
of first impressions on the group's productivity and efficacy: "Setting up that
dynamic . . . has a lot to do with how the committee works." He claimed
that if committee members are discouraged, frustrated, or confused from the
start, the group may never achieve the cohesive and productive environment
necessary to accomplish the committee's goals. The expectation that work
will be assigned to committee members and completed by an agreed-on time
is essential. As Sharon stated, "I don't like when I come back to committees
where people are like, 'Oh yeah, I did say I was gonna do that' and then we're
all waiting on something or behind." Missed deadlines compound quickly
and can lead to frustration.

Drawing on extant resources for meeting management (see *Harvard
Business Review*, 2016a; Streibel, 2007) and conversations with administrators and faculty, I found the following expectations to be helpful to establish
at the outset, and they should periodically be reinforced:

- *Meeting schedule:* Review meeting schedules and attempt to schedule
  committee meetings as far in advance as possible. Schedules are subject to change as members take on additional work or conflicts arise.
- *Attendance:* Stress that members are expected to attend (in person or
  virtually if necessary) or send their comments or deliverables to the
  chair if they expect to be absent.
- *Agenda:* Emphasize committee meetings will stay on topic and agenda
  items must be proposed in advance or at the end of the committee
  meeting.
- *Preparation:* Encourage members to read committee materials in
  advance of committee meetings to maximize the use of meeting time.
- *Committee work:* Stipulate that all members should anticipate some
  work outside of the committee (provide an estimate if possible), and
  deadlines should be strictly observed. If deliverables or action items
  cannot be completed on time, committee members should notify the
  committee chair or committee manager.
- *Management:* Note that the chair or cochairs of the committee
  will intervene as necessary to mediate conversations and maintain
  momentum.
- *Decorum:* Ask members to refrain from using or monitoring cell
  phones, tablets, and other devices for the duration of the committee
  meeting unless they are being used for committee work. Urgent phone

calls should be taken outside of the meeting space. An interesting side note: Four researchers found that just having access to our cell phone, even if it's not being used, reduces our ability to be fully engaged and limits cognitive capacity (Ward et al., 2017).

- *Disagreement:* Stress that disagreement is anticipated, and members are encouraged to share their opinions no matter how contentious, but this should be done so respectfully.
- *Confidentiality:* Reaffirm that committee members are expected to use discretion when discussing committee work and refrain from discussing sensitive topics outside of the committee to avoid unnecessary external pressures.

Research has demonstrated that established or implicit processes are essential to team success (Hackman, 1987); should this not also hold true for committees? If so, why are we not more deliberate in how we manage committee meetings? One could argue that colleges and universities are resistant to adopting more businesslike functions and object to the rigorous rules of decorum and management that are associated with business meetings, but the consequences of not adopting proven meeting management techniques are regrettable. I believe we can employ more stringent rules of engagement in committees and still maintain the collegial and vibrant environment that reflects the innovative spirit of higher education. Committees can still produce novel solutions to unique problems using conventional meeting management techniques. After all the business world does it all the time. We have the good fortune of being able to cherry-pick which aspects of business acumen we want to integrate into our organizational strategies.

Committee Logistics

Perhaps you are familiar with the acronym TEAM (together everyone achieves more). J. Richard Hackman, a distinguished Harvard University professor who researched teams, revealed the fallacy of this mantra and instead said, "Research consistently shows that teams underperform, despite all the extra resources they have. That's because problems with coordination and motivation typically chip away at the benefits of collaboration" (Coutu, 2009, p. 98). Often, the frustration with committees stems from the lack of foresight, planning, and basic logistics such as scheduling meetings, providing read-ahead materials, taking minutes, and tracking action items.

It is important to draw a distinction between committee management and committee leadership. Bennis and Nanus (1985) differentiated leadership and management in this way: Leadership is doing the right thing; management is doing things right. Kevin conceptualized committee leadership as a process manager: "It's not about deciding the outcome of the committee; it's about making sure that the committee is actually being efficient and effective in regard to everybody's time." Typically, the committee expects the chair to assume the roles of both committee leader and committee manager (let's ignore the fact that most chairs end up doing most of the work as well). Practically, committees require two dedicated positions; one is dedicated to committee leadership, and a separate position is appointed to handle the administrative functions that are arguably as important to the committee's success as its leadership and member participation. With a sports team, the coach is responsible for the team's performance; meanwhile, the manager is responsible for getting the team where it needs to be with all the right equipment and resources. Ultimately it is the chair's responsibility to ensure that logistical issues are addressed or, as Steve put it, "The one who sets the committee up is the one who is heading it up."

Ideally the person appointed to the committee's administrative position—let's call them the committee manager—will be familiar with and apply basic project management strategies. There are four principal logistical needs that should be addressed by the committee manager to provide administrative assistance to the committee. The logistical issues that need attention are as follows:

1. Schedule committee meetings
2. Create and distribute meeting agendas and materials in advance of each meeting
3. Manage attendance
4. Maintain meeting minutes and action items

Scheduling

Administrators and faculty maintain busy schedules, which demands significant lead time for them to prepare for and find time to attend committee meetings. As one faculty member mentioned, just because they receive a meeting invitation doesn't mean that they are available to attend despite the implied expectation. Meetings should be scheduled as far in advance as possible; 2 weeks at a minimum. Many administrators and faculty require an even longer lead time. Ideally committee meetings will be scheduled on a routine basis (e.g., first and third Thursdays at 9:00 a.m.) throughout the year to allow organizers to reserve committee meeting times months in advance. Scheduling applications such as Microsoft Outlook allow quick and easy access to committee member calendars and the ability to confirm attendance or absences. A permanent meeting location should be arranged to avoid the logistical difficulties of finding a new space for each meeting.

Meeting Agendas and Materials

While scheduling a meeting with our director of strategic communications to discuss our institution's crisis communications plan, I noticed that Microsoft Outlook includes the following in the notes section of each appointment: "Make this event meaningful. Add an agenda." Microsoft Outlook's designers imply that a meeting without an agenda is worthless. As Kim stated,

> You don't just show up (a) without an agenda, which is something that really makes me crazy, or (b) thinking that you can just have faculty of all people sit around and talk about something without any sort of guiding direction to lead toward a decision.

All committee meetings should be preceded by an agenda. Agendas do not need to be formal documents; an email or notes in a calendar invitation will suffice.

If there are multiple agenda items, consider designating or allotting time for each agenda item so that each topic receives the appropriate amount of attention, encourages members to be brief and concise, and also demands that committee leadership hold members accountable to the agenda and their allotted time. If topics require more time, consider removing select agenda items to avoid potential frustration regarding perceived lack of progress. Allocating adequate time to each topic can also avoid perceived slights to topic owners if some issues are rushed while other topics dominate the committee's time. If necessary, poll the committee to determine which topics are most important, make those the priority, and adjust future agendas accordingly. Committees should receive meeting agendas a week in advance of each meeting.

A common complaint that I heard from administrators and faculty is the lack of communication and information they receive before the initial meeting and in between meetings. The "out of sight, out of mind" nature of committee work can result in a loss of momentum that can lead to setbacks between committee meetings unless members are consistently engaged via email or maintain contact with their fellow committee members. An uninformed assembly and lack of continuity consume valuable time to refresh the committee's collective memory of the issues, progress, and outstanding action items. Prior to each meeting, preparatory materials, an agenda, and a reminder or list of action items should be distributed to the committee. All correspondence with the committee should occur at least 1 week, preferably 2 weeks, prior to scheduled meetings. Sharon has found that this level

UNDERSTANDING UNIVERSITY COMMITTEES

of preparation greatly increases the value of committee meetings. She sends an agenda in advance of each meeting to confirm committee meeting dates, recapitulate what the committee will do, and thank members for their service.

Attendance

Taking attendance should not resemble roll call; instead, absent members should be noted discreetly (although their absence will be obvious to everyone on the committee) so that the committee chair can follow up with them as necessary. Members who frequently miss meetings should be encouraged to identify an alternate. When members are noted to be out, alternates should be contacted and provided with the agenda and materials for the meetings they will attend. A brief premeeting conversation with the alternate member is often necessary to acquaint them with the issues and brief them on their role or expected contribution. When alternates are not appropriate, the committee chair may need to explore the option to appoint another suitable permanent member who is able to regularly attend committee meetings. Distributing an agenda or other communication prior to committee meetings can encourage attendance.

Meeting Minutes and Action Items

Another typical complaint that I heard from administrators and faculty is that nothing gets done in committees. In many cases, this is because work assignments are not clearly defined, and committee members are not held accountable for committee work in the same way that they feel obligated to complete their day-to-day responsibilities. Assigning tasks, documenting action items, and setting deadlines can encourage participation and productivity. Action items should be documented during each meeting when they are identified and tracked to ensure that responsible parties remain aware of their obligations to the committee.

Although it may seem patronizing to check up on professional administrators and faculty, most individuals appreciate a reminder of outstanding action items; first, because it helps those members save face in front of their colleagues, and second, most committee members are eager to complete committee tasks, and a little encouragement can go a long way toward maintaining momentum and accomplishing objectives on time. Follow-up should occur at least 1 week, or 2 weeks if possible, before the committee meeting to allow time for work on action items to be completed.

Kim remarked, "Successful committee meetings are like successful classes; you have to backward design them" to reach an objective. We should be deliberate about how we structure committee meetings and explicit about the group's goals, otherwise we run the risk of creating a vacuum where, as one faculty member stated, "people are just going to fill the air with words, because who better to talk than me right now, you know?" A simple planning tool that serves in place of a charter (think course syllabus) can address most of the logistical issues outlined previously and counteract the potential for committees to stray off topic. Figure 5.1 is an example of a committee planning tool, a "committee contract" if you will, that I developed from various resources that address meeting management techniques (i.e., Boudett & City, 2014; *Harvard Business Review*, 2016a).

This template is designed to encourage committee leadership to consider both short-term aspects (e.g., objectives, composition, and initial meeting topics) and long-term aspects (e.g., meeting frequency, committee schedule, and final deliverable) of the committee's work with an emphasis on meeting frequency and demands on committee members' time and effort. In addition, this template can be used to record action items and, if distributed in advance of each meeting, remind members of deadlines, references, and future meetings.

Meeting Length

Milton Berle (n.d.), a comedian, once remarked, "A committee is a group that keeps minutes but loses hours" (para. 1). Abuse of one's time seems to be a principal complaint concerning committee obligations. A desire for efficiency coupled with an increasing cost-conscious administration begs the following question: How much does a committee meeting cost? In higher education we don't typically think of committee meetings in terms of dollars per hour. Instead, we consider it to be the cost of doing business, but perhaps we should change our perspective on how we value our time. Here is why. According to the Bureau of Labor and Statistics (BLS), the average IHE administrator earns approximately $94,000 per year (BLS, 2017a); the average for faculty is $76,000 (BLS, 2017b). If the typical American employee works 2,087 hours in a year, the average cost of a 1-hour committee meeting is $407.50. Table 5.1 provides approximate costs of convening various combinations of administrators and faculty based on BLS salary data.

If we account for travel time to and from committee meetings, the conversations that occur before and after, delayed starts, and meetings that run over time, the actual amount of time allocated to a 1-hour committee meeting is likely closer to 2 hours. For every hour we spend in committees, we likely spend another hour preparing for each meeting—or at least we should. Add 30% for benefits and an additional hour for preparation and travel, and the average cost for a 1-hour committee meeting balloons to approximately $1,060!

Figure 5.1. Committee planning template.

Committee Name:

Committee Chair Name:	Phone: (___) ___-___ Email:
Committee Admin. Name:	Phone: (___) ___-___ Email:

Committee Charge/Goal:

Committee Objectives and Deliverables			
Objective	Deliverable	Deadline	Completed
1.		mm/dd/yy	☐
2.		mm/dd/yy	☐
3.		mm/dd/yy	☐
4.		mm/dd/yy	☐

Relevant Polices, Plans, Regulations, and Procedures	
Title	Agency or Document Owner
1.	
2.	
3.	
4.	

Committee Members			
Name	College/Department/Office	Email	Phone
1.			
2.			
3.			
4.			
5.			
6.			
7.			
8.			

Meeting Frequency: ☐ Weekly ☐ Monthly				
Date	Start Time	End Time	Location (Building/Address)	Room
1.				
2.				
3.				
4.				
5.				
6.				
7.				
8.				

(*Continues*)

Figure 5.1. (*Continued*)

Meeting	Action Items	Assigned To	Completed
1.mm/dd/yy	1a.		☐
	1b.		☐
	1c.		☐
	1d.		☐
2.mm/dd/yy	2a.		☐
	2b.		☐
	2c.		☐
	2d.		☐
3.mm/dd/yy	3a.		☐
	3b.		☐
	3c.		☐
	3d.		☐
4.mm/dd/yy	4a.		☐
	4b.		☐
	4c.		☐
	4d.		☐
5.mm/dd/yy	5a.		☐
	5b.		☐
	5c.		☐
	5d.		☐
6.mm/dd/yy	6a.		☐
	6b.		☐
	6c.		☐
	6d.		☐
7.mm/dd/yy	7a.		☐
	7b.		☐
	7c.		☐
	7d.		☐
8.mm/dd/yy	8a.		☐
	8b.		☐
	8c.		☐
	8d.		☐

Recommendations/Committee Closeout:

Note. Adapted from *Meeting Wise: Making the Most of Collaborative Time for Educators*, by K. Boudett and E. City, 2014, Harvard Education Press; *HBR Guide to Making Every Meeting Matter*, 2016a, *Harvard Business Review*.

TABLE 5.1
Financial Cost of Committee Meetings

Administrators	Faculty	Average Hourly Cost
0	10	$365.00
1	9	$373.50
2	8	$382.00
3	7	$390.50
4	6	$399.00
5	5	$407.50
6	4	$416.00
7	3	$424.50
8	2	$433.00
9	1	$441.50
10	0	$450.00

Standing committee meetings that are typically staffed by senior-level administrators and faculty obviously cost much more. More than one faculty member I spoke with recounted a routine faculty meeting composed of 50 or more people, of which only 6 people cared about the issue being discussed. You do the math! A group of business researchers discovered that one company was spending an incredible amount of money per year on a single weekly meeting. As a result, *Harvard Business Review* (2016b) created a free mobile application to calculate the cost of a meeting based on the salaries of attendees. This is a free and alarming exercise that can be used to drive home the importance of using committee time effectively. I suspect that you can recall more than one committee meeting that would be difficult to justify to taxpayers, parents, donors, alumni, and visitors who finance the institution's operations if they became aware of these costs and the seemingly fruitless nature of some meetings. The next time you convene a committee, or any meeting for that matter, consider the potential hourly cost and return on investment.

Some business experts suggest unique ways to maximize meeting time. One such way is to limit the amount of time allotted for meetings to 30 minutes. By limiting time, members should be more conscious of what must occur and less tolerant of tangents and distracting conversations. Steve spoke on behalf of most administrators and faculty: "If you can keep the meetings maybe to no more than about 30 minutes, that would be awesome, because we've got so much other stuff on our plate." We should think of meeting times in terms of a sprint versus a run (Bregman, 2016); we can travel the same distance in a shorter amount of time. Another way to maximize time is to hold a standing or walking meeting. This suggestion may not be appropriate for all groups, and careful attention should be paid to ensure that some members are not put in an uncomfortable position based on personal health issues. Another argument for shorter meetings is to allow time between meetings for travel to the next meeting. I often find myself booked in back-to-back meetings, which means I am expected to depart one meeting and arrive at the next instantaneously. Shortening committee meetings to 45 or 50 minutes allows members to tend to business and arrive at their next obligation on time. In any case, limit meetings to no more than an hour, stay on topic, end early if possible, and don't hold a meeting for the sake of holding a meeting. The next time you convene a committee, consider the following:

- Does your organization have explicit or tacit rules or norms around meeting management?
- If you could change two aspects of committee work, what would you do differently?
- What is your organization's or committee's tolerance for rigorous meeting management techniques?
- The next time you attend a committee meeting, try to calculate the cost of the meeting and evaluate the institution's and your own return on investment.
- Can you apply one or more of the strategies listed in this chapter without much effort and anticipate positive results?

Note

1. University of Montana: Academic Conduct Board; University of New Hampshire: Environmental Health and Safety Committees; Pepperdine University: University Retirement Plan Committees; University of Tennessee: Academic Affairs and Student Success Committee; Texas Tech University System: Audit Committee; New York University: University Compliance Steering Committee; Western Washington University: Sustainability Committee; San Jose State University: Business Continuity Steering Committee; Eastern Michigan University: Academic IT Advisory Committee; University of Iowa: General Charter for University Committees.

COMMITTEE LEADERSHIP

This chapter explores formal and informal leadership roles in committees, leadership styles, leading diverse committees, how leaders can help committee members establish their respective roles and voice, and strategies for countering unproductive behaviors. Research has established a relationship between leadership and behaviors that are conducive to committee work (Mayer et al., 2009; Piccolo et al., 2010); however, "the mechanisms through which these leader behaviors influence citizenship behaviors are not always clear" (P. Podsakoff et al., 2000, p. 552). The mechanics are not fully understood, and the influence of leadership styles on committee performance is obfuscated by environmental and organizational conditions (see chapters 3, 7, and 8) that serve as antecedents or moderators of organizational citizenship behaviors. Leadership plays a critical role, be it formal or informal, in committees to both shepherd the committee toward a goal and foster a cohesive and inclusive environment. As First Lady Claudia "Lady Bird" Johnson once remarked, "A committee is only as good as the most knowledgeable, determined, and vigorous person on it. There must be somebody who provides the flame, who furnishes the inspiration" (L. Nickson, 1970, p. 79). Without intentional leadership and planning, committee meetings can devolve into unproductive social events. As one faculty member remarked, in the absence of leadership, "you feel like you're just showing up for a meeting."

When it comes to university governance, leadership influences the effectiveness of small groups more than any other individual factor (Schuster et al., 1994). Typically, committee chairs do not possess formal authority over committee members and therefore must rely on a blend of leadership, negotiation, facilitation, and mediation tactics to shepherd the work of the

Portions of this chapter are derived in part from an article published online with *Inside Higher Ed* (Farris, 2017). Visit www.insidehighered.com/advice/2017/06/06/advice-improving-efficiency-and-effectiveness-committees-essay to view the article.

committee toward its goal. The greatest challenges to leadership exist in this gray space of responsibility without authority, especially when leaders are confronted by a membership of disparate objectives and contrasting personalities. J. Richard Hackman (2002) postulated that there are five conditions for effective teams: (a) The group operates and feels like a genuine team, (b) tasks are both engaging and meaningful, (c) there are processes in place to support the group's work, (d) the larger organization supports the group's goals, and (e) the group is provided with appropriate leadership or coaching. Adept committee chairs can facilitate conditions for committees to become effective teams by creating a climate in which committee members can thrive by promoting the ideals of teamwork, aligning committee work with individual members' interests and skills, negotiating with the larger organization for support, and exercising leadership in ways that account for member dispositions and followership.

The responsibilities of the committee chair are significant, and being appointed chair is an honor or a dubious distinction. Houston noted that it's "a tough job" with many responsibilities. In addition to accepting primary responsibility for doing the bulk of the committee's work, Steve suggested that the chair also assumes the position of "convenient whipping boy." The sometimes tumultuous eddy line between academic and administrative cultures also requires adroit leadership skills. The impact of leadership is unique to each leader–subordinate dyad (Dasborough & Ashkanasy, 2002); therefore, some leadership styles are more effective than others depending on committee dynamics, group composition, and work task. Steve acknowledged, "It definitely starts with leadership." I appreciate this comment, because Steve recognizes that committee leadership has a role in facilitating the performance of the committee but is not solely responsible for its performance. True, committee performance begins with leadership, but the mantle of performance and leadership is shared with the membership.

Leadership in committees is not "an inherently individual phenomenon" (Bennis, 1999, p. 72) but a collective effort in which we assume or defer judgment and leadership to those with the relevant expertise and authority. Salas et al. (2005) explained that team leaders are responsible for three aspects of group work: (a) cultivate, maintain, and adjust the committee's shared mental model; (b) monitor team, organizational, and external conditions to anticipate changes and adapt the group's efforts accordingly; and (c) set expectations and manage members' contributions based on their expertise and disposition. Leadership is the process of facilitating the interactions among committee members, mediating conversations, confirming viewpoints, soliciting counteropinions, fostering a cohesive environment, engaging marginalized members, and managing or overseeing the committee's administrative functions. Committee leadership and management are two distinct skill sets. A good committee chair will be proficient in both areas.

Shared leadership, also referred to as distributed leadership, collective leadership, or team leadership (Kocolowski, 2010), is an appropriate model to help us understand leadership in university committees. Leadership is a responsibility of each and every member. Collectively, and consistent with the shared leadership construct, members assume leadership roles as necessary to influence the group and move the committee closer to its goal (Carson et al., 2007; Morgenson et al., 2010). The transition of authority among committee members is accompanied by an expectation of individual action. Shared leadership tends to yield greater interpersonal relationships among members of a group (Pearce et al., 2004) by fostering a cohesive environment (Solansky, 2008), encouraging engagement (Lee-Davies et al., 2007), reinforcing collegiality and trust among members (Bergman et al., 2012), and improving group performance (Mathieu et al., 2015). I contend that the relationship between the chair and the committee is like that of a conductor and an orchestra. The chair should help each member understand their role as it relates to the other members on the committee and create an environment that encourages them to fulfill their respective leadership roles with sufficient enthusiasm as is necessary to accomplish the committee's work.

If we accept that each member of the group is responsible for exercising leadership, we must also acknowledge that leadership styles within the committee are likely to be diverse and potentially contradictory. Understanding leadership techniques employed by committee members can mitigate confusion, improve interpersonal dynamics within the committee, and facilitate work assignments. Some individuals prefer charismatic leadership styles (i.e., I'll follow you because I admire you), whereas others might be more responsive to operant or transactional leaders (i.e., I'll do the work because I'll receive something in return). The remaining sections of this chapter discuss specific leadership styles and functions desired by administrators and faculty.

Leadership Styles

Leadership styles are important to explore, as each committee chair and member is apt to exercise their own unique leadership style. Sharon observed that committee chairs and deans are often brokering committee work outside routine meetings to continue the work of the committee, which illustrates a multifaceted committee leadership approach: one leadership style in public, and a second done privately with individual committee members. Committee objectives will also dictate which leadership style is most effective. As Adam pointed out, "There are committees that are clearly established because they are intended to be consensus building or change agent proxies, and those leaders have to be the charismatic consensus-building types." Recognizing each member's respective style, including our own, can help committee members navigate tensions that might result from conflicting perspectives on which leadership styles are appropriate to the committee's goals.

What could be a book exclusively on leadership in university committees is abridged here. Table 6.1 provides a broad overview of 11 of the most common leadership styles documented in popular leadership texts (see Bass & Stogdill, 1990; Hughes et al., 2012; Northouse, 2018).

While any of these leadership styles may appear in committees, some forms of leadership have been shown to be more conducive to and promotive of organizational citizenship behaviors than others, primarily charismatic and transformational leadership styles. Charismatic leadership is one of the most effective means to elicit organizational citizenship behaviors (i.e., active engagement, compromise, and helping behaviors) in groups (Babcock-Roberson & Strickland, 2010; Den Hartog et al., 2007). In addition, charismatic leaders influence behavior by serving as a referent example and role model for desired behaviors and attitudes, providing direction and clarity amidst confusion or ambiguity, reconciling differences through articulation of a strategy, and motivating change through inspiration (Bass, 1985; Conger & Kanungo, 1988; Ehrhart & Klein, 2001; Jacobsen & House, 2001). Furthermore, leader expressions of organizational citizenship behaviors create a lingering positive effect throughout the organization by promoting expressions of organizational citizenship behaviors in subsequent business interactions beyond the initial leader–individual exchange (Ferreira et al., 2013).

Transformational leaders encourage organizational citizenship behaviors by creating an environment that engages individuals in meaningful work by manipulating task characteristics (Piccolo & Colquitt, 2006). Transformational leadership has the strongest impact on subjective assessments of job appeal (i.e., meaning, significance, intrinsic value, etc.), which in turn can encourage individuals to actively engage in committees to meet personal or group objectives (Purvanova et al., 2006). The influence of leadership styles in committees is moderated by the idiocentricity or allocentricity of the individuals within the group (Nahum-Shani & Somech, 2011). Allocentric individuals are more likely to respond to transformational leaders and desire to maintain harmony within a group, which translates into helping behaviors or compromise. Idiocentric individuals are likely to be motivated by leadership styles that are task oriented (e.g., autocratic or transactional).

TABLE 6.1
Leadership Styles

Leadership Style	Characteristics	Application	Drawbacks
Autocratic	Leaders make decisions based on positional authority and do not typically consider subordinate input. Subordinates are expected to accept the prescribed course of action. Autocratic leaders can exercise authority explicitly through verbal directives or subtly through intimidation and retribution.	• Decisions must be made quickly or under urgent conditions, and normal decision-making procedures cannot be observed. • Routine or simple work decisions	• Does not take others' opinions or needs into consideration • Tends to discourage or alienate other members of the group • Antithetical to the ideals of shared governance
Bureaucratic	Leaders subscribe to a process (e.g., rules, standards, standard operating procedure, etc.) and expect subordinates to adhere to "the rules." Organizational hierarchies and positional authority are important to bureaucratic leaders. This leadership process can be very rigid, may involve multiple gatekeepers, and might use checks and balances.	• Decisions pertain to regulatory or legal issues that carry a high degree of risk or liability. • Decisions must be justified with documentation that outlines the logic used to reach the decision.	• Stifles creativity and innovation • Focus is on the process, sometimes at the expense of expertise, pragmatic solutions, or experience
Charismatic	Leaders influence others by serving as a referent example for desired behaviors and attitudes, providing direction and clarity amidst confusion or ambiguity, reconciling differences through articulation of a strategy, and motivating change through inspiration.	• A committee or organization must navigate a difficult or unpopular period of change. • Buy-in for a new initiative is needed.	• Not sustainable; once leader is gone, motivation is likely to follow • Might be more focused on their performance as a leader than on the welfare or success of the group

Democratic	Leaders collect input from stakeholders, in a systematic or nonsystematic way, and use this information to exercise their responsibility to make a final decision. Leaders engage multiple stakeholders to ensure that a holistic perspective is taken and a fair decision is made.	• Inclusive of the group's opinions and ideas; tends to generate high-quality, thoughtful decisions. • Participatory process tends to elicit participation and ownership.	• Process can be time-consuming • Inclusive process might imply that all opinions are equally valued when only the opinions of a minority group are considered conversely, expertise within the committee may be overlooked or discounted.
Laissez-faire	Leaders are minimally involved in the committee's work and allow others to work autonomously. The French to English translation of *laissez-faire* is "let them be."	• Committee is highly experienced, and technical expertise is beyond that of the leader. • A high degree of freedom is needed to allow the committee to perform at its best.	• Difficult to monitor the committee process or hold individuals accountable to deadlines or for deliverables
Relational	Leaders focus their effort on developing relationships with and among committee members. Leaders are supportive, serve as mentors, and are looked to for advice. Interpersonal relationships and sense of belonging and purpose are propagated by the leader.	• Committees that are staffed by junior-level employees can benefit from developmental opportunities. • The atmosphere creates a strong desire to be part of the committee.	• Committee members do not typically desire mentorship or support. • Focus on individual development may detract from accomplishing the committee's work

(Continues)

TABLE 6.1. (*Continued*)

Leadership Style	Characteristics	Application	Drawbacks
Servant	Leaders prioritize the needs of others and strive to work in a manner that emphasizes collaboration and shared governance. Leaders lead by example and reflect the values, attitudes, and behaviors that are integral to the committee's goals.	• Supports shared governance and committee decision-making processes • Decision needs to satisfy a diverse group of stakeholders.	• Hesitancy to exercise command and control when needed
Situational	Leaders adapt to the committee's needs and situation by exercising different leadership styles that are appropriate for the challenge or environment. Leaders are adept at multiple leadership styles and leverage their leadership experience as necessary.	• Work is expected to be multidimensional and challenging. • Committee has a high degree of variability in experience and/or authority. • Flexibility	• Difficult to find individuals who are capable of effectively executing this leadership style
Task oriented	Leaders focus on the task and implement processes, technologies, and organizational structures to achieve their end goal. Objectives and individual roles are clearly defined or prescribed, and the leader maintains oversight and responsibility for the committee's progress.	• Complex challenges with tight deadlines • Committee desires efficiency and productivity.	• Can feel autocratic and discourage participation • Limits opportunities for creativity and innovation

Transactional	Leadership is based on the leadership–subordinate dynamic, which is defined by the nature and quality of emotional and material exchanges that occur between the two parties. Leaders engender trust from employees who perceive just treatment regarding rewards or consequences for their performance.	• Member roles are clearly defined, expectations are explicit, and individuals are held accountable for their performance.	• Requires the leader to have authority over award and disciplinary processes • Resembles management more than leadership
Transformational	Leaders encourage participation and productivity by creating an environment that engages individuals in meaningful work by framing or manipulating tasks in a way that makes them engaging and meaningful. Leaders provide inspiration to the committee.	• A high level of committee engagement is needed to accomplish assigned work.	• Focus may be the vision at the expense of details that are critical to the work.

It may be necessary to adjust leadership styles to match committee demographics or appoint new leadership that is adept at leading the committee in a manner commensurate with the committee's task and personalities.

My conversations with administrators and faculty indicate a desire for committee leaders to possess a more traditional and assertive style, one that clarifies the committee's task and individual member roles, encourages collaboration and participation, holds members accountable to action items, and confronts counterproductive behaviors (Farris, 2017). Administrators and faculty unanimously agree that strong and deliberative leadership plays a critical role in supporting, soliciting, and promoting active engagement in university committees. Some of the individuals I spoke with said that they desire committee leadership that provides boundaries to the committee and its members (Adam), takes a more aggressive leadership approach (Brent), identifies individuals to take on tasks (Nick), has a capacity to know how to get people to volunteer (Sharon), sets and upholds expectations for committee member performance (Brent), manages disruptive individuals (Sarah), calls out unproductive behavior (Steve), and actively facilitates committee discussions (Marleen). These statements are not a referendum on leadership styles as much as they are a desire for specific leadership outcomes.

Following an impromptu and contentious faculty senate meeting regarding a controversial topic at George Mason University, the senate gave a standing ovation to the chair for his leadership. During this meeting, Keith Renshaw maintained order, remained conscious of time, did not allow members to deviate off topic, silenced those who broke with decorum, facilitated debate, and called on members to be brief and focused. Renshaw's leadership was remarkable in that it was absolute, direct, tactful, humorous, and efficient. This performance is just one example of the ideal committee leader as defined by previous research, observations, and interviewees. Exemplary committee leaders

- remain sensitive to the idiosyncrasies and needs of each member;
- act ethically and demonstrate integrity;
- are cognizant of marginalized members and seek to engage them in the committee's work;
- strive for diversity of thought and dialogue;
- tactfully manage individuals who detract from the committee's efforts;
- hold committee members accountable to action items, schedules, and deliverables;

- establish relationships with and among committee members and foster relationships both inside and outside of the committee;
- negotiate on behalf of the committee with the organization or leadership for resources and support;
- provide transparency regarding decision-making processes and timelines; and
- facilitate meetings in a way that is respectful of members' time and effort.

These traits constitute the ideal characteristics that committee leaders should aspire to emulate across leadership styles. As formal and informal leaders in committees, we should periodically reflect on our individual leadership styles. This exercise requires sufficient emotional intelligence to recognize the subtle cues and expressions that convey the impacts of our behavior on our colleagues. Questions that can help identify committee leadership issues include the following:

- Under what circumstances do individuals struggle or thrive as leaders?
- What core values are expressed through leadership?
- How are leadership roles supported by the institution or others within the committee?
- How is feedback on leadership given or received?
- Does the committee's work require a particular leadership style?

One last thought on leadership styles: Not everyone is cut out to be a leader despite their best effort, ambitions, and position. Marleen summed it up best: "Not everyone who should be a leader is supposed to be a leader." Leadership and management training are two areas that most administrators and faculty agree that IHE can reap great returns in regard to organizational performance. As Kevin stated,

> Faculty are not trained on how to be team leads; they might do okay in a research team, but in terms of running a meeting or being an administrator, we are sort of flying blind, right! That does have a lot of implications for committees.

Some administrators and faculty who struggle in committees can nurture leadership skills through training and practice, while others may not. Identifying those who can lead and those who cannot will spare committees hours of frustration, not to mention the individual cost of placing someone in an untenable position. Committee leadership and management training is addressed in chapter 3.

Informal Leadership

It is erroneous to expect committee leadership to act as the group's governor, project manager, and most productive member. Instead, committee chairs should be supported by a pool of informal leaders who exhibit leadership when appropriate as issues ebb and flow across the boundaries of their expertise. The burden of leadership is not retained by the chair; rather it should be imagined as a baton that is passed to each member in due time, and when the baton is received, the member will exercise an appropriate and responsible level of leadership. Sharon explained that in committees "everyone has the capacity to lead." This of course requires each committee member to acknowledge their informal leadership role and assume leadership as the committee's work evolves and integrates with each member's respective area of expertise. Chairs can encourage leadership among committee members by appointing individuals to champion specific action items or lead individual projects.

For informal leadership to manifest in committees, space must be provided to allow it to evolve. An overbearing leader tends to discourage others from assuming informal leadership roles. Leader extroversion is inversely related to group member proactivity because of the dictatorial climate some extroverted leaders create (Grant et al., 2011). Informal leadership should be not only encouraged but also recognized and promoted. As noted previously, for some members, especially junior members, committees provide unique learning conditions and opportunities to mature leadership skills. What does informal leadership in committees look like? According to the administrators and faculty I spoke with, informal leadership takes many forms that include but are not limited to the following:

- Holding recognized leaders and others accountable to documented action items, deliverables, read-ahead materials, and timelines
- Clarifying committee objectives and goals
- Defending or supporting a colleague who expresses an unpopular opinion
- Mentoring fellow committee members who are new to the group or are unfamiliar with the committee's charge, group dynamics, or history
- Recognizing individual and committee achievements
- Moderating conflict or redirecting unproductive conversations
- Taking notes and distributing a synopsis of the meeting as a substitute for formal meeting minutes

- Recommending that agendas or dialogue be structured in a more productive way
- Taking the lead on a project and managing other members as necessary
- Being well prepared and modeling exemplary behaviors when leading a committee topic

Any member of the committee can implement these recommended best practices as long as the chair is agreeable to sharing leadership. Good committee leaders will recognize the contributions of members and provide room and opportunity for them to exercise leadership when appropriate. Furthermore, informal leadership in a committee is, essentially, an audition for future committee leadership positions. Committee members tend to remember those individuals whom they found to be productive, willing to serve, collaborative, collegial, and supportive. Conversely, those committee members who earn a reputation for being disagreeable, difficult, or indolent are less likely to be sought out to serve on future committees. Reputations precede us. When individuals are appointed to committee leadership roles, their past performance is likely to dissuade would-be committee members from being fully engaged if they have had negative committee experience or conflict with the individual in question.

Leading for Diversity

Staffing committees with individuals who represent the various communities within the institution seems an obvious first step in promoting diversity and aligns with the purpose of the committee; however, the real benefits of diversity in groups requires concentration on group dynamics and a willingness to consider new ontologies that may be radically different among group members. Although there are many benefits to be realized by forming diverse committees, research shows that diversity, if not managed thoughtfully, can detract from group performance (Jehn et al., 1999; McGrath, 1984; Riordan & Shore, 1997; T. Simons et al., 1999) resulting in out-group and in-group bias (Brewer, 1979; Levin et al., 2002) and potentially creating conditions for racism and sexism. A critical step toward promoting diversity within committees and institutions is to acknowledge that discrimination and bias are persistent issues in IHE. We must first embrace diversity as an issue and condition ourselves for the sometimes uncomfortable tenor of conversations on this subject.

Leading a committee requires marrying the tenets of project management, facilitation, advocacy, leadership, and followership while maintaining attention to inherent cultural, gender, ethnic, and racial biases. It is incumbent on committee leaders to address (individually or publicly, if appropriate) behaviors that might be perceived as hostile, discriminatory, or otherwise detrimental to group discourse and cohesion (e.g., microaggressions, domineering behaviors, hegemonic thinking, arrogance, and obtuse attitudes) and work to find commonality of ideas, purpose, and needs among committee members so as to minimize apparent or perceived differences. The following are recommendations to promote gender, ethnic, and racial diversity within organizations and committees through inclusive leadership practices (e.g., Chun & Evans, 2018; Stanley, 2006a; Stefani & Blessinger, 2017; Sweeney & Bothwick, 2016) that can yield the benefits associated with diverse groups:

- Be prepared to stand up to institutional leadership to justify your selection of committee members and their unique contributions.
- Provide mentorship or identify a mentor to assist new faculty and administrators who may be unfamiliar with organizational norms, challenges, and procedures.
- Appoint a critical mass of underrepresented faculty and administrators in committees to avoid microcosms of underrepresentation.
- Actively solicit, illuminate, and validate the perspectives and contributions of underrepresented faculty and administrators.
- Recognize and reward the contributions of faculty and administrators who promote diversity and inclusion.
- Ensure that committee members have the requisite training or experience to identify potential incidents of bias and discrimination.

Challenging traditional conceptions of gender, racial, and ethnic identities and organizational norms provides opportunities for novel solutions to organizational problems while simultaneously providing a more inclusive committee environment. As a result, we can attempt to rectify inequities in committees, and committee work can also serve as a positive force within IHE. Before a committee makes a recommendation or offers a solution, the committee must ask itself "How does this practice, policy, procedure, strategy, or program advantage or disadvantage members of our community?" If we accept my argument that committees are the pipeline and proving ground for institutional leaders, then committees play a crucial role in rectifying the inequities in our institution by offering unique opportunities for disadvantaged faculty and administrators to learn, lead, and leverage their experiences to affect organizational change.

Role Clarification

One administrator remarked, "Sometimes people are on committees and they might have opinions about things, but they are unclear about their roles or they are unclear about how they are supposed to bring their inputs or expertise to bear." Members who are unclear about their role in committees are less likely to volunteer for tasks, be actively engaged, or help others because they do not understand how their participation and effort will be received by the committee. Research shows that groups tend to perform better when individuals understand their adopted or appointed role as it relates to and benefits others within a group (Kayser, 1990).

Houston recognized that for IHE to operate, "there's a million things that are beyond the capacity of one person to do." Understanding how individual roles interrelate and defining responsibilities are essential to collaborative work in committees. In addition to understanding the purpose of the committee, it is essential that members have a clear conception of "the roles people [they and others] play or that need to exist in a committee" (Adam). Edmondson (2004) found that trust among group members can be fostered by addressing ambiguity regarding group member roles, authorities, work procedures, and objectives. Committee leadership should focus on helping members identify their respective roles and understand the boundaries of their participation. Creating a shared vision for the committee, which includes how members can and should contribute and interact, is one of the initial steps of building a cohesive environment. A shared mental model (Cannon-Bowers et al., 1995; Zaccaro et al., 2001) facilitates group work by creating an environment where members of the group can anticipate one another's needs, communication among members is profuse, and members are encouraged to come to the assistance of others (Salas et al., 2005). Indeed, research shows that self-managed groups tend to perform better when they can anticipate the demands of the group and are provided with a stable environment (Bunderson & Boumgarden, 2010), which justifies the investment in setting ground rules and defining committee member roles and responsibilities.

To abate confusion regarding the purpose and scope of the committee, members should be informed as to why they were selected, appointed, or asked to serve on the committee. It should be made evident by the chair how the objectives and goals of the committee align with each member's skills and expertise. Clearly articulating why the committee was convened and how members' interests are coupled to the success of the committee can improve participation and subsequently committee performance. Establishing individual member roles ensures that members understand expectations and boundaries for themselves and others and how to engage with other members of the committee. Brent suggested that ground rules establish a "safe space" and create conditions where individuals are "more apt to take risks" and engage in the committee's work. With clear rules of engagement, expectations, and objectives, committee members are more willing to actively engage because the mechanics and outcomes of their efforts are understood. In situations where roles are ambiguous, committee members are cautious about investing their time and energy because the results of their work are uncertain. Leadership can position a committee for success by helping members understand how they contribute to the committee's work and the informal roles they serve to promote teaming and participation (see the section titled Individual Roles in chapter 4, p. 69, this volume).

Teaming and Participation

Sarah recognized that committee leaders who are "conscious about involving people as much as they can" and try "to leverage the strengths of the people in the group as much as they can" are instrumental in creating a fruitful committee environment. Although it is uncomfortable for some people, calling on members to contribute to the discussion or holding conversations outside of committee meetings to solicit input may be necessary to elicit active engagement. Leaders who inspire teaming and participation mitigate dominant personalities and obstructionists by orchestrating a sense of equity among committee members. Sharon explained that leadership and members of the group can aggregate perspectives by exploring the context of seemingly disparate viewpoints:

> If someone makes a comment that feels like it's an outlier, it's not necessarily an outlier comment. Helping them understand how it's connected to the larger picture of what we're trying to address, especially on controversial topics, builds bridges between members to connect ideas and solutions.

Formal and informal leaders who moderate committee interactions provide opportunities for marginalized voices to engage in the committee. Nick noted that in any group "there are sheep and there are wolves"; the wolves tend to dominate the direction of the group. It is not uncommon for committees to be controlled by a minority of members or even a single individual. As one individual remarked, "How many times have you been on a committee and the same three people are talking and everybody else is sitting quietly and the chair doesn't attempt to draw the others in?" Leaders who encourage involvement and manage overbearing personalities can elicit valuable contributions that might otherwise be lost. Adam assumed that people who are marginalized by leadership or other members of the committee

> don't feel that their knowledge is valued, and their institutional capacity is valued, and they don't get any opportunity to get feedback. They tend to pull back. The effect is the committee goes down because people aren't receiving from the leadership that [their input and participation] is valued.

Promoting participation and encouraging faculty and administrator voices yield significant benefits to the committee by providing alternative perspectives, higher levels of engagement, distribution of workloads, and a positive and inclusive committee atmosphere that facilitates group cohesion. Creating a collaborative climate allows committees to explore issues in ways that are not possible when people are relegated to their respective areas of expertise. As one faculty member stated, "Asking people to bring observations and a different perspective can really help" develop amicable solutions. Another way to promote participation is to turn committee discussions, especially those that are not going anywhere, into working sessions. Sharon will occasionally pivot and ask the committee, "Hey, since we don't have a lot of items today, can we actually spend this next hour working?" This strategy may work for many but likely not all committee members. You may need to excuse one or two members who are not amenable to group work sessions. Working meetings provide alternative ways for members who may be uncomfortable in an open debate to engage in ways that have meaningful impact on the committee's work.

Some committee members may resist engagement and participation. There are a variety of reasons why a person may choose to not speak up in a committee meeting (e.g., disposition, fear of retribution, lack of trust, aversion to being the deviant member, or organizational politics that place a person's opinions in an untenable position). Silence or lack of participation should not be misconstrued to mean agreement or acceptance of the committee's goal, direction, or decisions. It may be necessary to engage those silent members of the committee outside of routine meetings to reveal the members' issues and perspectives.

Last, active engagement is what we strive for, but a fully engaged committee can lead to some challenges. As Kim pointed out, committee leaders need to know "how long to let debate go on before people start to get frustrated." There is a fine line between constructive engagement and talking "for 3 hours and realizing you are saying the same thing using different words because you are coming from different disciplines." This leads us to our next topic: identifying and dealing with unproductive behaviors.

Unproductive Behaviors

Another leadership trait that has a significant impact on committee performance is countering unproductive or disruptive behaviors. The individuals with whom I spoke suggested that chairs who are reluctant to actively manage committees contribute to the entropic climate endemic to many committees. One of the challenges that many committees face according to one administrator I interviewed is that organizations are not

> teaching administrators or managers how to deal with people who aren't pulling their weight; we just incentive them for getting stuff done so they keep going back to the high performers again and again and again, and you find situations where those people leave, or they get stressed out, or they get burnt out.

Instead of coaching administrators and faculty on how to be better committee members, we tend to tolerate unproductive behaviors at the expense of the committee. Many of the individuals with whom I spoke prefer that nuisance behaviors be confronted by the chair to spare the committee the anguish of sitting through unproductive or contentious committee meetings.

There are a variety of behaviors that distract or otherwise discourage committee members from engaging in committee work. Unproductive behaviors include grandstanding, bullying, disengagement, and disruptive behaviors (see the discussion on deviant behaviors in chapter 8, p. 139, this volume). Sporadic instances of disruptive behavior are expected and tolerated; however, chronic disruptive behaviors by one or more members can have negative effects on the committee. Members who consistently experience disruptive or unproductive behaviors tend to become annoyed, disgruntled, and mistrustful of the committee's leadership and subsequently begin to lose confidence in the committee's ability to accomplish its mission. Adam suggested that it is the committee chair's responsibility to manage and control committee members' interactions that stray into counterproductive conversations, stating that "if the leadership doesn't control that action among the group," there is a risk that members will "pull back" and become disengaged. Similarly, if one person is allowed to dominate the conversation or derail the committee, other members might begin to withdraw if they perceive their involvement as undervalued or discredited. Marleen also holds the chair ultimately responsible for committee members who exhibit unproductive behaviors: "We cannot fault that person; rather we need to fault the facilitator who allows it to happen." In some instances, disruptive behavior is so pervasive that other members disengage from the committee because they get tired of tolerating troublesome individuals.

Counterproductive behaviors also distract from the committee's agenda. Administrators and faculty are acutely aware of the time they spend in committees. Committee chairs who are disrespectful of the committee's time risk discouraging participation and potentially losing the respect of the committee's members. As Kevin stated, and others agreed, "Wasting my time is the worst thing you can do." Committees that do not remain on task or yield productive conversations irritate those who perceive the group's effort as a waste of time. Committee work is not necessarily perceived as optional, but people tend to prioritize their formal roles and responsibilities as defined by their job description ahead of committee obligations. Subsequently, where formal roles and responsibilities conflict with committee obligations, we become reluctant to make or compromise time for discretionary effort. One administrator I spoke with recalled a committee meeting that devolved into an irrelevant discussion: "I was at a staff meeting once, and we ended up having a 30-minute discussion about Twitter, and it had nothing to do with the reason why we were there." Subsequently, they resented their attendance and disengaged from the group. The potential for this administrator to be an actively engaged and contributing member of the committee was lost once they perceived the committee as a waste of time. These examples illustrate the important role committee leadership has in actively managing committee proceedings, conversations, and member behavior.

There are strategies to counter unproductive behaviors, many of which are similar to those actions that encourage teaming and participation; that is, actively managing conflict resolution, facilitating effective communication among members, showing tact and being respectful of all members' dignity, removing an unproductive or combative committee member from the meeting (exceptionally rare), and using humor to defuse tense situations. Steve recalled a meeting where faculty were chastised for catching up on grades and emails during a committee meeting. He said it felt a little like "a slap on the wrist" because they were expected to be present and engaged. He went on to say that the chair addressed the group's inattentiveness tactfully by addressing the group rather than specific individuals with a statement along the lines of "we've noticed that some people are working, and you need to be paying attention." Although it may have been an uncomfortable moment, the outcome brought the committee back on task and set expectations for future meetings.

While firm leadership strategies benefit committees and promote participation, they are impeded by the philosophy of shared governance and traditionally acquiescent committee leadership styles characteristic of many committee chair–committee member relationships. Countering unproductive behaviors requires skill, discretion, and diplomacy. Brent noted the challenges of exercising proactive and strong committee leadership:

If I am the chair of the committee, but I have no supervisory authority over this person, what do you do? How do I motivate you if you didn't do whatever you are supposed to do? You're over here and supervised by these people and . . . how do I somehow censure you or get you to be engaged?

It might be necessary to address counterproductive behaviors outside the committee on an individual basis or with the individual's supervisor; again, exceptionally rare. Rebecca Knight (2016), a business author who contributes to *Harvard Business Review*, offered advice for dealing with disagreeable individuals offline. Among her recommendations are the following:

- Ask the individual if you can discuss the recent committee meeting with them.
- Inquire about the individual's goals and objectives for the committee.
- Describe the disruptive behavior and perceived consequences on the committee's efforts.
- Explore why they feel the way they do or why they are expressing themselves in the potentially unconstructive way.
- Make specific suggestions on how to move forward and agree on the next steps.

If you peel back the prescriptive format of this process, it is essentially a performance improvement plan. Given that this skill is rarely practiced within committees and usually not innate, institutions should teach, cultivate, and promote these skills through professional development plans and committee training.

We can't have a genuine conversation about leadership without also discussing the principles of followership. Leadership and followership represent two sides of the leader–subordinate dyad; one cannot exist without the other, and any disparity in value becomes evident to leaders and followers alike (Shamir, 2012). In terms of group success, a willingness to be led is just as critical as an intention to lead. There are several factors that influence the leader–follower dynamic: personalities, impressions, our judgements of others, work tasks, and the context in which the relationship exists (Lord et al., 2001). All of these factors potentially exist in committees and influence the chair–member relationship. So what behaviors constitute good followership? Nick, who I perceive as an experienced and resourceful leader, recognized that occasionally leaders must assume the role of follower to support committees. He stated,

So, whatever I can do to help, even if that's shut up and sit back and relax and don't do anything. I try my best to see what is needed from my perspective and do that. If I am in charge, I take charge and try to get things done the way I see fit. I really try to meet the situation with the appropriate type of leadership or subordination as is required.

There are a variety of follower typologies that describe followership behaviors, but much like leadership, they are vast, disparate, and have nuanced overlapping characteristics. To summarize, the following behaviors constitute *good followership* as defined by extant research (Carsten et al., 2010; Chaleff, 2003; Kellerman, 2008; Kelley, 1988):

- Being open and receptive to leadership influence
- Observing directions provided by those in recognized positions of authority
- Offering constructive feedback to support the leader's and/or group's objectives
- Identifying leadership weaknesses and supplementing leadership strengths through informal leadership or action
- Facilitating positive relationships among leadership, the group, and the larger organization
- Adapting individual roles to the needs of the group or leadership
- Actively promoting a positive environment and defending the leader and/or group from dissent
- Pushing back against leadership when necessary to avoid unfavorable outcomes
- Being responsive, accountable, and self-actuating in a manner that supports the leader and group

These principles are not a call for abdication of our agency as experts in our respective fields! Instead, these behaviors are listed here to instigate thoughts on what it means to be a follower and draw attention to the important followership role we may need to assume and challenge us to consider how our actions support a positive leader–follower dynamic. It is rare to see followers recognized by an organization, but they are invaluable members of our organizations and easy to distinguish from other committee members. I am sure with some thought, you can identify a few of your colleagues who embody the characteristics of a good follower and can easily list ways in which they have contributed to your organization's success.

The next chapter focuses on the most salient individual characteristics that manifest in committees, but before we move on, consider how committee leadership is encouraged and practiced at your institution:

- What is your leadership style or styles, and in which contexts are you most successful as a leader?
- What types of leadership traits and personalities are celebrated at your institution?
- How important is positional authority in your organization, and how does your organization encourage informal leadership?
- When serving on a committee, can you identify followership behaviors; are those followers acknowledged; and, most important, how do you exercise followership across the various groups in which you serve?

7

COMMITTEE MEMBER
CHARACTERISTICS

This chapter explores the individual characteristics and work conditions that serve as antecedents to the roles individuals assume in committees. This could be the start of a long discussion on social, group, and identity theories; however, for the sake of brevity, let us agree that individuals form unique identity profiles in committees based on disposition and environment. Research suggests that group development is driven by the members' respective personalities and knowledge, the group's objectives, and external conditions (Morgan et al., 1993). We have discussed committee objectives and external conditions (i.e., political, cultural, and organizational); we must now turn our attention to the idiosyncrasies of committee members. In the following pages, we will explore just a few of the most prevalent antecedents and moderators of organizational citizenship behaviors in university committees.

Professional Identity

Committee work is practically inescapable in IHE, and as such expectations regarding participation and contribution are tacitly conveyed via social modeling. As committee members, most individuals feel a natural inclination or obligation to participate; however, the rules of engagement and specific behaviors that contribute to committee success are rarely if ever discussed, taught, or acknowledged. Sarah explained that expectations regarding committee work are implied by the observed behavior of her supervisor, which she interprets as an expectation to "participate fully, to do my part, to show up, to be respectful." The ambiguous parameters of what constitutes committee participation provide a wide margin of discretion in determining how we should engage in committee work (Schnake & Dumler, 2003; Tompson

& Werner, 1997). There are two primary ways by which individuals define their roles on a committee: First, how does their role on the committee fulfill formal job responsibilities? Second, what expertise do they possess that is germane to the committee's work?

As ambassadors representing specific functions of the institution, committee members are beholden to their departmental and positional responsibilities and authorities. For example, Adam understood that there is an implicit expectation to advance his department's goals when serving on committees; in other words, "Do I adequately represent our organization, our agenda? Am I able to compromise where it benefits the organization and make everybody look good?" Adam implied that he engages in discretionary effort (i.e., being actively engaged and compromising) to fulfill this responsibility. Nick emphasized, "Members of the committees are not just representing themselves; they are typically representing some organization or group" and as such feel an obligation to do justice to their department's needs. People who define committee responsibilities broadly or recognize committee work as a requisite function of their position are more inclined to be productive and engaged members of the committee because they perceive discretionary effort as necessary to success in their formal role. For example, Kevin found a committee that was convened to establish a new international campus was extremely effective and time conscious because "everybody had to contribute, because everyone was in charge of their own little piece" and clearly understood the relationship between the committee's work and their individual responsibilities. When an individual intuits a strong link between the committee's work and their area of responsibility, they are more inclined to exhibit active engagement, compromise, and helping behaviors. Even when a committee is related to one's formal role in the organization, if the committee's work is irrelevant to the department's objectives or an individual's personal ambitions, there is little incentive to be engaged.

Where participation is viewed as strictly obligatory or offered under duress, individuals tend to exhibit normative committee behaviors (see Table 2.1). As one faculty member stated, unless the committee's topic is germane to them or their field of expertise, they "kind of tune out" because "well this doesn't really concern me right now." As an administrator stated, if committee members "don't feel that the conversation is directly relevant to them, then they tend to think it's not a good use of their time." Administrators and faculty recognize that committees are integral to the idea of shared governance in IHE and accept committee duty as a necessary responsibility but tend to contribute less when the committee's work diverges from their professional obligations.

The second way our professional identity influences participation in committees is when we perceive ourselves as a subject matter expert or have a personal interest in the committee's work, regardless of whether the committee's work is related to our formal job responsibilities. This is consistent with existing research that found that people who are given opportunities to engage in interesting or satisfying work that is aligned with self-concordant goals demonstrate higher levels of discretionary behaviors (X. Chen, 2005). Brent recounted a situation when he was the junior committee member but the most informed member of the group. He understood that "if the committee work has something that resonates with me, or my experience, and my area of expertise, then that's probably a reason why I would feel more empowered to speak up." Understanding one's mastery of a subject moderates how individuals leverage their engagement in committees. When committee members perceive themselves as the subject matter expert on a committee, they admit that they feel a strong obligation to conform to the committee's performance expectations, which often results in doing discretionary work, showing leadership, and facilitating decisions.

Confidence derived from being a subject matter expert or exclusive holder of privileged information is a source of empowerment and positively influences levels of engagement. IHE are full of intelligent and well-educated individuals. An individual's knowledge and expertise are rarely universal or transferable. One faculty member I spoke with admitted some colleagues erroneously assume "I'm really a smart guy, and I really know my stuff. Therefore, if I go over there, I can be really smart over there too," operating under the assumption that his professional expertise in one field qualifies him to be a potential expert in other areas of institutional governance and administration. Perhaps, but this is likely not the case for most issues addressed by committees, particularly those that span organizational silos. The phenomenon of self-importance is not isolated to the academic side of academe; plenty of administrators think they have it figured out as well. Conversely, individuals who recognize that they do not have expertise in the business of the committee tend to play a more passive role. Some people consciously refrain from participating in committees when they feel that they lack the prerequisite knowledge to make informed contributions. As one administrator stated,

> I try to contribute where I think I have expertise. I do always try to be thoughtful and not to just give random opinions. . . . I have a lot of opinions about tenure track, but I don't give them because obviously I have never been on tenure track.

Most individuals affirm that they self-regulate their contribution in committees based on their knowledge of a subject. If committee issues do not touch on the participant's knowledge base, they tend to reserve their effort for those subjects that are more pertinent to their role and responsibilities.

It is important to note that an individual can be committed to different aspects of their work. Bishop et al. (2005) found that an individual's commitment to a group within the organization is independent from commitment to the organization in general. For example, faculty may take a greater interest in matters pertaining to their field of expertise than the governance of the institution (Benson & Brown, 2007; May et al., 2002). Furthermore, faculty have greater autonomy to engage and disengage in organizational governance procedures as they see fit (Lawrence & Ott, 2013). As a result, faculty are more inclined to engage in committees when they perceive that their expertise will be respected and their contributions will be impactful (Birnbaum, 2004). Much is written about how institutional service is a distraction from teaching and research; however, research reveals that faculty allocate 8.22 hours per week to institutional service (Lawrence et al., 2012). This research also revealed that faculty service tends to increase over time. As one faculty member stated, "Assistant professors are shielded as much as possible from those roles because you're never going to get tenure on the basis of a great service record, period." In this case, senior faculty are expected to fill service roles and mentor junior faculty to prepare them for their future service obligations, which include committee obligations.

Tension may arise between individual objectives and what is best for the group or institution when the committee's goals do not align with an individual's conceptions of what suits their respective discipline or expertise. It is critical to tease out the connection between the committee's work and the members' responsibilities or expertise. If these connections cannot be made, the composition of the committee may need to be adjusted. By helping members establish identity by forming opportunities through leadership roles and participation, we are also solidifying their respective roles within the committee. At worst, when committee participation is obligatory, beneficial discretionary effort (i.e., active engagement, compromise, and helping behaviors) is not necessarily discouraged but offered with less frequency and enthusiasm.

Personality and Disposition

Some people are predisposed to exhibit organizational citizenship behaviors (Barrick & Mount, 1991; Borman et al., 2001; Organ, 1994; Organ &

Ryan, 1995; Roberge et al., 2012). According to research, organizational citizenship behaviors are expressions of the following personality traits: courtesy, agreeableness, and conscientiousness (Borman & Motowidlo, 1997; Moorman et al., 1998; Organ, 1988; Van Scotter & Motowidlo, 1996). The moderating effect of personality on discretionary behavior and the subsequent effect on group performance can take many forms. For instance, individuals who are conscientious, extroverted, and agreeable facilitate engagement, compromise, and helping behaviors within groups through the expression of employee voice (LePine & Van Dyne, 2001). Hough (1992) and Mount et al. (1998) provided additional evidence that these three personality traits support cooperative or helping behaviors in independent meta-analytical studies. Next is a discussion of the most prevalent dimensions of personality documented in organizational citizenship research: conscientiousness and agreeableness.

Groups with conscientious members who endeavor to collaborate tend produce a higher quality product in greater quantity than comparable groups that lack conscientious members (P. Podsakoff et al., 1997). Conscientious individuals tend to exhibit behaviors such as dependability, integrity, and acting with concern for others or the organization (Erdheim et al., 2006). Individuals who are cognizant of how their behavior potentially affects others (i.e., high self-monitors or emotionally intelligent individuals) tend to regulate their behaviors in accordance with group norms, are considerate of others, and are more likely to engage in citizenship behaviors (Blakely et al., 2003; M. Snyder, 1987). Steve summed up his interactions with other committee members in this way: "I want to treat them as I'd want to be treated."

According to my interviews, people who are conscientious of how their behavior affects others consciously engage in helping behaviors. For example, in Steve's department he and his fellow conscientious colleagues were "looking for ways to take the pressure off each other at difficult moments." Sarah captured the value of conscientious people to committees and how they use organizational citizenship behaviors to create a cohesive environment:

> To me, probably the best committee members are people who can be self-reflective, that they have some self-awareness, that they have awareness of other people, that they understand that personality affects how people work together. . . . They, at least, understand the value and tremendous potential in working as a true group and are trying to pull everybody together.

Brent agreed that conscientiousness is a critical component of well-functioning committees. He argued that committee members should "have a good amount of emotional intelligence" to manage interpersonal interactions in committees. He does this by "being a nice guy," maintaining and promoting "positive energy and a sense of humor, and having an openness to meet people where they are" socially and professionally. Being aware of others and how interpersonal interactions influence committees requires effort and is often premeditated, an idea summarized by one of the administrators I interviewed:

> Professionally and personally, one thing that I have been trying to do more when I go to a committee is I am trying to be a lot more observant and thoughtful about what's actually happening around me and how I am trying to contribute to it.

Agreeableness is broadly defined as friendliness and the ability to work well with others in a harmonious fashion (Konovsky & Organ, 1996). Individuals who rate high in tests of agreeableness tend to demonstrate organizational citizenship behaviors at a higher frequency than those who rate low on agreeableness (Ilies et al., 2006; Neuman & Kickul, 1998). In general, friendly, positive, and outgoing individuals engage in organizational citizenship behaviors more frequently than morose, dissatisfied, or reclusive individuals. Positive impressions or likability of in-group members influence the degree to which other members express affective behaviors that manifest as person-to-person acts of support (Isen & Baron, 1991). Day and Carroll (2004) hypothesized that individuals who rate high in emotional intelligence and perceive the group in a positive light lead to affective responses that include organizational citizenship behaviors. Openness to experience, extraversion, conscientiousness, and agreeableness are also positively related to citizenship behaviors in diverse groups (Roberge et al., 2012). Furthermore, individuals who have strong positive relationships with their colleagues tend to behave in a manner that benefits members of their network to include helping behaviors (Ilies et al., 2009).

We should also acknowledge that some people just aren't cut out for committee work. As one person I spoke with admitted, "I'm not a meeting guy. I've never been a meeting guy. In a perfect world, this is my temperament, too; just leave me alone and let me do what I'm good at, right?" This level of self-awareness is extremely valuable but only if it is taken into consideration by supervisors and committee leaders. In summary, if a person is likable, pleasant, agreeable, and conscientious, chances are they will be a more productive asset to the committee than a disagreeable, pertinacious, or socially inept individual. A faculty member once told me that social science sometime results in discovery of the obvious; this is one such instance.

Gender, Race, and Ethnicity

In 1974, Sandra Bem conducted research on self-identified, positive, valued personality traits to expose conceptions of masculine or feminine gender roles. Gender roles that are learned, conditioned, and reinforced by family, peers, education, and society manifest in committees in ways we may not be aware of. Table 7.1 is adapted from Bem's initial sex role inventory and is provided here to illustrate dispositional characteristics that might be observed in committees.

As much as we may want to resist or deny these stereotypes, research shows that they persist to this day (Donnelly & Twenge, 2017); however, research also reveals an ongoing gradual shift in gender identities as both men and women migrate toward more androgynous traits (Twenge et al., 2012). For example, women are less likely to identify with traditionally feminine characteristics and are instead beginning to identify with masculine characteristics more frequently. It is also important to note that that these gender traits are not mutually exclusive; instead, they are independent. Individuals can express feminine and masculine traits simultaneously or along a spectrum spanning seemingly opposite behaviors (Bem, 1974). One of the barriers to women and men adopting fluid gender roles in committees is judgment by our colleagues. Women are often admonished or penalized for adopting masculine traits, while men face few or no repercussions for exhibiting feminine and gender-neutral traits. This double standard is yet another form of gender discrimination that persists in higher education.

TABLE 7.1
Bem's Inventory of Masculine, Feminine, and Gender-Neutral Sex Roles

Masculine	Feminine	Gender Neutral
Leadership	Compliant	Helpful
Aggressive	Affectionate	Reliable
Analytical	Compassionate	Happy
Assertive	Considerate	Truthful
Competitive	Sympathetic	Friendly
Dominant	Gentle	Adaptable
Forceful	Understanding	Tactful
Independent	Loyal	Sincere
Risk taking	Yielding	Solemn

Note. Adapted from "The Measurement of Psychological Androgyny," by S. Bem, 1974, *Journal of Consulting and Clinical Psychology, 42*(2), 155–162.

If we examine Bem's (1974) record of gender traits in its totality, I believe we can agree that a committee composed of individuals who exhibit predominantly feminine and gender-neutral characteristics is more likely to produce a cohesive and inclusive atmosphere than one described as aggressive, assertive, dominant, forceful, and independent. Indeed, Bem (1974) suggested and hoped that the "androgynous person will come to define a more human standard of psychological health" (p. 162). This is not to say that we should challenge our peers to be someone they are not; rather the inventory is provided here to help us diagnose and appreciate the various dispositions that constitute a committee and value the complexity of interpersonal relationships among individuals with potentially disparate personalities. You might consider asking yourself which traits best describe your personality and how your behaviors might be perceived, accepted, or rejected by others. We should also create a mental index of who exhibits which characteristics and how they conflict with other dispositions in the committee that preclude, moderate, or discourage participation. With this insight and information, we can begin to identify group dynamics that demand attention and leadership to encourage equal participation and promote marginalized voices.

In chapter 4 the potential organizational benefits of diverse committees are outlined, and in chapter 6 strategies for leading diverse committees are recommended to create an inclusive climate to yield the benefits of gender, racial, and ethnic diversity. Despite genuine attempts to establish an inclusive committee, social injustices precede us and may complicate our efforts. Research shows that racially and ethnically diverse teams tend to perform poorly compared to heterogenous teams, at least initially, because of apparent differences in perspective and experiences (S. Jackson & Joshi, 2011). Over time, diverse teams learn to appreciate and assimilate the various perspectives that initially fractured the group to outperform nondiverse groups (Harrison et al., 2002; Hoever et al., 2012), but this transformation requires an understanding of underlying diversity issues. There are several confounding issues stemming from racial and ethnic inequity that are obstacles to assembling a successful diverse committee. For example, research shows that underrepresented individuals in groups

- talk less frequently than the majority White male members because of real or perceived power imbalances (Levin et al., 2002);
- are the subject of implicit behaviors used by the dominant group to maintain control over group processes (Harper, 2012);
- maintain a social identity that is uniquely different from that of the predominant group or institutional identity norms, which can lead to a sense of alienation (Turner et al., 2011);

- focus on relational aspects of the work task, whereas White members tend to focus on procedural or structural elements, which can create conflict (Mor Barak et al., 1998);
- can be unaware of racism, discrimination, or bias affecting themselves or others (Dovidio, 2001; Stanley, 2006b); and
- feel pressure to contribute more service work to the institution than their White colleagues, which can lead to increased stress and burnout (Fries-Britt et al., 2011; O'Meara et al., 2017).

Research indicates that diversity in groups begins with observable surface-level demographic differences (e.g., complexion, gender, ethnicity, and language) then gradually transitions to attention to deep-level differences (i.e., attitudes, philosophies, and values) as members get to know each other (Harrison et al., 1998, 2002). In other words, over time and with frequent interaction, committees integrate, appreciate, and leverage individual contributions stemming from diversity as members come to understand one another on a personal and professional level. This evolution occurs as individuals adjust their attention from personal goals to collective goals that transect individual differences (Ely & Thomas, 2001). Appreciation of diverse viewpoints and how individuality benefits committees requires proactive leadership and a genuine investment of effort to see beyond our individual perspectives in order to yield the benefits diversity affords.

An example of deep-level gender differences that influence committee dynamics is evident in how trust is perceived, gained, or given among committee members. Trust among committee members has a significant impact on group dynamics, group efficacy, and productivity. Research shows that high levels of trust among group members encourage participation in group work, are associated with expressions of organizational citizenship behaviors (Self et al., 2011), improve communication (G. Jones & George, 1998), and moderate relational conflict (T. L. Simons & Peterson, 2000). One of the interesting findings from my initial research on university committees is the difference between women and men regarding the locus of trust in committees. Among women and men, high levels of intragroup trust within committees tend to encourage citizenship behaviors; however, women appear to be primarily concerned about their ability to trust others, whereas men seem to be focused on how others (individuals or the organization) trust them. Table 7.2 provides transcript excerpts from my original study on organizational citizenship behaviors that illustrate the difference between women's and men's perceptions regarding the locus of trust.

TABLE 7.2

Female Versus Male Locus of Trust in Committees

Female	Male
• Trust that person	• Trusts me
• Trust level of you	• Trust that I am
• Trust their making hard decisions	• Trusts me
• Trust her	• Trust and confidence that they put
• Trust where he's going	in me
• Certain people whom I feel I	• They trust me
cannot trust	• It's an implied trust [in me]
• Trust and respect your colleagues	
• Trust in that group	
• Trusting each other	

When we are armed with this information, it is not difficult to appreciate how group dynamics and discourse affect individual members differently. Understanding how to build trust, a critical component of group cohesion, is contingent on our ability to discern minute or practically imperceptible dispositional nuances among committee members. There are many other conclusions about our colleagues' competency, potential, attitudes, and intentions that we infer (correctly or erroneously) from their disposition that influence group dynamics. The purpose of this section is to illuminate the potential ways that committee members' identities and dispositions can moderate participation and offer information that can be useful in diagnosing obstacles to member engagement. Acknowledging gender and ethnic dispositional variety in committees is necessary to ferret out discriminatory, offensive, or insensitive conduct. Fortunately, these stereotypes are challenged by many faculty and administrators as modern concepts of gender, equity, and social justice take root in IHE. The ideal committee environment is an androgynous environment that pays equal credence to traditionally masculine and feminine attitudes and behaviors. A study of demographically diverse groups conducted in 1996 found that "groups with high levels of androgyny across all members made higher quality decisions than did groups with low levels of androgyny. Moreover, androgyny demonstrated unique predictive strength beyond the separate effects of masculinity and femininity" (Kirchmeyer, 1996, p. 659). This is not to suggest that committee member differences should be normalized but rather to suggest that members should strive to expand their capacity to promote and appreciate the various gender roles members assume and the contributions each role contributes to the committee's work. With this evidence, committee chairs and members are justified to consider ways to propagate the exploration of identities and roles in order to create a diverse and inclusive committee environment to reap the results of blending gender and ethnic differences (see the section Leading for Diversity in chapter 6, p. 103, this volume).

Work Conditions

There are a variety of work conditions that influence participation in committees. How we feel about our job, our commitment to the organization, and our capacity to be engaged are some of the most prevalent variables in determining our ability or desire to engage in committee work. The following sections provide a brief overview of these aspects of our work lives.

Workload

Our capacity to be engaged, how we feel about our job, and our commitment to the organization are some of the most prevalent variables in determining committee participation. My conversations with administrators and faculty suggest that there is a reservoir of discretionary effort that we choose to allocate to committee work. Research confirms that time constraints and workload are two of the primary predictors of faculty citizenship (Bellas & Toutkoushian, 1999). As one administrator stated, "I personally tend to exceed performance requirements when I am pretty confident that I have the subject matter expertise or the ability and time, the capacity, to actually do work." Marleen affirmed the challenge of balancing committee work with day-to-day responsibilities: "Obviously committee work means that you have work to do. . . . You need to have the autonomy" to manage routine workloads and the obligatory or discretionary effort required by committees. Committee members also consider personal obligations, extracurricular activities, volunteer obligations, and responsibilities at home in their calculation of how much effort they can spare for committee work. As Sarah stated, "I am teaching in addition to my job . . . so choices that I make in my job will influence my participation in committees." Marleen framed the conflict between committee engagement and routine work obligations elegantly and identified the need for organizations to consider the existing workloads of individuals in committee composition and committee expectations:

> There has to be at least one person who has a little bit more time to make those things happen because I think recognizing that everyone has a full-time job, the committee work is in addition to, very often, and that can sometimes be a hindrance to its results. So safeguarding that a little bit. Who will be given the time to do all the extra [work] . . . when it's clear the group cannot really have the time?

Kevin has researched the issue of human capital and discovered that most organizations do not take a holistic account of various demands on faculty time. He stated that while faculty tend to be sensitive to their workloads, teaching expectations, or research requirements, managers are not asking the important questions such as, "I would like for you to serve on this committee, but before you say yes, I need to know specifically where those hours are coming from." When the burden of committee work is not fully understood at the outset, individuals resist engagement in order to maintain a margin of flexibility in their work schedules for unexpected events. The art of balancing current and potential work obligations is best summarized by Brent: "I am cognizant of not taking on extra work, because you know one hazing incident, one Title IX incident, one student crisis, can take up my day."

Motivation to serve on committees is further complicated by conflicting priorities. As another faculty member admitted, "So in theory, our jobs are teaching, service, and research. For us, its research, research, research, research, research, teaching, and as little service as you can possibly get away with." If you are in a position or period of work that demands more time than you can spare for committee work, you might recommend a colleague who has similar expertise, has more capacity for committee work, or is seeking a professional development opportunity. This person might be more capable of providing the meaningful contribution needed by the committee. There also continues to be an imbalance in workload distribution throughout IHE, with unrepresented faculty and women routinely dedicating more service time than their White male counterparts (O'Meara et al., 2017). It is important that we remain mindful of this inequity to avoid perpetuating discriminatory work practices by asking already overburdened colleagues to serve on committees. A forthright conversation about one's ability to serve on a committee and competing work priorities can spare both the member and the committee potential hardship.

Job Satisfaction and Commitment

Job satisfaction is "the perception that one's job fulfills or allows the fulfillment of one's important job values" (Henne & Locke, 1985, p. 222) and the positive emotional state that results. The relationship between job satisfaction and exhibition of organizational citizenship behaviors is documented by numerous studies (Bateman & Organ, 1983; Ilies et al., 2006; Lee & Allen, 2002; LePine et al., 2002; Organ & Ryan, 1995), and some scholars maintain that it is the most important moderator of organizational citizenship behaviors (Dalal et al., 2012). Happy faculty and administrators make better committee members. Job satisfaction and organizational commitment (both normative and affective commitment) help establish expectant behaviors (E. Morrison, 1994). Individuals who have high affective commitment to the organization are more likely to adopt broad definitions of their jobs to include organizational citizenship behaviors as implied expectations of their position. Satisfied individuals perceive active engagement in organizational governance, compromise, and helping their colleagues as part of their job. Most everyone I spoke with confirmed that job satisfaction is an important predictor of their level of engagement in university committees. Sarah provided the most succinct response regarding job satisfaction and effort in committees:

> I would say that if I am not feeling particularly satisfied in my job at a certain period, usually that's going to have to do with the things I've said: Is there trust or feeling that we are appreciated or that I am appreciated, that there is meaning in being here? I think that definitely affects my level of engagement.

Brent also recognized the relationship between job satisfaction and his performance in university committees: "If I am satisfied with my job, I am more likely to be engaged and involved in committee work, or if I am not well in my job or I am experiencing dissatisfaction, I am more likely to be disengaged." Expectations for faculty to participate in institutional governance, teaching, professional service, and community engagement all contribute to perceptions of job satisfaction. When these stressors exceed faculty tolerances for work stress, job satisfaction declines (Neumann & Finaly-Neumann, 1990; Sanderson et al., 2000). It is easy to imagine that committee obligations might be the first place to look for opportunities to reduce workload.

Commitment is differentiated from job satisfaction in that commitment is a measure of an individual's sentiments about the organization as a whole and the enduring impression it makes, whereas job satisfaction tends to fluctuate with the immediate or transient aspects of one's job that change over time (Mowday et al., 1982). The longer a person is affiliated with an organization, the more likely they are to develop a sense of organizational commitment. The relationship between job tenure and propensity to be engaged in organizational governance and civic activities is curvilinear. Affective commitment and expressions of organizational citizenship behaviors rise and crest at approximately 10 years (Ng & Feldman, 2012). Meyer et al. (2002) described three forms of commitment within organizations: affective (emotional attachment/dedication to organization), continuance (cost benefit of leaving/staying with the organization), and normative (obligation to remain with the organization). Lee and Allan (2002) argued that affective commitment elicits organizational citizenship behaviors because it implies a willingness or desire to perform rather than an obligation or duty, which is the foundation of normative or continuance forms of commitment. This hypothesis is consistent with other research that found that people who perceive their relationship with the organization as a covenantal relationship are more likely to express organizational citizenship behaviors than those who see work as a means to an end (Van Dyne et al., 1994). Higher degrees of commitment tend to produce higher levels of engagement in committees to include exhibition of organizational citizenship behaviors. Understanding a person's commitment to the organization can help us identify and select members to serve on committees who are more likely to fit the profile of the ideal committee member.

Organ (1994) argued, "Leaders of organizations must take pains to manage the context of work in such a way as to meet with widely prevalent norms of fairness, if their organizations require volumes of discretionary contributions for survival" (p. 467). Ensuring that faculty and staff feel valued and satisfied with their work is critical to promoting job satisfaction and commitment, which in turn encourages behaviors that are conducive to committee work. As committee chairs and colleagues, we may not have the ability to affect changes to member job satisfaction, but we might be able identify those individuals who are struggling with low job satisfaction or commitment issues and moderate our expectations accordingly.

Individual Motivation

Why do some individuals show up and provide their best performance in some committee meetings but are reluctant to engage in others? The five motives documented in organizational citizenship behaviors research include compliance, challenging, instrumental, prosocial, and task motives. Motives for engaging in committee work can be separated into two general categories. The first general category is a desire to help a specific individual or the group borne from a concern for the welfare of others. Individuals who place high importance on or value personal relationships are more apt to engage in prosocial behaviors. Prosocial motivations tend to be more prevalent in collectivistic (allocentric) teams and are expressed by actions and activities intended to help other people. The second general category of motivation includes the remaining motives (compliance, challenging, task, and instrumental), which are often found in individualistic (idiocentric) groups that are motivated by a desire to help the organization or self (Finkelstein, 2010; Lai et al., 2013).

We will focus on the three most prevalent motives for engaging in committee work—prosocial, task, and instrumental—however, a brief discussion of challenging and compliance motives is warranted, as you may encounter these motives in committees. Some individuals are engaged in committees because they are motivated by a desire to improve the organization and its performance (N. Podsakoff et al., 2014; P. Podsakoff et al., 2000). Farh et al. (2010) argued that challenging the organization can generate healthy debate that ultimately leads to more creative solutions to problems and subsequently better outcomes. Steve observed that the liberal arts tend "to advocate for critical thinking even if it goes against the party line" but only insofar as it improves the education of students in a manner that is consistent with the institution's values. You may observe these challenging behaviors on committee and mistake them for critical or defamatory assessments of the institution when in fact it is a challenge to improve. Other members of the committee may be reliably engaged members because they feel a strong sense of duty to the organization. For example, Houston recognized that all faculty have a service obligation; that is, "service that you do at the department level, it's just important to get it done." These individuals are motivated by a desire to comply with institution norms and expectations. They are present and playing their part because they must; ". . . it's just something one must do" (Steve). This is not to suggest that these obliged members are less engaged than any other committee member; they may in fact be the most productive members of the committee if they perceive active engagement as an institutional norm or expectation. It is important to note that a person can be motivated by more than one aspect of the committee's work. For example, Kevin stated that he is most engaged when "I am passionate about the issue of faculty mentoring, I get to connect with others across campus, and I learn something. So for me that's a total win." In this example, Kevin illustrated the importance of task, social engagement, and professional growth opportunities in driving his engagement in committees.

Prosocial

A considerable amount of research on organizational citizenship behaviors is oriented around positive and altruistic expressions of helping behaviors that derive from personality constructs such as conscientiousness, agreeableness, openness, and extraversion (MacKenzie et al., 2011). Prosocial motives are characterized by compassion and regard for others' well-being that manifest as acts of assistance. There are two unique themes underlying prosocial motives: one, a desire to maintain existing friendships and relationships, and two, a conscious effort to build unity and community within the committee. Both themes are strong motives for engaging in organizational citizenship behaviors and seem evenly balanced in terms of inspiration and importance to committee members. When asked why people help colleagues on committees, responses included the following: "It could be because I like them and I want them personally to have more growth opportunities and I can see a way to help them do that" (Sarah); "When someone is a good colleague [who] probably needs my expertise" (Nick); and "It could be the individual relationship that I have with that person" (Brent). The statement that best summarized prosocial motives was provided by Adam: "The whole time it was like, I know this is important for them, but this isn't nothing for me, for my organization. I like the people so much that I'm willing to continue to do something that doesn't justify my time." Similarly, Sarah commented that personal relationships have a significant influence on her willingness to help others. Her motives stem from affective emotions and concern for her colleagues' welfare:

> So, relationships are part of it, and wanting them to know that I care enough about what they are doing, and again not from a devious perspective or anything like that, but it's like you know, I care about what you're doing. It's important that we work well together. I want to give you what you are asking of me.

Helping behaviors motivated by prosocial tendencies also appear to be much more literal in that they are often conducted in response to a verbal request for help from a colleague. For example, Adam said,

> The motivations for helping a colleague are the work relationships where you are supportive of each other. So you're on the committee or your colleague might call you in and say, "Hey I know you're somebody who could be helpful. I am really trying to get these things happening with this committee and can you help?"

The second underlying theme behind prosocial motives is a desire to build unity or maintain harmony within the committee. Individuals with prosocial motives acknowledge that their efforts ultimately lead to more efficient and productive committees. As Marleen stated, a sense of unity "encourages some level of cohesion because certain people in a group know each other better or work better or are on the same page and then will find it easy to volunteer" to take on committee work. Some committee members possess an inherent desire for community and civility that motivates them to be more engaged in the committee's work. For example, Sarah stated that her motivation to help others is driven by her compassion for others:

> Some of it is the more human part of me I guess, where I sense if there are people who are being discouraged from participating, when I feel like they have a lot to offer, and there are other people with much stronger personalities that override them. I think that we lose opportunities by shutting certain people down.

Prosocial motives typically result in person-to-person acts of kindness or assistance that stem from existing relationships with or compassion for other members of the committee. Prosocial motives tend to exist in committees that have been meeting for some time or among committee members who have a long history of working together inside and outside of committees.

Task

Coleman and Borman (2000) proposed an alternative motive for engaging in advantageous behaviors in committees that is focused exclusively on the committee's work. Task-oriented organizational citizenship behaviors are extra-role behaviors that are performed in the interest of completing a task that reflects strong job dedication. Houston put it in much simpler terms. Regarding committee work he stated, "You're not going to be there unless you have an interest in the problem [the committee is trying to solve]." Personal interest in the committee's work and feeling empowered by the work of the committee are aspects of committee tasks that encourage engagement. Individuals might also become engaged in order to pursue their curiosity or interest in an area in which they feel that they have expertise or desire additional knowledge. For example, Brent observed that members of his department "step up in areas that they have an interest. . . . Somebody stepped up and wanted to take on the assessment instrument because they had an interest in doing an assessment and working with data and things of that nature." Most individuals I spoke with suggested that they expend more effort when they perceive the work of the committee as having a profound or wide-reaching impact on their respective institutions (e.g., sexual assault policies, university-wide academic programs, and student welfare issues). Kevin also stated that he is a willing and eager committee member when he understands how the committee's work is "critical to the operation of the university" even if he has no personal interest in the issue.

Last, engagement in a committee is driven by the outcome of the committee. Houston noted that there is often a high level of engagement in general curricular requirement committees, "because everybody wants to have some service course that everybody takes." There are implications for the academic department, potential budget implications, teaching loads, space assignments, and so on that might be a function of enrollment figures. In these instances, the task is directly relevant to future success and as such is a strong motivator to be a fully engaged, prepared, and contributing committee member.

Instrumental

Instrumental motives produce behaviors that are a means to an end (e.g., impression management, power attainment, visibility, and personal advancement) and that have some utility or benefit for the person offering. I found that most individuals have three distinct instrumental reasons for engaging in committee work: First, they desire visibility and personal advancement; second, they use their effort in committees to influence others or the committee to satisfy a personal agenda; and third, they engage in committee work to garner future favors from others.

Impression management is the predominant form of instrumental motives. Impression management comes from a conscious or an unconscious effort to make a favorable impression on supervisors or colleagues through one's personal performance. Some reasons administrators and faculty engage in committees is they "don't want to look stupid in front of the dean," want to show "commitment to the organization," want to improve supervisor appraisals and "make an impression," want to "get visibility," and want to demonstrate "value to the institution." Brent provided an honest assessment of instrumental organizational citizenship behaviors:

> Although people probably don't want to say "I am doing this because I want to look good in front of my colleagues," maybe that is it. I have charged up the hill on a committee or two because I wanted to leave a good impression for the vice president or someone like that.

When individuals are in highly visible committees, the importance and power of impression management increases as a motive. Sarah suggested that people looking for personal advancement or to impress superiors might "look for opportunities that would demonstrate the behavior of something [i.e., some position] more responsible." For example, one faculty member I spoke to said, "I am going up for promotion this year, so I'm going to give as much as possible, volunteer." Individuals are more likely to be actively engaged in committees, offer assistance to others, and compromise when there is the potential that their actions will be perceived as benevolent, serving the organization or otherwise viewed as positive by those whom they wish to impress. Last, some people suggested that helping behaviors constitute a form of currency to obtain future favors from others. As one person put it, "You scratch my back, I scratch yours." Some forms of participation constitute a strategy of quid pro quo. When a person offers to help another person, reciprocity is implied. In one instance an administrator admitted they actively participated in a committee for the sole reason of "somewhere down the line it's kind of a 'you owe me one.'"

One of the nuances of impression management and instrumental motives is that they appear to diminish throughout a person's career. Some of the individuals I interviewed admitted that impression management was a conscious effort earlier in their careers. Adam shared that when he began working in higher education, he was on a handful of committees that he felt had no intrinsic relevance or value to him personally but "they sure looked good on paper." He said,

> I would openly admit it. I mean a lot of the decisions I made in the first 10 years of doing this were [based on] how does this look or benefit my next step as a career. The altruism thing is great, but it doesn't pay my bills, doesn't put food on the table.

Although instrumental motives sound premeditated and manipulative, instrumental motivation likely occurs on a subconscious level. As Brent stated,

> I don't know if there is a conscious way of saying, "Gee I am only going to do this because I am going to get something or it's going to make me look good." Maybe some people do. I don't necessarily know if I do.

Despite the negative connotation of instrumentality, instrumental motives are not necessarily malicious or harmful to the organization; they can, in fact, be just as beneficial to the organization as behaviors driven by prosocial or task motives. Committee members can possess one or more motives for engaging in committee work. For example, when discussing his motives for engaging in committee work, Adam said, "I think what's in it for me is probably number one; number two is probably what's in it for my program or mission focus." He went on to say that the third motive he considers is his "personal relationship with whoever is asking about the committee or driving the committee."

The committee's task is often cited as the most motivating aspect of committee work that encourages active engagement, compromise, or helping behaviors. In committees, we tend to act in our own self-interest and place the good of the group, organization, or others (in roughly this order) second but not always. How can we create an environment that encourages an allocentric mind-set? How do we foster collaboration in committees and encourage committee members to consider the needs of the organization ahead of their own ambitions? Nick, the director of an academic program, defined his attitude toward committees in the following way:

> I want to make them [the committee chair] a success and the organization a success. So, whatever I can do to help, even if that's shut up and sit back and relax and don't do anything. I try my best to see what is needed from my perspective and do that. If I am in charge, I take charge, and try to get things done the way I see fit. I really try to meet the situation with the appropriate type of leadership or subordination as is required.

This chapter only scratches the surface of what could be a tome on group psychology. You can likely name three or four additional personality traits, work conditions, motives, and pet peeves that occasionally crop up in university committees that either derail a meeting or contribute to the group's success. This chapter is intended to provoke self-reflection and stress the importance of self-awareness during committee work. It is easy to identify the faults of others; however, it much more difficult to critically reflect on our own behavior. Consider the following questions:

- Whom do you like to serve with on committees, and why?
- How do you balance positional, personal, and committee obligations? Where does committee work rank on your list of priorities?
- How would your colleagues describe your committee member identity?
- How self-aware are you when you work in groups? Can you acknowledge one or more of your own personality traits that are conducive to or hinder group work?
- Do you subscribe to an allocentric or idiocentric mind-set, and how does this skew your perception of others or committee work?
- What is your motivation for serving on committees (prosocial, task, or instrumental motives)?

8

COMMITTEE GROUP
DYNAMICS

This chapter explores group dynamics in committees and some of the prevalent dimensions that influence committee performance. In a review of literature regarding groups in IHE, Bess and Dee (2008b) suggested that leaders should "understand more fully how group variables are related to individual motivation and to organizational effectiveness" (p. 325). An extensive body of research exists regarding behaviors that are conducive to group tasks and organizational performance (e.g., Coleman & Borman, 2000; George, 1990; Organ, 1988; Stone-Romero et al., 2009; Van Scotter et al., 2000). Sandelands and St. Clair (1993) explored the concept of work groups and discussed the inherent identity duality in groups that are expressed by "a multiple of persons and a single entity" (p. 423). In other words, the performance of committees is a product of the cumulative effort of committee members and a reflection of the resultant collective group culture.

We tend to assume that the principal determinant in predicting a group's performance is the intellectual abilities of committee members, but research shows that interpersonal dynamics are equally, if not more, important to group productivity than individual effort (Woolley et al., 2010) and group leadership. Efforts to regulate group work through administrative procedures and process cannot surmount the powerful influence of interpersonal dynamics on committee productivity (Kezar & Eckel, 2004). Scholars challenge the academic community to investigate the mechanics of group dynamics in order to maximize productivity. Foote and Tang (2008) suggested, "Researchers and practitioners need to identify efforts that work towards increasing commitment of team members, thereby increasing organizational citizenship behavior in the organization" (p. 933). Identifying individual, group, and organizational characteristics that encourage constructive committee behaviors is the first step in developing strategies to mitigate dysfunction and improve committee performance.

Team building begins when a committee convenes and must be fostered throughout the life of the committee. The first few committee meetings are critical in creating an atmosphere that is conducive to collaboration, trust, and cohesion. Kim recognized the importance of starting off on the right foot and attempts to establish a cohesive climate that starts with icebreakers. She has learned that "you have to be intentional about building a sense of collective spirit" to garner the most from committees and their members. Relationships will form naturally over time; however, interpersonal relationships need opportunities to form. Engineering opportunities for committee members to build relationships outside of day-to-day work routines such as social gatherings, professional development programs, off-site team-building sessions, or group travel can strengthen interpersonal relationships and improve camaraderie. Special attention should be given to the relationships that evolve, devolve, and stagnate over the life cycle of the committee, and action should be taken to ensure that these relationships do not eclipse or detract from the work of the committee. Strong interpersonal relationships can moderate the potential task conflicts that result from the "personalities, lots of energy, and debating" (Sharon) that can dominate some committee meetings. What follows is a brief discussion of cohesive committees, dysfunctional groups, and the deviant behaviors that can discourage participation or prevent progress in committees.

Cohesion

Cohesion is a measure of the collective commitment of group members to both one another and the group's efforts (Zaccaro et al., 2001), which is essential to group performance (Lott & Lott, 1965). The administrators and faculty I spoke with described cohesive committees as highly collaborative, efficient, and well-functioning groups that share a sense of purpose, direction, and camaraderie. Cohesive committees are easy to identify. Marleen said, "If you are on a very good committee, you know what that looks and feels like." Cohesive committees, according to Nick,

> actually like working with each other, they don't always agree, but they like
> working with each other, and if they like working with each other, they
> like to discuss things, they like to talk it through, and then get things done

Steve finds his committee experiences enjoyable because the members "genuinely like one another," "have fun," and "have each other's backs." A cohesive attitude results in a group with "a strong enough sense of community in that team; in those committees, anybody would feel comfortable engaging with this person or trying to address that particular issue" (Sarah). Sharon defined a *cohesive committee environment* as one in which members "give each other permission to think out loud" and explore ideas without consequences, and members build dialogue on one another's statements rather than attack differing ideas. A results-driven, collaborative, and friendly atmosphere spawned by a cohesive climate is a compelling reason to be more engaged. Research supports this observation. Individuals who perceive a team as highly effective are inspired to be engaged in the group's work (Bandura, 1995). Brent explained how cohesive committees promote discretionary effort: "If other people are in the room and they are spirited or fired up, I am more likely [to be actively engaged], just because of the energy in the room."

Committee composition is also a significant factor in measures of group cohesion (Barrick et al., 1998). Group cohesion is a function of intermember familiarity and ability to work effectively with one another. Sharon observed that the productivity of a committee is a product of "the energy of the team, and who knows who." Adam recognized, "It's much more relaxing to know you're going to a meeting with somebody that you know you can work well with." Previous experience working with other committee members nurtures a cohesive environment by providing insight into member reliability, professionalism, and expertise, which garners trust among committee members. As Marleen explained,

> You already know that these people are committed, highly competent, very professional, and when they say they're going to do a certain task they will follow up and follow through. There is definitely a respect for each other's knowledge and expertise. That, I would say, is a highly functional group.

Evidence from my initial study on committees supports existing research that shows group solidity and trust positively influence discretionary positive behaviors in committees by generating social capital, a sense of camaraderie, and cohesion, which translates into increased levels of performance (Borman et al., 2001; LePine et al., 2008; Nielsen et al., 2009; Organ et al., 2006). Cohesive committees establish a self-sustaining cycle of organizational citizenship behaviors through a process of reciprocity and social exchange, a phenomenon identified by previous organizational citizenship behavior scholars (Deckop et al., 2003; Ehrhart & Naumann, 2004). Furthermore, research has found that helping behaviors contribute to a positive attitude and affection for the team and other group members (Barsade, 2002; Kelly & Spoor, 2007; Spoor & Kelly, 2004), which is instrumental in sustaining a cohesive committee climate and promoting organizational citizenship behaviors.

Exploring the purpose of the committee and refining the committee's objectives can help elucidate relationships between and among members of the committee, uncover interdependencies, and reveal common ground, which serve to support cohesive committee environments. Research shows that high levels of task interdependence positively contribute to measures of group cohesion (C. Chen et al., 2009). Ultimately committees should strive to create a shared mental model of the group's responsibilities, rules of engagement, and sense of purpose to which all members subscribe. Trust among committee members also has a significant impact on committee group dynamics and subsequently group efficacy and productivity. Researchers have long studied the effect of trust on group dynamics in teams. Principal findings indicate that high levels of trust among group members encourage participation (Self et al., 2011), improve communications (G. Jones & George, 1998), and moderate relational conflict (T. L. Simons & Peterson, 2000).

Cohesive groups yield conditions that are conducive to active engagement, compromise, and helping behaviors. George and Bettenhausen (1990) suggested that group-level organizational citizenship behaviors are a product of three variables: group cohesion, socialization, and leadership. Committee chairs, as the group's official leader, have the primary responsibility for manipulating the various contextual variables to promote cohesion and socialization; however, members share an obligation to promote the ideals of cohesive teams through their behavior, communication, and effort. There are many articles and business consulting firms that claim to have the secret recipe for building cohesive teams. Cohesive groups result from deliberate orchestration, management, and something else that can't be qualified. The coincidental mix of the right personalities, tasks, timing, spirit, abilities, and motivations adds up to what members of exceptional groups refer to as "something special." We can't prescribe the "something special," but we can break down some common characteristics of cohesive teams that you should look for and attempt to foster in committees. Group traits commonly found in cohesive teams include the following:

- Members share a common sense of purpose and mission.
- Success is acknowledged and rewarded.
- Individuals feel accountable to the team and hold others responsible for their roles.
- There is a high degree of trust and mutual dependence among the group.
- Conflict is valued and constructive.
- Members communicate (convey and listen) effectively.
- Individual roles are defined, respected, and used appropriately.
- Members build connections that transcend conventional professional relationships.

To the extent that we can, we should attempt to choreograph committees in a manner that promotes these ideals of cohesive groups.   .

Dysfunction

Most administrators and faculty agree that committee composition is the most important factor in predicting dysfunction or cohesion in a committee. One person I interviewed argued, "Ineffective committees are not the fault of the committee; it's either the mandate of the committee or the composition . . . . That's the number one thing." As Marleen pointed out, "Some committees are just by nature going to be very cohesive and coherent, and others are just dysfunctional from the get-go, and sometimes you notice you're on one and there's nothing you can do." She went on to explain that personal agendas, work ethic, communication styles, and personalities coalesce in committees, and if these factors don't work in harmony, "all of that can put [the committee] on a dysfunctional path." Specific behaviors that lead to dysfunction are disengaged committee members, vitriolic disagreement, self-absorbed committee members, and obstructionism. Collectively, dysfunction decreases committee members' propensity to exercise organizational citizenship behaviors by negatively influencing participants' assessments of the committee's purpose, its composition, and its prospects for success. Persistent deviant behaviors reflect an inherent sense of dysfunction, which subsequently discourages many committee members from being fully engaged in the committee. Steve distilled dysfunctional committee behaviors into one astute maxim: "Dysfunction is any action that makes the committee go longer."

Disengaged members derail committee progress through passive obstructionism and dampen the positive collegial cohesive climates that breed organizational citizenship behaviors. Disengagement can take many forms. Some examples include not attending meetings, arriving late, leaving early, acting disengaged, being distracted by technology, or engaging in other work in the presence of the committee. Marleen observed that disengaged committee members can take a committee "off track quickly if there're a lot of people that are pulling it down as dead weight." Nick observed, "In most cases, if someone on the team is not being effective, it not only affects that individual, it affects the team." Disengaged members also detract from the committee's work. For example, members who are unprepared require attention from the committee chair or others to provide them with information and materials that should have been understood or read in advance. Digressions from the group's agenda to accommodate unprepared or disengaged members are a source of frustration to others. Houston pointed out that faculty have only so much tolerance for committees that use faculty time unproductively. As he said, "Anything that's robbing the clock and is not necessary, [faculty] are not going to fall for that." When individuals are frustrated by the committee's progress or lack thereof (i.e., group inertia), they tend to reserve their effort for more worthwhile endeavors, and the committee suffers as a result.

Group incongruities discourage positive discretionary behaviors by hindering committees from developing a sense of community, cohesion, and camaraderie. This is not to suggest that the committee is ineffective. Beneficial behaviors may persist despite group incongruities, but discretionary efforts do not appear to be as profuse as they are in cohesive committees. The most common result of group incongruities (i.e., disagreement, disengagement, grandstanding, and obstructionism) is group inertia. Group inertia is a condition wherein committees are unable to make progress or come to consensus, or as one faculty member put it, "We got together, but we didn't get anything done." Inertia dampens organizational citizenship behaviors because people perceive their efforts, both in-role and discretionary, as futile. Administrators and faculty admit that when they witness a committee's inability to come to a decision or make a recommendation "over and over again . . . pretty soon, they just shut down because you can't seem to get past it" (Sarah). One administrator wondered why organizations tolerate this abuse of faculty's and administrators' time and effort; they stated, "After a while, it becomes you're meeting with 20 people and the same issues get discussed and ultimately you're still doing it the way that you did before. Then you really don't need my help, right?"

The power of group inertia on engagement is reinforced by the fact that group momentum has an equally powerful and opposite positive effect. Nick explained the influence of committee momentum on individual effort:

> When you have been frustrated by lack of action, or there is a problem that has been bothering you and finally, it looks like there is movement potential, then I think people are willing to try something and step out and start doing things.

Kim has had similar experiences with the committees she manages and has witnessed the value of progressive committees. Several of her colleagues have stated, "I love being part of this committee because we get so much done." She is quick to point out that committee progress is "not random, it's by design!" Combating dysfunctional behaviors requires tact and diplomacy and may require assistance from other committee members to curb deleterious participants.

Deviant Behaviors

One administrator lamented, "One of the least effective things for me and what probably drains my interest in a committee project experience is when the leader is not willing to address issues that are impeding progress or to deal with them honestly." During my conversations with administrators and faculty, they described the following types of behavior that consistently rankle committee members and decrease committee efficacy: (a) the overly ambitious individual who volunteers for everything, or the overachiever; (b) the individual who is only interested in propagating their personal agenda or grandstanding; (c) the bad apple who spoils the meeting for everyone; and (d) the curmudgeon, or obstructionist, who erects barriers to every possible solution. Members who are overzealous, obstructive, disagreeable, or disengaged negatively influence the climate of the committee and prospects for its success.

Overachiever

Sarah was the first to identify this phenomenon when talking about group dynamics: "I mean you can have your engaged [committee member] that goes 150% almost to the point of annoying." She went on to characterize overly engaged members as the person who speaks up at every meeting regardless of the topic and relevance to their role: "There has never been a meeting where that person hasn't said something, and usually, it's something, not just a question, it's always a comment, always this always, always, always." An administrator I spoke with had a similar experience but was on the receiving end of someone else's ire. During a social function he was confronted by a colleague and told "You! You're making us all look bad." In this case, the administrator was proactively advancing the goals of the institution, and as a result his peers were expected to follow suit. He was merely doing what he thought was best for the institution, to the chagrin of his colleagues.

We might appreciate the person who volunteers to take up the work of the committee, but if it's taken to extremes, it can breed resentment among members of the committee. Bachrach et al. (2006) found evidence that helping behaviors can be perceived as an affront to one's autonomy or abilities to work independently. For example, one administrator said that they reacted negatively to unsolicited assistance and interpreted their colleague's unwelcome assistance as "taking over." As the subject matter expert, they felt it was their responsibility and thought to themselves, "This is my job, back off, let me do my job." Bradley et al. (2012) found that conflict can result when individuals feel that someone else is poaching in their field of expertise or perceive that they have not been recognized as the rightful subject matter expert. Although we want to encourage volunteerism in committees, it may be necessary to temper some members' enthusiasm to avoid creating conflict or perceived slights.

Grandstanding

Kim suggested that one of the most disruptive behaviors in committees is "a person who doesn't understand how much space they are taking in the room," or as Kevin put it, members who "spout about whatever they want to spout about" without regard for the committee or its objectives. We have all experienced the dominant member who misses no opportunity to engage in self-promotion or "who loves to hear the sound of their own voice" (Steve). Adam suggested that it is the committee chair's responsibility to manage and control committee member interactions in order to protect members' respective ideas and positions: "If the leadership doesn't control that action among the group," there is a risk that members will "pull back" and become disengaged because they feel either that they are not "a part" of the committee or that their contributions are not appreciated. Similarly, if one person is allowed to dominate a conversation, other members may begin to withdraw. Failure to confront counterproductive and/or disruptive behavior has a negative impact on committee climate. In some instances, disruptive behavior is so dominating that other members "have to acquiesce" because they get tired of engaging with the troublesome member. Acquiescing in one administrator's experience means giving up, disengaging from the committee, or expediting the committee's work so as to avoid further interaction with the disruptive member.

Bad Apple

The most alarming aspect of group incongruities is the power and influence one individual can have on the committee's performance. As Adam stated, the tenor of a group is often "driven by one individual usually within the group; you either accept that or don't accept that, and then you either shift away from the person or shift toward that person." Houston also pointed out, "It's possible for a very small minority to derail the process for a lot of people." Perhaps the most damaging impact of disengaged members on committees is the potential for their recalcitrant behavior to serve as a catalyst for establishing detachment, poor attitudes, combative dialogue, or other negative conduct as a normative committee behavior that pervades the rest of the group. As Marleen stated, disengaged committee members impede the collective effort of the group, and as Adam attested, this affects all members and potentially becomes the focus of attention and locus of effort. Bad apples discourage positive discretionary behaviors by hindering committees from developing a sense of community, cohesion, and camaraderie. Committees that are plagued with these issues are not necessarily ineffective; however, the effort required to move the committee's work forward is stymied by the negative behaviors of others, which can discourage active participation. The adverse impact of group incongruities on committee member inclinations toward discretionary behavior is further evidence that committee composition must account for an individual member's social disposition as well as their formal position and responsibilities.

Obstructionist

Obstructionist behavior in committees has a discernable impact on participation in committees by introducing a sense of futility and frustration that slowly erodes the will and effort of committee members. Furthermore, obstructionism inhibits the creation of a cohesive committee environment and can erode cohesive committee climates already in existence. Sarah, Nick, Marleen, and Adam noted that individuals who are difficult to work with introduce feelings of antipathy among committee members and for the committee's work in general. The effect is a reduction in active engagement among committee members due to the lack of progress, conflict, and annoyance produced by the person acting (consciously or unconsciously) as an impediment to the committee's progress. Obstructionists corrode the cohesive environment of committees through negativity and constant opposition to the spirit of the committee by "shooting down ideas" (Sarah), adopting a "this is how we have done it" mentality (Sharon), and being "passive aggressive" (Nick). The epitome of obstructionism is captured by this administrator's insightful statement:

> If you think about all the people who are negative, who sort of bring this notion of negative energy to a group or an office, [you realize] how much time that takes away, psychological time that takes away from you to deal with somebody who is negative.

The level of effort necessary to manage, engage, evade, or educate obstructionist individuals also detracts from committee progress and productivity. In Adam's experience, obstructionists are "a 100% hindrance to moving forward . . . . That slows everything down because not only are you having to justify a vision . . . you also have to fend off this person." In some instances, the individual may not be aware of their disruptive behavior and may be unaware of their effect on the committee. Nick suggested that obstructionism is more than just being ignorant, arrogant, or persistent; instead, obstruction is a premeditated strategy. He said, "The effort that you are going to put into derailing whatever it is, is probably more than whatever effort you are putting toward the committee. It takes work." *Contrarian* is another term to describe a person engaged in obstructionist behavior. Houston suggested, "If that person is strong-willed enough, that can lead to bad outcomes" for the committee.

Sporadic instances of disruptive behavior are expected and tolerated; however, chronic disruptive behaviors by one or more members can have lasting negative effects on the committee's proclivity to be fully engaged. Members who experience disruptive or unproductive behaviors may become annoyed, disgruntled, and mistrustful of the committee's leadership and eventually lose confidence in the committee's ability to accomplish its tasks. I suspect that you can identify one or more of these behaviors in a committee you are currently serving, and if not, one or more of these profiles is likely coming to a committee near you. Early diagnosis and intervention can prevent hours of frustration. As discussed in the previous chapter, ideally strong leadership will tactfully counter these behaviors to foster an inclusive and collegial environment.

Conflict

Disagreement among committee members is inevitable given the individual expertise, interests, and juxtapositions inherent in bringing a diverse constituency together; however, disagreement that devolves into unconstructive debate jeopardizes committee progress. Unmoderated and uncivil disagreement leads to frustration, discouragement, and group inertia. How disagreements are presented, mediated, and resolved has a tremendous influence on a person's willingness to participate in committees. Research suggests that when conflicts arise, members may engage in avoidance behavior in order to complete assigned tasks (De Dreu & Van Vianen, 2001). One administrator I spoke with said that a subgroup of a committee met routinely outside of the published committee meetings to avoid working with a member with whom they could not trust the information discussed in committee. Conflict, if it is not managed properly, can sideline one or more crucial members of the committee, which naturally affects the committee's performance and outcomes. Adam shared an honest assessment of how people behave when they become caught up in the emotional aspects of the committee and lose sight of the larger issues:

Depending on the type of personality people have, especially how sensitive you are to relative or perceived offenses or rudeness in a meeting, those sorts of behavioral things, some people just don't like it and are distracted enough by that that they're now not engaged in the meeting.

Language plays a key role in all conflicts. How we communicate in committees can exacerbate or mitigate conflict. For example, Kevin pointed out that statements like "I don't agree" can come across as "you're stupid" to some individuals. Careful attention should be given to the words we use particularly when addressing other members of the committee directly. Sharon shared her approach of approach of "I never feel like I'm in the business of convincing; I'm in the business of providing opportunity for us to find a space to engage, to try to have a healthy conversation." Attention to constructive language (let's not forget that active listening is a critical component of communication) requires effort and practice. This skill can reap rewards in all professional environments. Each committee will establish its own language over time, but it may be necessary for individuals or committee leadership to intervene, clarify, restate, and interpret communications in committee, particularly if individuals appear offended or discouraged by one another's comments.

There are essentially two types of conflict that occur in groups: relational conflict, which is conflict that occurs a result of personality differences or interpersonal dynamics, and task conflict, which is borne from disagreements about how a task is managed or executed. Adam's previous statement illustrates how individuals become discouraged when they perceive themselves as being attacked, treated unfairly, or otherwise subjected to the emotional ire of another committee member. This is an example of relational conflict. Sarah provided an example of task conflict, recalling a time when she disagreed with the actions of the committee, which led to a sense of disenfranchisement:

> It was really, really hard for me to do the work and to be invested and to be excited. I couldn't. I couldn't be excited because I just thought I so totally disagree. That was an instance where dealing with disagreement and conflict, I mean we were supposed to be using this process and everything for doing it, it didn't work, and at some point, I was like I don't care.

Nick admitted that despite the collegial atmosphere of his organization, if a disagreement arises, the issue ultimately becomes a question of "group dynamics and personalities." Conflict often results when we do not fully understand the needs of our colleagues or the impact of our ideas on their respective roles or department functions. Sharon explained that territorial disputes and selfishness can create fertile ground for conflict. By unpacking each committee member's respective priorities, reservations, and tolerances for change or additional workload, we can begin to define a problem set and a corresponding solution set that respect the boundaries and needs of all members. This process requires time and adroit facilitation to define each member's respective positions and concerns. It is not enough to simply understand another's position or perspective; it's critical that each member's concerns are respected by the committee. Transparency grants members with opportunities to disclose the details of their reservations, which serves two purposes: One, transparency validates the members' position, and two, transparency educates other members of the committee on the details of organizational processes likely not familiar to them, which supports the concept of committees as social learning systems (see chapter 1).

Research shows that conflict can decrease productivity and erode group member satisfaction (De Dreu & Weingart, 2003; Saavedra et al., 1993). When conflict becomes unproductive, strategies to resolve group conflict should be employed. Some proven methods for resolving group task and relational conflict based on group research (Bess & Dee, 2008a; Kuhn & Poole, 2000; Levi, 2014; London & London, 2007; Tjosvold, 1989) are outlined in Table 8.1.

Some of the topics discussed previously such as positive group dynamics, committee composition, clarification of roles, and establishment of clear objectives can mitigate conflict; however, latent organizational conflict might continue to undermine committee efforts if not ferreted out and exposed. Tjosvold (1989) identified two conflict management strategies: competition and cooperation. The competitive style focuses on individual success, resolving differences by challenging others, and dominance of majority opinions. In contrast, the cooperative style requires a balance of self-interest and concern for the group. Cooperative conflict management focuses on integrating diverse viewpoints, collaborating, and creating mutually beneficial outcomes. Naturally, the cooperative model tends to be more conducive to group work (Alper et al., 2000). A successful conflict management strategy is contingent on creating a committee environment that is tolerant, respectful, and considerate of diverse opinions. Each committee will develop its own tolerance for conflict and conflict management techniques. It may be necessary to discuss conflict management explicitly to determine the committee members' preferences for conflict resolution strategies.

Although conflict carries a negative connotation, it is extremely important to exposing issues hidden in the recesses of the committee's work.

TABLE 8.1
Task and Relational Conflict Management Strategies

Task Conflict Resolution	Relational Conflict Resolution
• Establish rules of engagement and procedures to resolve conflict that are justified by regulations or agreed on by the group (i.e., conflict resolution model).	• Allow committee members ample time to express their opinions and concerns.
• Define the problem and competing needs, resource constraints, or objectives.	• Encourage active listening and feedback loops to clarify statements or sentiments.
• Develop defined and mutually established criteria to assess committee recommendations and solutions, and measure proposals against the criteria rubric.	• Explore how the committee's task affects each member's unit or area of expertise, and attempt to find common ground.
• Break the task into components and examine each component for areas of agreement or disagreement to find common ground, and route out barriers to consensus.	• Curtail conversations or cancel meetings that become personal or destructive, and take a break if necessary.
• Provide training or evidence to support proposed solutions, and provide contradicting evidence where it exists to contrast pros and cons of each option.	• Periodically poll committee members individually to gauge their level of satisfaction and identify relational conflict issues.
• Explore multiple options that include all desired outcomes or as many as possible.	• Continuously reorient the committee to the issue, and attempt to create distance from the members and the task at hand.
• Vote or use nominal decision-making techniques to reach a resolution.	• Consider rotating responsibility for process management or committee governance to provide opportunities to gain an alternative perspective.
• Ask for external assistance to provide guidance and consultation.	• Discuss interpersonal conflict privately outside of the committee or mediate a meeting of two members in conflict.
• Step back and reevaluate the problem, and reframe the problem if possible.	• Restructure the committee if relational conflict persists to the detriment of the committee.

Patrick Lencioni's (2004) book *Death by Meeting* tells a fictitious tale of a group of executives who struggle with weekly meetings and risk losing control of their company as a result. In the book, the executives discover that conflicting ideas and opinions are not only the secret to a productive and engaging meeting but also the fastest path to the ideal solution. If managed correctly, conflict can actually increase productivity, improve outcomes, and bolster committee member engagement (Tjosvold, 1997). For example, task conflict can stimulate creative thinking and ultimately better results in some groups (De Dreu & Van de Vliert, 1997; T. L. Simons & Peterson, 2000). It should be noted that relational conflict does not yield the same benefits as task conflict. Relational conflict should be addressed through conflict resolution strategies; there is no silver lining to a group of individuals who do not work well together.

There are two conditions to ensure that conflict is constructive rather destructive. The first is a psychologically safe environment in which members feel comfortable sharing their opinions, thoughts, needs, and ideas without fear of retribution or judgment from other committee members (Bradley et al., 2012; Edmondson, 1999). The second is an adept leader who can effectively manage conflict and engineer constructive conflict if needed (D. Nickson et al., 2012). I was once asked to give a presentation on building effective teams to a statewide professional association. During my preparations I reached out to Kevin for assistance, and he recommended that I explore the concept of perspective taking as a central theme. Perspective taking is "the active cognitive process of imagining the world from another's vantage point or imagining oneself in another's shoes" (Ku et al., 2015, p. 79). Perspective taking seems like a simple concept, but it requires a concerted effort and genuine commitment to mediating disagreement. The challenges of understanding one another in committees can stem from our respective idiosyncrasies and our knowledge of the institution and expertise. As Kim observed, faculty and staff often

> know their own unit very, very well and therefore think they know exactly how the institution runs. It turns out that just because it runs this way in [one department] doesn't mean that's how it runs in other departments. In fact, the differences are vast. Part of the perspective taking and listening mind-set is having everyone understand that the way it works in their world isn't actually the way it works in everybody's world.

Possessing the ability to step back and look at a committee issue objectively and holistically can be more difficult for some than others. Adept committee leaders and members will find ways to encourage perspective taking by challenging assumptions in ways that promote exploration and dialogue.

Ku et al. (2010, 2015) cataloged a variety of benefits that perspective taking offers individuals and groups. The benefits of perspective taking include improved interpersonal relationships, increased capacity for cognition, better conflict resolution, enhanced communication, increased collaboration, and heightened ethical decision-making. They went one step further to argue that perspective taking is a mechanism that "helps individuals effectively navigate a world filled with mixed-motive social interactions" (Ku et al., 2015, p. 95). Many of the challenges we encounter when working in groups are a function of how well we listen. Perspective taking is arguably a prescription for many of the challenges encountered in committees. Before we explore the evolution of committees, think back on your committee experiences and consider these questions about group dynamics in the committees on which you have served:

- Have you been involved in a committee that you would describe as cohesive? What were the characteristics of this committee, and what was the driving factor in creating the cohesive climate?
- Have you experienced a dysfunctional committee? What created the sense of dysfunction, and what actions, if any, were taken to combat the group's dysfunction?
- Are there behaviors, other than those discussed in this chapter, that are disruptive or otherwise counterproductive?
- How are conflicts resolved in committees at your institution? Does institutional culture influence committee climate, tolerances for disruptive behaviors, or conflict resolution strategies?

9

COMMITTEE LIFE CYCLE

S tephen Covey (1989), author of *The Seven Habits of Highly Effective People*, said that we should "begin with the end in mind" (p. 97) when tackling a new endeavor. Regarding committees, we often focus on the beginning: who should be on the committee, and what the committee needs to do. Once the committee is formed, we tend to become hyperfocused on outcomes at the expense of attention to maintaining and nurturing the committee. The real work in committees is bookended by the most discernable committee events: the moment the committee is formed and those occasions when the committee produces an output. It is this in-between space that is the focus of this chapter. There are critical processes that occur along the spectrum of committee development that warrant our attention, if for nothing more than to help us understand where we are within the committee life cycle and establish reasonable performance expectations based on the maturation of the committee.

Evolution of a Committee

The concept of forming, storming, norming, and performing was developed by Bruce Tuckman in 1965. Tuckman later revisited his idea and added a fifth phase: adjourning, the process of decommissioning a group (Tuckman & Jensen, 1977). Tuckman argued that groups mature through a sequence of phases that are characterized by specific individual and group behaviors. If we remain cognizant of the forming, storming, norming, performing, and adjourning phases of committees, we might be able to adjust our performance and expectations to suit the situation. Figure 9.1 is adapted from Tuckman's original work, and it shows that group maturation is a function of time. Starting from inception, committees move through progressive phases until, it is hoped, they become high-functioning teams.

Figure 9.1. Committee maturation.

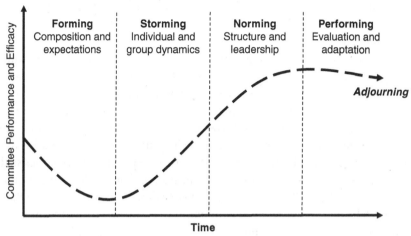

Note. Adapted from "Developmental Sequence in Small Groups," by B. Tuckman, 1965, *Psychological Bulletin*, 63, 384–399.

Although these phases seem prescriptive and straightforward, the actual process of building cohesion and the sense of camaraderie that typifies exemplary work groups often takes a more convoluted route based on the group's task, membership, environment, and other internal or external characteristics (Morgan et al., 1993). As discussed earlier, there are any number of issues that may derail a committee: people, motives, politics, job satisfaction, and resources, just to name a few. External factors and conflict among members can also prevent committees from transitioning from one stage to the next (Gersick, 1988; Richards & Moger, 2000). Some committees successfully navigate the pitfalls of small group maturation and accelerate through the forming, storming, and norming phases, especially if they have experience working with one another. Unfortunately, many committees attempt to rush from the forming phase to the performing phase without giving the group adequate time to cycle through the critical storming and norming periods that are essential to building healthy working relationships, establishing trust, and learning how to effectively resolve disagreements. This model oversimplifies the complexities inherent in group work, but it's a convenient and concise means of classifying typical behaviors exhibited throughout the life cycle of teams, groups, and committees. Understanding which phase a committee occupies can help us diagnose the challenges that prohibit progress and identify leadership opportunities. Furthermore, this model is useful for helping us understand our performance in committees and why we may exhibit or observe certain behaviors and sentiments affecting the committee. Following is a brief discussion of each phase. As you read through each phase, think about your committee experiences. Can you align your experiences with one or more of the phases outlined in the following paragraphs?

Forming is the process of getting to know one another, establishing rules of engagement, and beginning to understand the relationships between members of a team. This is the period when the basics of team building discussed earlier are so critical, and it starts, as Sharon pointed out, with "let's make sure we all know who we are" and why each person is present, especially if the committee represents a cross section of the institution. Researchers stress that time is critical to developing some of the beneficial group characteristics such as trust, communication, procedures, and norms that can lead to cohesion (Kozlowski & Ilgen, 2006) and must be considered when evaluating where a group falls on the spectrum of cohesion (Greer, 2012). If significant effort is not invested in this first and most crucial stage, the committee will have a more difficult time navigating the next two cycles (storming and norming). As a result, committee efficacy is likely to be poor. During the forming stage, members may experience anxiety or confusion about their roles or the group's objectives, communications may be forced or dominated by one or two individuals, and members may be hesitant to be fully engaged until they understand more about their fellow committee members' motives, expertise, and disposition.

Storming is the second stage in this model and is characterized by group conflict (moderate or intense, which can be healthy) and potential resistance to the group's goals, setting personal boundaries, and determining where others' boundaries exist (i.e., personality, competency, expertise, etc.). During this phase careful attention should be given to resolving disagreements regarding the committee's direction or goals, alleviating tension and conflict among committee members, adjudicating territorial disputes, fostering communication within the committee, helping members self-define their roles, and finding opportunities for members to establish their areas of expertise. To stave off a potential committee collapse, committee chairs and committee members alike should give careful attention to fostering an inclusive climate within the committee through leadership and exploration of the unique skills and perspectives each member contributes to the committee (see the section Leading for Diversity in chapter 6, p. 103, this volume). The storming phase is arguably the crux of the committee experience. Committees tend to diverge in one of two directions once the group enters the storming process: The committee either successfully negotiates these challenges and establishes a positive group dynamic marked by a cohesive environment, effective communication, collaboration, and engagement, or the committee begins the long descent into the quagmire of group inertia until the committee is able to reconcile competing priorities, establish a common goal, and clarify member roles. Formal leadership and informal leadership are critical during this phase to marshal the committee through these potentially turbulent times.

Norming is the phase during which teams solidify roles, procedures, and communications processes. At this phase, interpersonal dynamics have played out, and individual idiosyncrasies are integrated into how the committee operates. During this phase, committees are transitioning from surface-level superficial diversity issues to a deeper understanding of individual identities and skills. Norms become universal (or nearly universal), accepted rules of engagement that are influenced by the committee's leadership, informal leaders, and members of the committee and promoted through training or discussion and reflective of the institution's culture (Druskat & Wolff, 2001). Obviously, this process takes time and begins from the moment the committee forms. When new members join the committee, they are likely to introduce a new element to the committee, and as such, committee norms will bend and adapt around the new member's influence. During the norming phase, committee members are likely to reinforce their expertise, show deference to others, shift from an assertive posture to one of curiosity and inquiry, and begin modeling behavioral trends adopted or established by the group (e.g., reliability, discourse, group temperament, humor, etc.).

The performing phase is the period during which group and individual goals are reconciled, when members are sufficiently motivated, and when the committee discovers how it can perform best with the available resources and expertise. During this phase, the committee has come to terms with its task, individuals accept and perform their responsibilities, and each member executes their roles accordingly. Groups that are performing are adaptable, procedures and processes are engrained, and effort has shifted from learning how to work together as a team to completing the work at hand. This is the penultimate level of committee performance during which time committees work effectively as a team and produce high-quality outputs in using a collaborative and efficient process.

Last, the adjourning phase is the period during which the committee begins the process of disbanding. This phase results from a task being completed, dissolution of the committee, or one or more influential members leaving the committee. Effectively, losing touch with a well-functioning team or group member with whom a bond is formed can lead to a sense of sadness and loss (Tuckman & Jensen, 1977). During the adjourning phase, members may be melancholy, apprehensive, reflective, and perhaps even a little sad that their work in the committee is complete. I suspect many people will ask themselves, "Is it possible to lament the end of a committee?" I have. I sincerely enjoyed a committee on space utilization and scheduling that I was tasked to chair. I enjoyed working with each member of the committee. Our conversations were lively and productive, every member was engaged, and we knew that we were taking on and potentially solving an important problem that affected the entire institution. Serving on this committee was fun, rewarding, and impactful, and I was disappointed that I was unable to continue working on this committee.

Committee Workflow

We tend to imagine committee work as a linear decision-making process, much like an assembly line. At each meeting, the committee works toward a goal in a stepwise solution; each meeting brings us closer to the end. In reality the pathway of committee work is less direct and rarely systematic. Many committees experience delays, regressions, setbacks, and repetitious meetings with periodic bursts of productivity. Marks et al. (2001) studied the episodic nature of productivity in work groups and illustrated group work as steps that are a function of inputs, processing, and outputs that produce or require a new set of inputs that demand yet another round of processing. Groups transition to new phases of productivity between meetings and potentially regress to previous stages depending on new inputs, new information, member preparations, new members, changes in the task's scope or objectives, and other internal and external factors. This process can occur once for simple tasks or reoccur as many times as necessary to accomplish the group's goal. Research shows that group effort and productivity ebb and flow over time (Gersick, 1988). What this feels like to some members is a one step forward, two steps backward routine. Figure 9.2 (see pp. 154–155) illustrates the incremental, episodic, and hypothetical regression that might occur through the committee's decision-making process. Figure 9.2 is adapted from the original work of Marks et al. (2001).

If we take all of this into consideration, we see the progress of a committee is anything but linear and predictable. Instead, committees tend to follow a rambling course over a dynamic organizational landscape. This process can be further complicated by organizational constraints, membership turnover, the time-consuming group maturation process, and group dynamics. Like the path of a moth, erratic and seemingly inefficient, committees eventually reach their destination. Figure 9.2 is intended not to instill a sense of futility but rather to offer perspective on a phenomenon we often fail to appreciate. With practice we can improve the committee's course by creating order and purpose through leadership, task clarification, and defined committee procedures.

Decision-Making in Committees

Eventually a committee will reach a decision. The quality of that decision is dependent on the various issues, opportunities, and challenges discussed heretofore. Much like the life cycle and temporal nature of committees, decision-making in committees should progress through a logical, albeit somewhat meandering, process. Unfortunately, the path to a conclusive decision is fraught with traps and distractions. Reaching a decision in committee can be a long and arduous task punctuated by conflicting agendas and new appealing objectives that seem worthy of pursing; however, many of the shiny objects that are brought to committee only obfuscate the committee's goal. There are several strategies that are useful to tactfully interrupt the focus on extemporaneous issues. One technique used by an administrator I spoke with is to use a code word such as *fuzzy bunnies* to identify concerns that demand attention but in another venue. Fuzzy bunnies are adorable and innocent but irrelevant to most conversations. The second strategy is to employ a "parking lot"; that is, a record (usually a sticky pad stuck to the wall of the room or whiteboard) to keep track of topics that warrant further discussion but are not germane to the present conversation. Parking lot issues may be appropriate for the committee to address later or be referred to the appropriate office, committee, or individual for resolution.

How committees reach a decision may seem like wizardry, but all committees use one or more decision-making models or techniques. The decision-making model or technique used by a committee is driven by the task, leadership, and committee membership. Ideally, the process for reaching a decision will be explicitly laid out with the committee before work begins. One of the challenges to decision-making techniques in committee is that all processes must necessarily be participatory, otherwise why convene the committee? Some decision-making models lend themselves to participation better than others, and it may be necessary to blend one or more decision-making strategies to resolve issues brought to committee. Table 9.1 outlines common decision-making models that can be employed in committees.

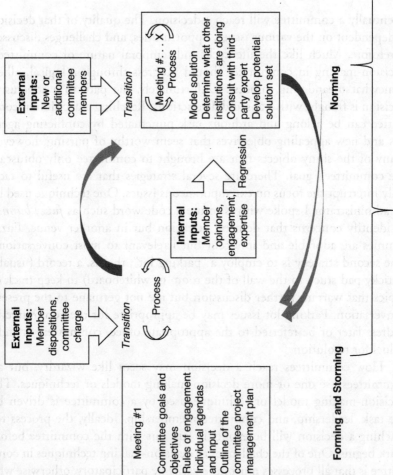

Figure 9.2. Temporal nature of committee work.

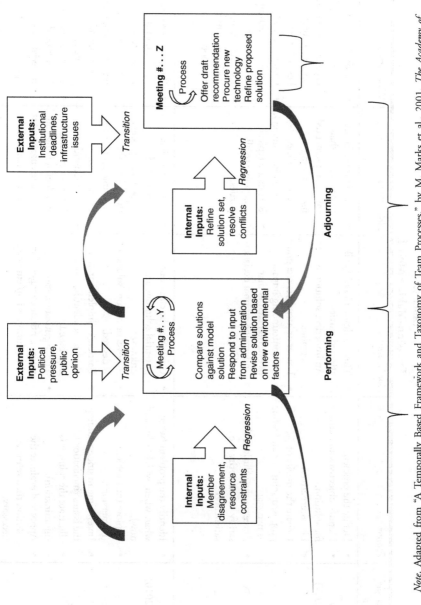

Note. Adapted from "A Temporally Based Framework and Taxonomy of Team Processes," by M. Marks et al., 2001, *The Academy of Management Review, 26*(3), 356–376.

TABLE 9.1
Decision-Making Models

Decision Model or Technique	Process	Application	Advantages	Disadvantages
Bounded rationality (Simon, 1957)	• Define the problem. • Identify objectives and criteria for solution. • List alternatives. • Debate the merits of proposed solutions and refine as necessary. • Agree on the solutions that satisfy the majority (i.e., satisficing).	• There is desire to satisfy all affected parties. • An imperfect solution is acceptable. • Leader or members recognize the confounding impact of external factors that undermine rational decision-making.	• Solutions are limited to only those that can be implemented using existing resources (time, information, money). • Results are typically acceptable to all parties.	• Limited information, resources, or cognitive capacity to consider all options may eliminate the best solution. • Outcomes are based on group satisfaction rather than best fit. • External forces influence decisions, which can result in suboptimal outcomes.
Creative (Proctor, 2010)	• Identify the problem (who, what, when, which, why, and how). • Explore the problem (immersion). • Invest time in understanding the issues (incubation). • Illustrate the solution(s) (illumination). • Apply and evaluate the solution then refine as necessary.	• Goals may be clear, but potential solutions are unknown. • A novel or custom solution is desired. • Barriers to implementation need to be identified and negotiated. • The organization can tolerate minor changes after the solution is implemented.	• It is an iterative, flexible, and unbounded process that allows for multiple options to be explored. • The unbounded nature of creative problem-solving can promote engagement and ownership of the issue.	• Process can require significant time to formulate solutions. • If the process is unstructured, it can become frustrating for some members. • Solutions may be infeasible if not bounded by material, financial, or other operational constraints.

Delphi (Dalkey, 1969; Dalkey & Helmer, 1963; Delbecq et al., 1986)	• Survey instrument is distributed to stakeholders to define and refine the problem. • Results are evaluated, and a new survey (or interview) is conducted to pursue lines of inquiry based on member input. • Process repeats until consensus is reached.	• Multiple experts (from the same or different fields) with potentially different ideas must agree on one outcome. • It can be used to consolidate divergent viewpoints. • Group cannot convene face-to-face.	• It avoids any face-to-face conflict between experts. • It encourages independent thought and analysis. • The method is more effective at reaching consensus than committee discussions.
			• Process requires a person adept in survey methods. • It requires considerable administrative time and effort. • Bias can be introduced by the person administering the survey.
Nominal (Delbecq et al., 1986; Van de Ven & Delbecq, 1971)	• Each member states the problem in writing. • Problem statements are cataloged. • Solutions are proposed by each member and collectively discussed one at a time. • Solutions are refined and evaluated. • A silent vote is taken to determine the outcome.	• A wide variety of potential solutions is desired. • Each member is allowed ample time to evaluate and reflect on the problem and potential solutions. • All opinions are weighted equally. • The process of documentation encourages commitment, accountability, and ownership of the problem.	• It is a highly structured process. • It can avoid conflict. • The absence of domineering voices or popular opinions allows individuals to engage in unbounded creative decision-making. • It mitigates some of the challenges of managing interactive groups.
			• Rigid process can stifle collaboration and adaptability as the problem evolves. • This method is antithetical to traditional conceptions of what constitutes a committee meeting. • The emotional significance of a decision may not be conveyed.

(Continues)

TABLE 9.1. (*Continued*)

Decision Model or Technique	Process	Application	Advantage	Disadvantage
Rational (Eriksson, 2011)	• Recognize a problem. • Identify all potential options. • Systematically evaluate all options. • Select the option that best addresses the problem based on available evidence. • Implement the selection solution and monitor performance.	• Impact of decision or outcome is a critical institutional priority. • There is desire for the best solution versus the best possible solution. • The committee has unfettered access to information and resources.	• It typically results in the best possible outcome. • Committees that are granted wide latitude to select the best option are likely to be more engaged. • Evidence-based decision-making lends itself to objectivity and impartiality.	• It does not consider the desires of individuals; instead the solution is driven by an objective assessment of the problem. • Process requires time to identify and evaluate all options. • Scarce resources (e.g., money, infrastructure) may need to be allocated to implement the solution.
Ringi (Ala & Cordeiro, 1999; Hattori, 1978; Maccoll, 1995)	• Intense discussion occurs formally and informally to root out and define a problem. • Written documents are generated outlining a problem and proposed solution. • The document is circulated (vertically and horizontally) within the organization. • Members provide anonymous edits and comments. • Cycle is repeated until consensus is reached.	• It avoids face-to-face meetings and conflict at the most difficult stages of decision-making. • It allows all members to be included and voice opinions. • Members can gather information and input from other members of the organization who are not members of the committee.	• It allows members to be independent thinkers without fear of upsetting their friends or colleagues. • The decision-making process is documented for future reference.	• This method is antithetical to traditional conceptions of what constitutes a committee meeting. • This process requires time and someone to manage the document and version control and assimilate opinions. • The authors of the documents typically control the conversation and have decision-making authority.

Bounded rationality is the most common decision-making strategy used by committees. This model is straightforward and consistent with higher education's ideals of collegiality and, to a degree, the scientific method: suggest a solution, explore all possibilities, reach a decision in consideration of all variables, test the decision through implementation, and refine as necessary. Furthermore, one can argue, as I do in chapter 1, that the heuristic environment of committees is an invaluable experience that benefits both organizations and individuals. Bounded rationality provides members with opportunities to be engaged in the committee's work in ways that nominal decision-making techniques do not. The decision-making process that I observe in committees most often is a hybrid of bounded rationality and creative decision-making models.

Some of these decision-making models might seem improbable in committee settings because they rely on unconventional methods, like anonymous voting, written position papers to facilitate debate, or a rigid systematic voting process, that seem antithetical to traditionally open, semistructured committee meetings; however, research shows that blending nominal decision-making and interactive strategies can produce better decisions and do so more efficiently than many other decision-making models (Van de Ven & Delbecq, 1971). Furthermore, nominal methods are particularly helpful in larger committees because nominal processes tend to moderate the open debate that becomes untenable as groups get larger. Perhaps we can migrate away from the traditional round the table, knuckles dug into the mahogany, heated discussion and circular conversation to a more methodical approach that includes a structured process involving documented opinions and tangible artifacts to propel the committee toward its objective. Naturally, the decision-making model should fit the problem at hand. Despite our best efforts to attain the best outcome, there are a number of confounding phenomena that can confuse decision-making efforts that are worth mentioning.

Consensus

How many times have you heard the term *decision by consensus* in higher education? Contrary to popular opinion, group consensus does not mean that everyone agrees on the same outcome. Consensus simply means that all concerned parties have a role in determining the outcome and understand how it is reached. The result may not be everyone's preference, but it is generally recognized as an acceptable solution. What likely happens in most committees is an alternate form of normative decision-making theory that includes democratic and consultative processes. Democratic decision-making is exactly what you imagine it to be: A group convenes to discuss and formulate proposed solutions that are later put to a vote, and the preferred solution is advanced to the appropriate authority. Consultative decision-making involves getting input from each member of the group, processing proposed ideas, and formulating a decision based on the members' input. Consultative decision-making does not necessarily involve collaborating so much as collecting opinions and ideas from the group to create a solution that satisfies most members of the group (assuming the leader respects the members' input and adheres to their wishes). Both decision-making techniques include a period of negotiation to solicit and integrate member ideas; nevertheless, the result is likely to leave one or more members unsatisfied. Consensus in higher education is essentially a form of collegial democracy.

Garbage Can Model

If we apply the garbage can model (Cohen et al., 1972) to higher education functions, we must acknowledge the anarchistic nature of our organizations and that procedures for finding solutions to problems do not mirror the systematic decision-making theories and techniques listed previously. Instead, the garbage can model presupposes that decision-makers have limited and/ or sporadic involvement in the decision-making process and therefore may not fully understand the complexity of the problem. The slurry of problems, solutions, stakeholders, and available opportunities that coalesces in the decision-making process constitutes a garbage can from which decisions are extracted without leaning on rational decision-making schemes (Cohen et al., 1972). What results are solutions that are not based on the problem; rather the problem justifies the solution and vice versa. When a perceived problem aligns with an existing solution, the two are married regardless of the legitimacy of the problem or appropriateness of the solution. In the garbage can model, problems are resolved based on available solutions, so the work begins without fully understanding what the problem is and what is required to satisfy the organization's needs. Instead, the institution applies a seemingly viable solution to a problem not because it is appropriate but because it is expedient and available, and the problem helps justify the solution. Think of this process as decision-making done in reverse.

Abilene Paradox

The Abilene paradox (Harvey, 1988) is a situation in which members of a group do not communicate their position, decide on outcomes individually, and avoid confrontation to maintain harmony. The result of this condition is a solution that satisfies no one. Harvey (1988) went so far as to suggest that groups trapped in the Abilene paradox actually generate solutions that are contradictory to the needs of the organization and individual group members. Put simply, the group is ineffective. It defeats itself by failing to engage in the discourse and deliberation that are necessary in group decision-making. This phenomenon tends to result from members' reluctance to challenge proposed ideas for fear of repercussions or creating discord. It can also result from the perception that efforts to sway the group's presumed position will be insubstantial or futile. Tension and frustration are typical by-products of this seemingly innocuous phenomenon. Group members leave the situation feeling unsatisfied, disappointed, and unhappy with the outcome. The next time you abdicate your position and go with the flow for what you perceive to be for the benefit of the committee, think again. What if everyone else is doing the same thing? You have just entered the Abilene paradox!

Groupthink

The Abilene paradox is similar to groupthink in that individuals want to avoid conflict to maintain harmony; however, the difference between the two is that groupthink occurs as a result of leadership, external pressure, and group norms (e.g., discourse, cohesiveness, tolerance for opposing viewpoints, etc.) that play out in a social context (Parks, 1999), whereas the Abilene paradox is an individual dilemma that occurs silently within each member. Groupthink encourages members of a group to conform to the dominant voice or idea, objections are discouraged (implicitly or explicitly), and the results are often flawed in some capacity. Deviant members, external observers or evaluators, and the encouragement of diversity of opinion can counteract groupthink. Recall that healthy conflict is critical for not only reaching the best solution but also promoting committee member engagement.

It is incumbent on the committee chair to maintain transparency throughout the process and provide justification for how the committee reaches its decision. As members of the committee, we should be cognizant of these decision-making traps and act to avoid the garbage can model, Abilene paradox, and groupthink. Addressing these issues may require a sidebar conversation with the committee chair or in extreme cases an intervention by senior leadership.

Committee Diagnostics

Periodically, committees should be surveyed for feedback on the committee's performance. This informal process should focus on ways to improve the committee, with specific emphasis on goals, relevance of the committee's charge, work procedures, distribution of effort, and potential challenges. The life cycle of committees, the temporal nature of committee work, and interpersonal relationships make it difficult to accurately diagnose the impediments to committee progress. Committee charge, composition, and performance are interrelated and interdependent to the degree that adjusting one facet will have repercussions on all other elements of the committee. Figure 9.3 illustrates the interconnected relationship of key aspects of committees discussed previously.

Group evaluations are common among production and project management teams in the business world; a similar process might be employed to evaluate the performance of committees. Anonymous surveys can provide valuable information to committee chairs and the organization on how committees can be managed or retooled to be more effective. Evaluations should assess the committee on at least three dimensions: design of the committee's task, group performance (e.g., leadership, cohesion, collaboration), and individual contributions. For example, evaluations could be used to identify organizational support issues or external pressures that impede the committee's effort. Although this may not be well received by committee members, I imagine that participation, contributions, and the quality of committee work will drastically improve if a formal assessment of committees is implemented.

Drawing on results from a study on ad hoc committees, researchers concluded that "people do not examine the implications of their governance process" (Hartley & Wilhelm Shah, 2006, p. 89). Committees, and many other governing bodies, occasionally fail to adequately monitor the results of their decisions, to the detriment of the organization. Committees should

Figure 9.3. Committee diagnostics.

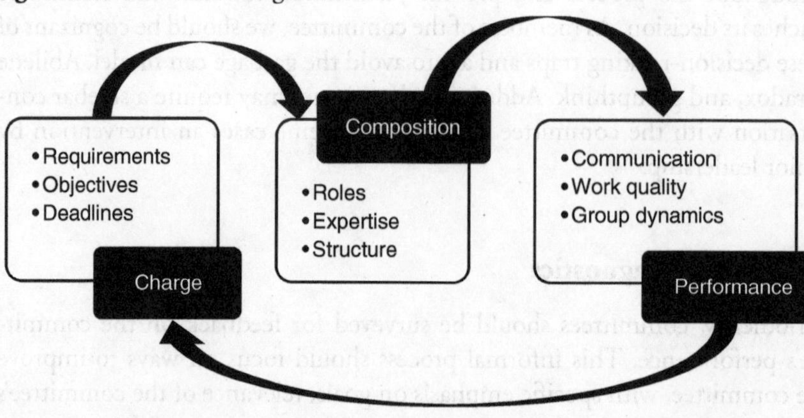

- Requirements
- Objectives
- Deadlines

Charge

Composition
- Roles
- Expertise
- Structure

- Communication
- Work quality
- Group dynamics

Performance

not only evaluate their performance but also assess the outcome of their work. Committees that disband too quickly or move on to more pressing topics risk creating a minefield for future administrators and faculty if an assessment of the committee's work is not conducted. The responsibility for decision-making comes with an obligation to chaperone that action to an acceptable conclusion. This responsibility should be clearly articulated to the committee and spelled out in committee charters. Committees should periodically revisit the decisions and programs under their purview to determine if their outcomes are durable, appropriate, effective, and legitimate. A simple assessment using focus groups, field audits, examination of relevant documents, or other performance metrics defined by the committee when the proposed solution is implemented will suffice. If necessary, topics should be reintroduced to the committee for refinement when deficiencies are noted.

Restructuring an Existing Committee

The life span of teams is finite. Every so often the group needs to be restructured. Committees become less effective over time because of burnout, lack of new perspectives, and deterioration in team performance. Research shows that membership change can reduce conflict, improve output, and contribute to group cohesion (Arrow & McGrath, 1993). Ad hoc committees that convene for a finite period may not require reshuffling of committee membership or experience a high degree of turnover; however, the membership of standing committees scheduled to meet indefinitely will likely change because of promotions, retirements, departures, and even the occasional removal of a committee member. For example, Sharon shared an instance where she turned down a committee chair position because she felt the topic needed "somebody else's voice" to do justice to the committee's work. A desire for new perspectives, replacement of a deviant member, and changes to the committee's charge may also precipitate a reorganization of committee membership. In some cases, new leadership is necessary to keep the committee moving forward.

Initiating change in committee composition should be done strategically with the same intention and care used to recruit new committee members. If it is determined that the committee's composition is the root of the committee's struggles, one or more members may need to be removed, or the committee may need to be rebooted. The introduction of a new member can and often does interrupt the committee's momentum, modifies the committee's culture, and changes group dynamics (perhaps radically). New members are often disadvantaged because they are not afforded time to acclimate to the committee and are likely unaware of the committee's social, oratorical, and political history. Therefore, it may be necessary for the chair to meet with the new member to provide historical context, explain the purpose of the committee, set expectations, and outline the committee's rules of engagement. Some of the administrators and faculty I interviewed voluntarily took responsibility for onboarding new members by meeting with them outside of the committee to discuss the committee's work, providing counsel when asked, and offering to help new members on assigned tasks. Although it is seldom done officially, chairs may elect to appoint a mentor to assist the new member through the first few committee meetings.

Although governing boards typically have procedures for removing members by way of a formal process, committees often lack the process and stomach to forcibly remove a member, but it does happen. For example, Marleen, an experienced human resources administrator, once asked for someone on a search committee to be removed because they had violated the institution's confidentiality notice. More typically, we tend to tolerate deviant behaviors to the detriment of the committee. With foresight, committees can be equipped to deal with difficult or ineffective members by outlining performance expectations and procedures for removing individuals in committee charters or institutional policies and procedures. For example, Santa Clara University's (2016b) University Policy Committees Charter states that an appointed member on a chartered university policy committee may be removed by the University Coordinating Committee after three unexcused absences. If you must replace a member of the committee, consider asking an adjunct faculty member. There is growing concern about the plight of adjunct faculty and their diminished status in IHE despite their instrumental role. Research shows that inclusion of adjunct faculty in shared governance and organizational decision-making is improving, but inequities still exist (W. Jones et al., 2017).

The second form of restructuring involves changing the committee's charge. Altering the charge, expanding the scope, or adding responsibilities of the committee can create frustration among committee members. If the committee's charge is modified, membership should also be modified accordingly. Furthermore, expect Tuckman's (1965) forming, storming, norming, and performing process to reset. By changing the committee's charge, one is effectively creating a new committee; however, the committee will retain much of the interpersonal and group dynamic norms as artifacts from their time working together on the previous task. Redirecting committee effort requires a transition period that can be facilitated by observing fundamental change management strategies. The following steps are a synopsis of Kotter's (1995) widely referenced eight-step process:

1. Identify demand: Gauge interest, desire, and group tolerance for the proposed change. Initiate dialogue around the issue to gather information about the impact and potential challenges to change.
2. Find and organize supporters: Identify champions within the group and across the organization to help facilitate and promote change. Leverage stakeholder interests to solicit buy-in and participation.
3. Provide clarity and vision: Work with the group and organization to develop a clear and concise explanation of the problem and proposed solution.
4. Market the idea to the organization: Communicate this vision to stakeholders to establish expectations and prepare the organization for implementation.
5. Address potential challenges: Identify stakeholders, processes, and technologies that might be impediments to success. Engage those that may challenge the solution and seek to find a mutually amicable solution or way to avoid conflict.
6. Find immediate success: Recognize small wins that bring the group and organization closer to the final objective. Use small changes to build momentum to sustain systematic change.
7. Refine change: Gather feedback as changes are being implemented to determine the impact of proposed strategies or solutions. Modify the solution as necessary to account for unforeseen challenges or needs.
8. Establish the new normal: Maintain effort to entrench the changes within the organization using a top-down and grassroots approach. Weave changes into existing programs, policies, and procedures wherever possible.

The principles of change management apply to not only redirecting the efforts of the committee but also, critically, the execution of the committee's charge.

One last thought on committee service. Kim Eby stressed the importance of recognizing individual service on committees. She routinely distributes handwritten thank-you cards to her committee members, provides gift cards, and celebrates committee accomplishments. Members of standing committees are acknowledged annually, and ad hoc committees are celebrated when they accomplish their goal. I admire Kim's recognition of the invaluable contribution her colleagues make to her institution and her commitment to ensuring that they are appreciated. It is no wonder she has a reputation for being an exceptional committee chair and colleague. Steve said that it's not uncommon for him and his colleagues to periodically recognize one another for service to committees via email or in person. Many administrators and faculty perceive service on a committee as a thankless job. Committees can be recognized in any number of formal, informal, private, or public ways; for example, institutional newsletters, websites, or functions, to name a few. Recognition highlights not only the individual contributions of committee members but also the importance of committee work to institutional performance, which may inspire others to be more engaged.

10

CLOSING THOUGHTS

How does an organization create the right conditions for committees to thrive? What can we do as committee chairs or members to encourage levels of commitment and dedication found in high-performing teams? We have discussed some of the organizational, leadership, and independent characteristics that can be instituted to encourage committee engagement, but how are these efforts choreographed? Shaping a committee is a lot like working on your golf swing or learning how to bake bread. You should tinker with only one aspect of the committee at a time lest you confuse which cause results in which effect. Challenges to evolving committees into high-functioning, effective, and productive teams include our historical conception of committees, their role in our organizations, and how they are managed. As Kevin stated,

> Once you have norms and patterns in place, it's very difficult to change them. You have to have very specific people, typically leaders, who take on very specific behaviors in order to make those changes. Most leaders in organizations don't do that, and so it's the inertia of the organization that is reflected in a lot of committees.

In their book *Hot Groups*, authors Lipman-Blumen and Leavitt (1999) argued that highly effective work groups are difficult to orchestrate. Instead, they suggested that several conditions must align through design and to some extent chance to yield ultra-high-functioning teams, task forces, committees, or work groups. These groups are characterized by a "preoccupation with their tasks" (p. 27) and "have a sense of higher purpose, of embarking on an ennobling mission" (p. 28). The work of the committee is only half of the equation; we also need to be thinking about group dynamics. Steve found that his committees band together because "we are very collegial, and we know we're in this together. We know we're like suffering under the same weight, and we want to help one another."

An issue that warrants attention because of its importance to societal, organizational, and individual welfare is how committee chairs and members identify and address institutional constructs that disadvantage members in committees and discourage participation in university committees. IHE are catalysts for sociopolitical change. Through our work in institutional governance, we can begin to transform conceptions of gender roles and the nature of work and begin to rectify injustice. How can committees support this change? We begin by appointing women and underrepresented faculty, administrators, and staff to chair committees; we discuss our committee experiences to identify potential incidents of bias, discrimination, or norms that create challenges to engagement; we work to create a psychologically safe and inclusive committee environment that encourages and respects diversity of perspective and opinion; we challenge normative behaviors that produce predictable outcomes; and we remain cognizant of how our words, actions, and expectations might be perceived by or influence others in the committee.

LePine et al. (2008) argued, "Scholars have not been able to offer many clear recommendations to managers regarding ways to improve the functioning and effectiveness of teams in their organizations" (p. 274). One of the aims of this book is to help explain the social and professional dynamics within committees and the strong moderating effect group composition and interpersonal relationships can have on the effort and conduct of committee members. While we can manipulate some variables to yield better results from others around us, I prefer to use individual performance as our unit of analysis. In other words, we should examine our performance and model those behaviors that we desire from others. As Steve stated, much of what we do to improve the performance of committees is about "policing yourself."

Although this book cannot prescribe a treatment for the committee that ails you, it does outline practices that can mitigate some of the challenges you might encounter in a committee and help you diagnose potential problems and identify possible solutions. One of the challenges committees face is that they are not subject to scrutiny the way that other aspects of our work lives are critiqued. Most administrators and faculty don't assess committee work the way, for example, projects, organizational processes, or individual performances are evaluated. The common sentiment that I encountered was that the issue of committee efficacy is largely ignored. One faculty member I spoke to admitted that they "haven't ever had a conversation about it as a thing; it's just what one does" and that the evaluation and attention to committee performance "does represent an opportunity for value."

In this book, I attempt to describe the phenomenon of university committees and provide opportunities to reflect on our individual performance, critique committee experiences, and discover ways to improve committee work. I expect that much of what has been discussed resonates with you and your role within higher education. The experiences relayed by the contributors to this book appear common throughout higher education, and you likely have anecdotal evidence to support the conclusions presented herein. Much of this research originated from my doctoral dissertation on organizational citizenship behaviors in university committees. My initial study was the first of its kind, and two remarkable events occurred. First, interviews, which I expected participants to find tedious, were lively and engaging conversations. Second, I was surprised that nearly everyone I spoke to was critically reflecting on their committee experience for the first time. From this experience, I deduced that the mechanics of committees are largely ignored. In subsequent conversations about my findings and with some gentle prodding from my colleagues, I became convinced that a book on committees might find an audience with university administrators and faculty and contribute to the making of 21st-century IHE.

In the process of writing this book, I conducted a significant amount of research on committees, organizational citizenship behaviors, and group dynamics. What I find most interesting is that the results of my research mirror research that has been conducted in the business world; however, it was not until I began writing this book that I discovered myriad similarities between committee performance and phenomena documented in extant team, small group, and professional development research. One of the things that surprised me most was the alignment between my discussions with administrators and faculty and existing handbooks regarding meetings, teamwork, and leadership commonly used in the business world. For example, I was halfway through the first draft of this book when I read the *HBR Guide to Making Every Meeting Matter* (*Harvard Business Review*, 2016a). This experience helped validate what I have observed, discovered, and attempted to convey in these pages.

While I was researching this topic, it occurred to me that no one has attempted to define or acknowledged how the changing landscape of higher education threatens the viability of multidisciplinary committees. In higher education the ideas of a meeting, a committee, an advisory board, and a task force tend to get confused. I argue that we need to appreciate the nuance of group gatherings, apply an appropriate title, and assign corresponding expectations. As stated previously, most administrators and faculty do not have the requisite training or experience to effectively manage a committee. Should we not include committees among various group modalities commonly addressed by leadership and management texts? Much of what we do in higher education could be managed by means of a traditional task force or even meetings that don't have to rise to the level of a committee. Levi (2014) suggested that teams are "used to solve every organizational problem, regardless of whether they are an appropriate way to organize the work" (p. 34). Kim also lamented the abuse of committees. She recognized that there is "variability in what level of inclusiveness and investment" is needed for each institutional challenge and that a degree of "common sense or discretion" should be exercised when considering a new committee. This might seem ironic given the title of this book, but I suggest that organizations should discourage the formation of committees whenever possible. Committees should be reserved for those issues that are complex, cross functional, are evolving, and demand persistent attention. Most of the challenges we face day-to-day do not demand this level of participation. Instead, organizations should encourage meetings and task forces or assign the project to an individual and then vet the results through a standing committee or appropriate authority.

Another challenge that I believe will affect the way committees are used in the future is resource constraints. For example, reductions in state funding and responsibility-centered management budget models might encourage departments to become insular and less receptive to collaborative ventures that have the potential to affect department budgets. Internally, departments may wrestle for control of specific functions to adapt to their respective needs without thinking about the long-term implications on governance structures or the larger institution's welfare. If colleges, departments, and units become independent of the larger organization, how does this newfound freedom erode traditional governance structures, or, alternatively, does it create opportunities to establish a more methodical and systematic means of collaboration? Much is written about the differences between the administrative and the academic divisions in higher education. I attempt to identify some of these dissimilarities in the context of committees without driving the wedge deeper. One thought that occurred to me during my interview with Sharon was that most academic committees (e.g., curriculum review, admissions, promotion and tenure, etc.) have existed in some form since the dawn of higher education and share similarities across institutions. History serves as a blueprint for academic committees and departmental governance structures. Procedure, roles, behaviors, attitudes, expectations, and outcomes are guided by the legacy of faculty governance that is woven into the fabric of higher education. In contrast, many administrative committee functions are the result of emerging trends, new regulations, and changing economic conditions. The dynamic and sometimes frenetic nature of administrative committees (especially those convened under duress to address immediate risks or regulations) introduces new circumstances that are not accounted for in the institution's memory. Treading into the frontier of higher education governance, which many progressive institutions are attempting to do, has cascading effects on how committee members engage and execute their responsibilities. Both forms of committees are essential to institutional governance; however, each form places different demands on member engagement, tolerances for idiosyncratic behavior, and preferred leadership traits. Administrator and faculty attitudes toward committees are different as a result of their upbringing within the organization. These differences should be respected, leveraged, and married when possible.

In addition to exploring how committees do and do not function, I also posit that committees are essential components of administrator and faculty development, learning, and promotion. The general premise of this book is that we, regardless of our position and authority within a committee, are responsible for shaping the committees on which we serve and are individually accountable for the committee's success. As informal leaders, followers, participants, and peers, it is our obligation to evaluate our performance and adapt to the climate of the committee. We should strive to apply our capabilities, learning, and expertise where necessary to subtly pilot committees toward a more efficient and rewarding experience by being self-aware, actively managing our individual performance, and demanding the most from our colleagues. Each committee will have its own unique membership profile, political issues, resource constraints, and challenges; however, these issues can be effectively negotiated with a little attention to the social dynamics, logistics, leadership, and personal performance issues addressed throughout this book. The concept of equifinality suggests that the same outcome can be produced by following multiple pathways. We must begin to consider how we can adapt to the needs of our respective organizations in ways that increase productivity while simultaneously enriching our knowledge and social networks. I argue that committees are the gateway to future success in higher education, and if we are determined to succeed in our role as administrators and faculty, we will make a conscious and focused investment in our committee work.

Last, the chorus I hear most often in higher education today is that there is never enough time to get the work done. Managing committees and engaging in committees, as laid out in this book, require an investment that many of us cannot afford. Instead, we may need to look at specific aspects of our performance or committee management that will yield the greatest return on our effort. For example, focusing on agenda distribution and tracking action items might be a reasonable expectation and an excellent place to start transitioning committees toward a more regimented process if your organization has not done so already. Taking time to talk through some of the points raised previously (e.g., individual roles, committee objectives, professional development, individual leadership and followership styles, etc.) as simple discussion topics can serve as a catalyst for reframing how we and our colleagues conceptualize our committee experiences.

Methodology and Participant Biographies

I conducted an extensive literature review to weave together research on small groups, teams, organizational citizenship behaviors, and what little research does exist on committees. The quotes used throughout this book are excerpts from face-to-face interviews with administrators and faculty from seven different institutions and 10 different professional disciplines. All interviews were audio recorded, transcripts were created from the recordings, and interview data were analyzed using phenomenological methods proposed by Moustakas (1994). Through this process, I attempted to "develop a composite description of the essence of the shared experience" (Creswell, 2013, p. 76) as described by individuals who participate in university committees. Naturally there are some limitations to the information provided in this book. Phenomena revealed through interviews are limited to those environmental and social conditions that interviewees acknowledge as real and meaningful. There are without doubt many contextual and social elements of committee work that subtly act on personal behavior that never register with interviewees and are therefore inconspicuous omissions in this work. Also, because this work is the first to examine committees as a unique phenomenon, a broad perspective was necessary to explore the variety of experiences, environmental conditions, social dynamics, and motives related to committee engagement. This effort does not lend itself to detailed examination of any one aspect of committee work; instead, this book is intended to reveal characteristics of committees and individual behaviors that illustrate patterns based on scientific methods that withstand subjective and analytical scrutiny but nevertheless warrant further investigation.

This book would not have been possible without the candid, thoughtful, and genuine reflections provided by the administrators and faculty I interviewed. Interviewees were offered an opportunity to keep their identity and their institution anonymous. Throughout the book, I took the liberty of redacting names when I suspected that statements might be misconstrued or bring unwanted attention to that individual or reflect poorly on their respective institution. The administrators and faculty quoted extensively throughout this book graciously offered their time and insights to help us understand committees. Their biographies are included in an About the Contributors section at the end of this book.

Virtual Committees

Shortly after submitting the final manuscript for this book to Stylus Publishing, the world began grappling with COVID-19, and institutions of higher education (IHE) struggled to implement safe ways to maintain governance and deliver instruction during a period of uncertainty and rapidly evolving conditions. At the time of this writing, I have not been on campus in 6 weeks, and I have not met with any of my colleagues face-to-face for nearly a month, yet the important work that we do continues. I want to address virtual committees in the context of my previous work to help us navigate, what is for many of us, a novel committee experience.

In addition to putting pressure on existing committees, the COVID-19 pandemic precipitated many new committees and subcommittees to help IHE address the unprecedented challenges of transitioning instruction to alternate virtual formats; shifting student and employee support to online services; and continuing the governance of the institution with our faculty, administrators, and students distributed across cities, states, and the world. If there was ever any doubt that committees are indispensable to the governance of IHE, COVID-19 proved that committees are the cornerstone of institutional innovation and management.

I discovered that there are some benefits to holding virtual committee meetings coupled with an equal amount of challenges that warrant our attention. The work of virtual committees is no less important than traditional face-to-face committees, perhaps more so during difficult times, and therefore requires the same level of scrutiny, consideration, and support as traditional in-person meetings. Virtual committees can take many forms. "Most 'virtual' teams operate in multiple modes: sometimes face-to-face, sometimes via electronic communication, sometimes interacting with each other directly, and sometimes working as individuals" (Kimble, 2011, p. 7). This short appendix is intended to serve as supplemental material to the information provided throughout *Understanding University Committees* to help us navigate virtual committees; an organizational construct that will become a ubiquitous and indispensable facet of university governance and organizations in the future (Gilson et al., 2015).

In my experience, the metamorphosis of in-person committees to a virtual body illuminated the links between committee members and their connections to other areas of expertise within the institution (see Figure 1.2 in chapter 1) and emphasized attention to committee composition (see chapter 4). Working remotely highlighted some of the ideas contained early in the book in chapter 1, namely the benefit of committees in their capacity as social networking systems, social learning instruments, and double-knit organizations that bind our organizations together. The social aspects of committees cannot be underestimated from either a personal or an organizational perspective. Committees are the forum where our relationships are formed and maintained, but there are some drawbacks to a virtual organization. Many of the faculty and administrators that I spoke to during the COVID-19 pandemic remarked that the intensity of working virtually does not compare to office life. The constant connection can become a serious detriment to our well-being if unchecked. Just as it is important to lay ground rules in committee meetings, it is also important to set expectations and boundaries for virtual committees (see chapter 5).

Reading through past research, using my own experience, and gathering feedback from my colleagues at George Mason University, I have cataloged some of the predominant challenges and benefits of virtual committees for our consideration.

Challenges

- Engagement: Participants may be distracted by other work during a virtual meeting (Wasson, 2004). Virtual meetings provide unique opportunities to disengage and hide clandestine activities!
- Socialization: Building group identity and shared mental models can be more difficult in a virtual environment. As a result, intragroup trust, camaraderie, discourse, and productivity may suffer (Hallier & Baralou, 2010).
- Technology: Just as there is always "that guy" in every group who does not seem to understand emotional intelligence, there is always some people in a virtual meeting who are technologically inept, uncomfortable using collaborative technology, or competing with their teenager for bandwidth. Virtual meetings are subject to technological disruptions which can derail progress and engagement (Laitinen & Maarit, 2018).
- Harassment: Harassment and discrimination in virtual environments can take many forms that may not be readily apparent to the perpetrator or others at the expense of the recipient who may struggle with how to resolve virtual abusive behavior (Roehling, 2017).

Benefits

- Better results: Research shows that "virtual teams tend to take more time to make decisions but also generate a higher quantity of unique ideas compared to face-to-face teams" (Schmidtke & Cummings, 2017, p. 662).
- Convenience: Many of the obstacles to meeting in person are eliminated, namely scheduling space, allowing for time to get to and from the meeting, and arranging audiovisual technology (and support for some). Convenience often results in better attendance and if managed properly, better participation (Bergiel et al., 2008).
- Cost-effective and sustainable: Chapter 3 quantifies the financial cost of holding an in-person meeting. Virtual meetings not only eliminate the time lost in transit to and from a meeting but also reduce the carbon footprint of our organizations (Cascio, 1999)
- Richer information: Virtual meetings that are supported by collaborative technology often allow for greater exchange of information and visuals in real time that increases engagement, productivity, and the quality of committee outputs (Smith, 2014).

As recommended in chapter 9, opportunities to build a sense of community must be orchestrated if they do not occur naturally. Many of the virtual committee meetings I attend are preceded by a period of banter and conversation that is both off topic and explicitly nonproductive, or so it may seem. For example, I attended a meeting of deans that became a comparison of university-themed hats and regalia, and a staff meeting morphed into a pet show. These are examples of how we can place the human aspects of committees ahead of our work for the benefit of our members and ultimately the group by laying a foundation that creates psychological safety, promotes engagement, encourages discourse, and fosters relationships, all of which are shown to contribute to the construction of cohesive committee environment and maintain the social fabric of our organizations. Creating a sense of community and inclusion is even more important to virtual committees because the distributed nature of virtual teams hampers efforts to build a shared identity (Hallier & Baralou, 2010; Kimble, 2011; Sohrabi et al., 2011).

Strategies for Virtual Committees

There are specific recommendations that can facilitate the execution and efficiency of virtual committees. Following are some strategies to manage virtual meetings. Some are from the experts that have studied this topic, and some are lessons I learned recently.

- Offer a virtual meeting tool kit: Provide guidance and resources to your organization regarding institutionally supported virtual meeting applications. Explicit instructions on how to establish and access an account may be helpful, as well as tutorials on use and guidance on the types of technology (e.g., WiFi bandwidth, video cameras, security settings, etc.) that are needed to facilitate a smooth virtual meeting.
- Provide committee fundamentals: Virtual meetings demand all the accoutrements of in-person gatherings to yield a productive and efficient meeting. An agenda, read-ahead materials, action items, and shared documents should be distributed in advance and attached to the meeting invitation to allow easy access. The conduct of committee meetings should adhere all of principals shared throughout the book (chapters 3–8), with special attention to building community.
- Build community: Find creative ways to build a sense of community among committee members. Start meetings with a brief social conversation or other activity to spark dialogue. My daughters occasionally crash my virtual meetings, which has led to introductions of family members and conversations that never would have occurred in face-to-face meetings. Some late evening meetings have evolved into virtual happy hours!
- Use video: Whenever available, use video-enabled virtual meeting applications (e.g., WebEx, Zoom, GoToMeeting, Blackboard) to provide a semblance of being physically present. Video helps communications by transmitting visual cues, body language, and reactions that are an essential components of intragroup communications (Bos et al., 2002; Miles & Hollenbeck, 2014). Video can also discourage people from engaging in distracting behaviors.
- Use graphics to facilitate meetings: Use a virtual white board or shared document to capture the committee's comments, ideas, and action items for all members to see to facilitate the committee's work. Research shows that these practices increase engagement and productivity (Smith, 2014).
- Utilize the chat feature: Sidebar conversations can be distracting in a face-to-face meeting, but chat features in collaborative technology platforms allow tangential conversations to occur without disrupting the group's work. Chat features can also be used as parking lots to record issues or questions that need attention in the future, again without slowing the momentum of the committee.

- Make better decisions: Virtual committees provide unique opportunities to explore nontraditional decision-making models (e.g., Delphi, Ringi, and nominal models; see chapter 9). Consider using new or a mixture of decision-making models that leverage collaborative technology and maximize the use of your committee's time and effort.

Leadership

Lastly, I would like to address leadership in virtual committees. Gibbs et al. (2016) conducted a meta-analysis of virtual teams and discovered two key leadership issues; first, virtual teams "are seen as networked or self-organized forms that lack a formal leader [sounds like a committee to me] and may benefit from sharing leadership" (p. 593); and second, "a formal leader is necessary in virtual teams given the added challenges of building trust, commitment and team identity and managing and monitoring team progress in virtual teams compared to traditional teams" (p. 593). This is all to say that our behavior in a virtual committee may be much different than the leadership and followership styles we employ in person. Furthermore, leadership styles (see chapter 6) may need to shift when committees transition from in-person to virtual formats to account for changes in work processes, engagement, and group dynamics. For example, research has found that transformational leadership styles tend to be more effective in virtual environments (Purvanova & Bono, 2009). In this book, chapter 9 discusses the evolution and life cycle of committees. Disruptions to committee ecology precipitate an assessment of where your committee lies on the forming, storming, norming, performing spectrum (Tuckman, 1965) which will likely result in adjustments to committee leadership, management, and engagement strategies.

Understanding University Committees: How to Manage and Participate Constructively in Institutional Governance provides guidance to help constructively engage with our colleagues virtually or face-to-face. In my opinion, a virtual meeting will never be an adequate substitute for a face-to-face meeting, but perhaps that is because I am an extrovert. I have heard from my introvert friends and colleagues that they relish the opportunity to work virtually! I hope we can all learn from our virtual experiences and one another so that we can apply our new knowledge to building better virtual and physical IHE for the future.

REFERENCES

Acker, J. (1990). Hierarchies, jobs, bodies: A theory of gendered organizations. *Gender and Society, 4*(2), 139–158.

Ala, M., & Cordeiro, W. (1999). Can we learn management techniques from the Japanese Ringi process? *Business Forum, 24*(1–2), 22–25.

Allen, F. (n.d.). *Fred Allen: Quotes.* https://www.fredallen.org/quotes.html

The almanac of higher education 2019–20. (2019). The Chronicle of Higher Education. https://www.chronicle.com/specialreport/The-Almanac-of-Higher/267

Alper, S., Tjosvold, D., & Law, K. S. (2000). Conflict management, efficacy, and performance in organizational teams. *Personnel Psychology, 53*(3), 625–642.

Altbach, P., Gumport, P., & Berdahl, R. (Eds.). (2011). *American higher education in the twenty-first century: Social, political, and economic challenges.* Johns Hopkins University Press.

American Association of University Professors. (1966). *Statement on government of colleges and universities.* https://www.aaup.org/report/statement-government-colleges-and-universities

American Association of University Professors. (2013). *The inclusion in governance of faculty members holding contingent appointments.* http://www.aaup.org/report/governanceinclusion

Ancona, D., & Caldwell, D. (1992). Bridging the boundary: External activity and performance in organizational teams. *Administrative Science Quarterly, 37,* 634–665.

Argote, L., McEvily, B., & Reagans, R. (2003). Managing knowledge in organizations: An integrative framework and review of emerging themes. *Management Science, 49*(4), 571–582.

Arrow, H., & McGrath, J. (1993). Membership matters: How member change and continuity affect small group structure, process, and performance. *Small Group Research, 24*(3), 334–361.

Babcock-Roberson, M., & Strickland, O. (2010). The relationship between charismatic leadership, work engagement, and organizational citizenship behaviors. *Journal of Psychology, 144*(3), 313–326.

Bachrach, D., Powell, B., Collins, B., & Richey, R. (2006). Effects of task interdependence on the relationship between helping behavior and group performance. *Journal of Applied Psychology, 91*(6), 1396–1405.

Baer, M., & Frese, M. (2003). Innovation is not enough: Climates for initiative and psychological safety, process innovations, and firm performance. *Journal of Organizational Behavior, 24,* 45–68.

Bajdo, L., & Dickson, M. (2001). Perceptions of organizational culture and women's advancement in organizations: A cross-cultural examination. *Sex Roles, 45*(5–6), 399–414.

Baldwin, R., & Chronister, J. (2001). *Teaching without tenure: Policies and practices for a new era.* Johns Hopkins University Press.

Bales, R. (1950). A set of categories for the analysis of small group interaction. *American Sociological Review, 15*, 257–263.

Baltodano, J., Carlson, S., Jackson, L., Mitchell, W., & Madsen, S. (2012). Networking to leadership in higher education: National and state-based programs and networks for developing women. *Advances in Developing Human Resources, 14*(1), 62–78.

Bandura, A. (1995). *Self-efficacy in changing societies.* Cambridge University Press.

Bar, M., Neta, M., & Linz, H. (2006). Very first impressions. *Emotion, 6*, 268–278.

Barnard, C. (1938). *The functions of the executive.* Harvard University Press.

Barr, M. J. (1990). Growing staff diversity and changing career paths. In M. Barr, M. Upcraft, & Associates (Eds.), *New futures for student affairs: Building a vision for professional leadership and practice* (pp. 160–177). Jossey-Bass.

Barrick, M., & Mount, M. (1991). The big five personality dimensions and job performance: A meta-analysis. *Personnel Psychology, 44*(1), 1–26.

Barrick, M., Stewart, G., Neubert, M., & Mount, M. (1998). Relating member ability and personality to work-team processes and team effectiveness. *Journal of Applied Psychology, 83*, 377–391.

Barsade, S. (2002). The ripple effect: Emotional contagion and its influence on group behavior. *Administrative Science Quarterly, 47*(4), 644–675.

Bass, B. (1985). Leadership: Good, better, best. *Organizational Dynamics, 13*(3), 26–40.

Bass, B., & Stogdill, R. (1990). *Bass and Stogdill's handbook of leadership: Theory, research, and managerial applications* (3rd ed.). Collier Macmillan.

Bastedo, M. (2012). *The organization of higher education: Managing colleges for a new era.* Johns Hopkins University Press.

Bateman, T., & Organ, D. (1983). Job satisfaction and the good soldier. *Academy of Management Journal, 26*, 587–595.

Bejou, D., & Bejou, A. (2016). Shared governance: The key to higher education equilibrium. *Journal of Relationship Marketing, 15*(1–2), 54–61.

Belbin, R. M. (1993). *Team roles at work.* Butterworth-Heinemann.

Belbin, R. M. (2010). *Management teams: Why they succeed or fail* (3rd ed.). Butterworth-Heinemann.

Bell, S. (2007). Deep-level composition variables as predictors of team performance: A meta-analysis. *Journal of Applied Psychology, 92*, 595–615.

Bellas, M., & Toutkoushian, R. (1999). Faculty time allocations and research productivity: Gender, race and family effects. *Review of Higher Education, 22*, 367–390.

Bem, S. (1974). The measurement of psychological androgyny. *Journal of Consulting and Clinical Psychology, 42*(2), 155–162.

Bennis, W. (1999). The end of leadership: Exemplary leadership is impossible without full inclusion, initiatives, and cooperation of followers. *Organizational Dynamics, 28*(1), 71–80.

Bennis, W., & Nanus, B. (1985). *Leaders: The strategies for taking charge.* Harper & Row.

Benson, J., & Brown, M. (2007). Knowledge workers: What keeps them committed; what turns them away. *Work, Employment and Society, 21*(1), 121–141.

Bergiel, B., Bergiel, E., & Balsmeier, P. (2008). Nature of virtual teams: a summary of their advantages and disadvantages. *Management Research News, 31*(2), 99–110. https://doi.org/10.1108/01409170810846821

Bergman, J., Rentsch, J., Small, E., Davenport, S., & Bergman, S. (2012). The shared leadership process in decision-making teams. *Journal of Social Psychology, 152*(1), 17–42.

Berk, R. (2012). Meetings in academe: It's time for an "extreme meeting makeover!" *Journal of Faculty Development, 26*(1), 50–53.

Berle, M. (n.d.). *Milton Berle quotes.* https://www.brainyquote.com/quotes/milton_berle_382647

Bess, J., & Dee, J. (2008a). *Understanding college and university organization theories for effective policy and practice: Dynamics of the system* (Vol. II). Stylus Publishing.

Bess, J., & Dee, J. (2008b). *Understanding college and university organization theories for effective policy and practice: The state of the system* (Vol. I). Stylus Publishing.

Birnbaum, R. (1988). *How colleges work: The cybernetics of academic organization and leadership.* Jossey-Bass.

Birnbaum, R. (2000). *Management fads in higher education: Where they come from, what they do, why they fail.* Jossey-Bass.

Birnbaum, R. (2004). *Speaking of higher education: The academic's book of quotations.* Praeger.

Bisbee, D. (2007). Looking for leaders: Current practices in leadership identification in higher education. *Planning and Changing, 38*(1–2), 77–88.

Bishop, J., Scott, K., Goldsby, M., & Cropanzano, R. (2005). A construct validity study of commitment and perceived support variables: A multifoci approach across different team environments. *Group and Organization Management, 30*(2), 153–180.

Blakely, G., Andrews, M., & Fuller, J. (2003). Are chameleons good citizens? A longitudinal study of the relationship between self-monitoring and organizational citizenship behavior. *Journal of Business and Psychology, 18*(2), 131–144.

Blenko, M., Mankins, M., & Rogers, P. (2010). *Decide and deliver: 5 steps to breakthrough performance in your organization.* Harvard Business Review Press.

Bolino, M., Turnley, W., & Bloodgood, J. (2002). Citizenship behavior and the creation of social capital in organizations. *Academy of Management Review, 27*(4), 505–522.

Bolino, M., Turnley, W., Gilstrap, J., & Suazo, M. (2010). Citizenship under pressure: What's a "good soldier" to do? *Journal of Organizational Behavior, 31*(6), 835–855.

Borman, W., & Motowidlo, S. (1997). Task performance and contextual performance: The meaning for personnel selection research. *Human Performance, 10*(2), 99–109.

Borman, W., Penner, L., Allen, T., & Motowidlo, S. (2001). Personality predictors of citizenship performance. *International Journal of Selection and Assessment, 9*(1–2), 52–69.

Bos, N., Olson, J., Gergle, D., Olson, G., & Wright, Z. (2002). Effects of four computer-mediated communications channels on trust development. *Proceedings of the SIGCHI Conference on Human Factors in Computing Systems.* 30, 135–140. https://doi.org/10.1145/503376.503401

Boudett, K., & City, E. (2014). *Meeting wise: Making the most of collaborative time for educators.* Harvard Education Press.

Bowen, W., & Tobin, E. (2015, January 5). Toward a shared vision of shared governance. *The Chronicle of Higher Education.* https://www.chronicle.com/article/Toward-a-Shared-Vision-of/151041

Bradley, B., Postlethwaite, B., Klotz, A., Hamdani, M., & Brown, K. (2012). Reaping the benefits of task conflict in teams: The critical role of team psychological safety climate. *Journal of Applied Psychology, 97*(1), 151–158.

Braun, T., Ferreira, A. I., & Sydow, J. (2012). Citizenship behavior and effectiveness in temporary organizations. *International Journal of Project Management, 31*(6), 862–876.

Bregman, P. (2016, February 22). The magic of 30-minute meetings. *Harvard Business Review.* https://hbr.org/2016/02/the-magic-of-30-minute-meetings

Brewer, M. (1979). In-group bias in the minimal intergroup situation: A cognitive–motivational analysis. *Psychological Bulletin, 86*, 307–324.

Bunderson, J., & Boumgarden, P. (2010). Structure and learning in self-managed teams: Why "bureaucratic" teams can be better learners. *Organization Science, 21*(3), 609–624.

Bureau of Labor Statistics. (2017a). *Occupational outlook handbook, postsecondary education administrators.* https://www.bls.gov/ooh/management/postsecondary-education-administrators.htm

Bureau of Labor Statistics. (2017b). *Occupational outlook handbook, postsecondary teachers.* https://www.bls.gov/ooh/education-training-and-library/postsecondary-teachers.htm

Butler, J. (1988). Performative acts and gender constitution: An essay in phenomenology and feminist theory. *Theatre Journal, 40*(4), 519–531.

Cannon-Bowers, J., Salas, E., Tannenbaum, S., Mathieu, J., & Wiskoff, M. (1995). Toward theoretically based principles of training effectiveness: A model and initial empirical investigation. *Military Psychology, 7*(3), 141–164.

Carson, J., Tesluk, P., & Marrone, J. (2007). Shared leadership in teams: An investigation of antecedent conditions and performance. *Academy of Management Journal, 50*, 1217–1234.

Carsten, M., Uhl-Bien, M., West, B., Patera, J., & McGregor, R. (2010). Exploring social constructs of followership: A qualitative study. *The Leadership Quarterly, 21*(3), 543–562.

Cascio, W. (1999). Virtual workplaces: Implications for organizational behavior. In C. L. Cooper & D. M. Rousseau (Eds.), *Trends in organizational behavior, Vol. 6: The virtual organization,* (pp. 1–14). John Wiley & Sons Ltd.

Chaleff, I. (2003). *The courageous follower: Standing up to and for our leaders* (2nd ed.). Berret-Koehler.

Chen, C., Tang, Y., & Wang, S. (2009). Interdependence and organizational citizenship behavior: Exploring the mediating effect of group cohesion in multilevel analysis. *Journal of Psychology, 143*(6), 625–640.

Chen, X. (2005). Organizational citizenship behavior: A predictor of employee voluntary turnover. In D. L. Turnpinseed (Ed.), *Handbook of organizational citizenship behavior* (pp. 435–454). Nova Science.

Chun, E., & Evans, A. (2018). *Leading a diversity cultural shift in higher education: Comprehensive organizational learning strategies.* Routledge.

Cipriano, R. (2011). *Facilitating a collegial department in higher education: Strategies for success.* Jossey-Bass.

Cohen, M., March, J., & Olsen, J. (1972). A garbage can model of organizational choice. *Administrative Science Quarterly, 17*(1), 1–25.

Coleman, V., & Borman, W. (2000). Investigating the underlying structure of the citizenship performance domain. *Human Resource Management Review, 10*(1), 25–44.

Conger, J., & Kanungo, R. N. (1998). *Charismatic leadership in organizations.* Sage.

Copeland, R. (n.d.). To get something done, a committee should consist of no more than three men, two of whom are absent. Quotes. https://www.quotes.net/quote/41770

Cotton, J., Vollrath, D., Froggatt, K., Lengnick-Hall, M., & Jennings, K. (1988). Employee participation: Diverse forms and different outcomes. *Academy of Management Review, 13*(1), 8–22.

Coutu, D. (2009). Why teams DON'T work. *Harvard Business Review, 87*(5), 98–105.

Covey, S. (1989). *The seven habits of highly effective people: Restoring the character ethic.* Simon and Schuster.

Creswell, J. (2013). *Qualitative inquiry and research design: Choosing among five approaches* (3rd ed.). Sage.

Curseu, P., Kenis, P., Raab, J., & Brandes, U. (2010). Composing effective teams through team-dating. *Organization Studies, 31*(7), 873–894.

Dahlin, K., Weingart, L., & Hinds, P. (2005). Team diversity and information use. *The Academy of Management Journal, 48*(6), 1107–1123.

Dalal, R., Baysinger, M., Brummel, B., & LeBreton, J. (2012). The relative importance of employee engagement, other job attitudes, and trait affect as predictors of job performance. *Journal of Applied Social Psychology, 42*, E295–E325.

Dalkey, N. (1969). An experimental study of group opinion: The Delphi method. *Futures, 1*(5), 408–426.

Dalkey, N., & Helmer, O. (1963). An experimental application of the Delphi method to the use of experts. *Management Science, 9*(3), 458–467.

Daly, C., & Dee, J. (2006). Greener pastures: Faculty turnover intent in urban public universities. *Journal of Higher Education, 77*(5), 776–803.

Dasborough, M., & Ashkanasy, N. (2002). Emotion and attribution of intentionality in leader–member relationships. *The Leadership Quarterly, 13*(5), 615–634.

Davidson, M., & James, E. (2006). The engines of positive relationships across difference: Conflict and learning. In J. E. Dutton & B. R. Ragins (Eds.), *Exploring positive relationships at work: Building a theoretical and research foundation* (pp. 137–158). Lawrence Erlbaum.

Day, A., & Carroll, S. (2004). Using an ability-based measure of emotional intelligence to predict individual performance, group performance, and group citizenship behaviors. *Personality and Individual Differences, 36*(6), 1443–1458.

Deckop, J., Cirka, R., & Andersson, C. (2003). Doing unto others: The reciprocity of helping behavior in organizations. *Journal of Business Ethics, 47*(2), 101–113.

De Dreu, C., & Van de Vliert, E. (1997). *Using conflict in organizations.* Sage.

De Dreu, C., & Van Vianen, A. (2001). Managing relationship conflict and the effectiveness of organizational teams. *Journal of Organizational Behavior, 22*(3), 309–328.

De Dreu, C., & Weingart, L. (2003). Task versus relationship conflict, team performance, and team member satisfaction: A meta-analysis. *Journal of Applied Psychology, 88*(4), 741–749.

Delbecq, A., Gustafson, D., & Van de Ven, A. (1986). *Group techniques for program planning: A guide to nominal group and Delphi processes.* Green Briar Press.

Delgado, R., & Stefancic, J. (2012). *Critical race theory: An introduction* (2nd ed.). New York University Press.

Den Hartog, D., De Hoogh, A., & Keegan, A. (2007). The interactive effects of belongingness and charisma on helping and compliance. *Journal of Applied Psychology, 92*(4), 1131–1139.

Dierdorff, E., Rubin, R., & Bachrach, D. (2012). Role expectations as antecedents of citizenship and the moderating effects of work context. *Journal of Management, 38*(2), 573–598.

Dill, D., & Helm, K. (1988). Faculty participation in strategic policy making. In J. Smart (Ed.), *Higher education: Handbook of theory and research* (pp. 319–354). Agathon Press.

Donnelly, K., & Twenge, J. (2017). Masculine and feminine traits on the Bem sex-role inventory, 1993–2012: A cross-temporal meta-analysis. *Sex Roles, 76,* 556–565.

Doran, G. (1981). There's a SMART way to write management's goals and objectives. *Management Review, 70,* 35–36.

Douglass, J. (2015). The old, new and future American research universities in the age of privatization. In P. Gibbs, O. Ylijoki, C. Guzman-Valenzuela, & R. Barnett (Eds.), *Universities in the flux of time: An exploration of time and temporality in university life* (pp. 57–76). Routledge.

Dovidio, J. (2001). On the nature of contemporary prejudice: The third wave. *Journal of Social Issues, 57,* 829–849.

Drach-Zahavy, A., & Somech, A. (2001). Understanding team innovation: The role of team processes and structures. *Group Dynamics, 5*(2), 111–123.

Driskell, T., Driskell, J., Burke, C., & Salas, E. (2017). Team roles: A review and integration. *Small Group Research, 48*(4), 482–511.

Druskat, V., & Wolff, S. (2001). Building the emotional intelligence of groups. *Harvard Business Review, 79*(3), 80–90.

Dukerich, J., Golden, B., & Shortell, S. (2002). Beauty is in the eye of the beholder: The impact of organizational identification, identity, and image on the cooperative behaviors of physicians. *Administrative Science Quarterly, 47*(3), 507–533.

Eddy, P., & Vanderlinden, K. (2006). Emerging definitions of leadership in higher education: New visions of leadership or same old "hero" leader? *Community College Review, 34*(1), 5–26.

Edmondson, A. (1999). Psychological safety and learning behavior in work teams. *Administrative Science Quarterly, 44*, 350–383.

Edmondson, A. (2004). Psychological safety, trust, and learning in organizations: A group-level lens. In K. Cook & R. Kramer (Eds.), *Trust and distrust in organizations: Dilemmas and approaches* (pp. 239–272). Russell Sage Foundation.

Edmondson, A., Dillon, J., & Roloff, K. (2007). Three perspectives on team learning: Outcome improvement, task mastery, and group process. *The Academy of Management Annals, 1*, 269–314.

Ehrhart, M., Bliese, P., & Thomas, J. (2006). Unit-level OCB and unit effectiveness: Examining the incremental effect of helping behavior. *Human Performance, 19*(2), 159–173.

Ehrhart, M., & Klein, K. (2001). Predicting followers' preferences for charismatic leadership: The influence of follower values and personality. *Leadership Quarterly, 12*, 153–180.

Ehrhart, M., & Naumann, S. (2004). Organizational citizenship behavior in work groups: A group norms approach. *Journal of Applied Psychology, 89*(6), 960–974.

Ely, R., & Thomas, D. (2001). Cultural diversity at work: The effects of diversity perspectives on work group processes and outcomes. *Administrative Science Quarterly, 46*, 229–273.

Erdheim, J., Wang, M., & Zickar, M. J. (2006). Linking the big five personality constructs to organizational commitment. *Personality and Individual Differences, 41*(5), 959–970.

Eriksson, L. (2011). *Rational choice theory: Potential and limits*. Palgrave Macmillan.

Farh, J., Lee, C., & Farh, C. (2010). Task conflict and team creativity: A question of how much and when. *Journal of Applied Psychology, 95*(6), 1173–1180.

Farh, J., Podsakoff, P., & Organ, D. (1990). Accounting for organizational citizenship behavior: Leader fairness and task scope versus satisfaction. *Journal of Management, 16*(4), 705–721.

Farris, D. (2016). *Antecedents, moderators, and expressions of organizational citizenship behavior in university administrative committees* (Publication No. 1876048838) [Doctoral dissertation, George Mason University]. ProQuest Dissertations and Theses Global.

Farris, D. (2017, June 6). Not another committee: Advice for improving the efficiency and effectiveness of committees. *Inside Higher Ed.* https://www.insidehighered.com/advice/2017/06/06/advice-improving-efficiency-and-effectiveness-committees-essay

Farris, D. (2018). Organisational citizenship behaviour in university administrative committees. *Journal of Higher Education Policy and Management, 40*(3), 224–238.

Ferreira, A., Braun, T., & Sydow, J. (2013). Citizenship behavior in project-based organizing: Comparing German and Portuguese project managers. *The International Journal of Human Resource Management, 24*(20), 3772–3793.

Finkelstein, M. (2010). Individualism/collectivism and the volunteer process. *Social Behavior and Personality, 38*(4), 445–452.

Foote, D., & Tang, T. (2008). Job satisfaction and organizational citizenship behavior (OCB): Does team commitment make a difference in self-directed teams? *Management Decision, 46*(6), 933–947.

Fries-Britt, S., Rowan-Kenyon, H., Perna, L., Milem, J., & Howard, D. (2011). Underrepresentation in the academy and the institutional climate for faculty diversity. *Journal of the Professoriate, 5*(1), 1–34.

Fugate, A., & Amey, M. (2000). Career stages of community college faculty: A qualitative analysis of their career paths, roles, and development. *Community College Review, 28*(1), 1–13.

Fulton, R. (2000, May–June). The plight of part-timers in higher education. *Change,* 38–43.

Gander, M., Moyes, H., & Sabzalieva, E. (2014). *Managing your career in higher education administration.* Palgrave MacMillan.

Gant, J. (2011). Towing the gender and race lines in academe: A practitioner's perspective. In V. Yenika-Agbaw & A. Hidalgo-de Jesus (Eds.), *Race, women of color, and the state university system* (pp. 1–13). University Press of America.

Gasman, M., Abiola, U., & Travers, C. (2015). Diversity and senior leadership at elite institutions of higher education. *Journal of Diversity in Higher Education, 8*(1), 1–14.

Gayle, D., Tewarie, B., & White, A. (2003). *Governance in the twenty-first-century university: Approaches to effective leadership and strategic management.* Jossey-Bass.

George, J. (1990). Personality, affect, and behavior in groups. *Journal of Applied Psychology, 75,* 107–116.

George, J., & Bettenhausen, K. (1990). Understanding prosocial behavior, sales performance, and turnover: A group-level analysis in a service context. *Journal of Applied Psychology, 75*(6), 698–709.

Gersick, C. (1988). Time and transition in work teams: Toward a new model of group development. *Academy of Management Journal, 31,* 9–41.

Gibbs, J., Sivunen, A., & Boyraz, M. (2016). Investigating the impacts of team type and design on virtual team processes. *Human Resources Management Review, 27*(4), 590–603. https://doi.org/10.1016/j.hrmr.2016.12.006

Gilson, L., Maynard, M., Young, N., Vartiainen, M., & Hakonen, M. (2015). Virtual teams research: 10 years, 10 themes and 10 opportunities. *Journal of Management, 41*(5), 1313–1337. https://doi.org/10.1177/0149206314559946

Goldstein, I., & Ford, J. (2002). *Training in organizations: Needs assessment, development, and evaluation* (4th ed.). Wadsworth.

Grant, A., Gino, F., & Hofmann, D. (2011). Reversing the extraverted leadership advantage: The role of employee proactivity. *Academy of Management Journal, 54*(3), 528–561.

Gratton, L., & Erickson, T. (2007). Eight ways to build collaborative teams. *Harvard Business Review, 85*(11), 100–109.

Greer, L. (2012). Group cohesion: Then and now. *Small Group Research, 43*(6), 655–661.

Gregory, S. (2001). Black faculty women in the academy: History, status and future. *Journal of Negro Education, 70,* 124–134.

Griffin, R. (2012). In the salon: Black female faculty "talking back" to the academy. *Women and Language, 35*, 75–79.

Griffin, R., Ward, L., & Phillips, A. (2014). Still flies in buttermilk: Black male faculty, critical race theory, and composite counter storytelling. *International Journal of Qualitative Studies in Education, 27*(10), 1354–1375.

Guarino, C., & Borden, V. (2017). Faculty service loads and gender: Are women taking care of the academic family? *Research in Higher Education, 58*(6), 672–694.

Gumport, P. (2012). Strategic thinking in higher education research. In M. N. Bastedo (Ed.), *The organization of higher education: Managing colleges for a new era* (pp. 18–41). Johns Hopkins University Press.

Guzzo, R., & Dickson, M. (1996). Teams in organizations: Recent research on performance and effectiveness. *Annual Review of Psychology, 47*, 307–338.

Hackman, J. (1987). The design of work teams. In J. Lorsch (Ed.), *Handbook of organizational behavior* (pp. 315–342). Prentice Hall.

Hackman, J. (2002). *Leading teams: Setting the stage for great performances.* Harvard Business School Press.

Hackman, J., & Vidmar, N. (1970). Effects of size and task type on group performance and member reactions. *Sociometry, 33*(1), 37–54.

Hallier, J., & Baralou, E. (2010). Other voices, other rooms: Differentiating social identity development in organisational and pro-am virtual teams. *New Technology, Work and Employment, 25*(2),154–166. https://doi.org/10.1111/j.1468-005X.2010.00245.x

Harley, D. (2008). Maids of academe: African American women faculty at predominantly White institutions. *Journal of African American Studies, 12*(1), 19–36.

Harper, S. (2012). Race without racism: How higher education researchers minimize racist institutional norms. *Review of Higher Education, 36*(1), 9–29.

Harrison, D., Price, K., & Bell, M. (1998). Beyond relational demography: Time and the effects of surface- and deep-level diversity on work group cohesion. *The Academy of Management Journal, 41*(1), 96–107.

Harrison, D., Price, K., Gavin, J., & Florey, A. (2002). Time, teams, and task performance: Changing effects of surface- and deep-level diversity on group functioning. *Academy of Management Journal, 45*, 1029–1045.

Hartley, M., & Wilhelm Shah, S. (2006). The tenuous legitimacy of ad hoc decision-making committees. In P. Eckel (Eds.), *The shifting frontiers of academic decision-making: Responding to new priorities, following new pathways* (pp. 75–92). Praeger.

Harvard Business Review. (2016a). *HBR guide to making every meeting matter.* (2016). Harvard Business Review Press.

Harvard Business Review. (2016b, January 11). Estimate the cost of a meeting with this calculator. https://hbr.org/2016/01/estimate-the-cost-of-a-meeting-with-this-calculator

Harvey, J. (1988, Summer). The Abilene paradox: The management of agreement. *Organizational Dynamics*, 17–43.

Hattori, I. (1978). A proposition on efficient decision-making in the Japanese corporation. *Columbia Journal of World Business, 13*(2), 105–111.

Helgesen, S. (1995). *The web of inclusion: A new architecture for building great organizations.* Currency/Doubleday.

Henne, D., & Locke, E. (1985). Job dissatisfaction: What are the consequences? *International Journal of Psychology, 20*(2), 221–240.

Hobbs, W. (1975). Organizational roles of university committees. *Research in Higher Education, 3*(3), 233–242.

Hoeller, K. (2014). *Equality for contingent faculty overcoming the two-tier system.* Vanderbilt University Press.

Hoever, I., van Knippenberg, D., van Ginkel, W., & Barkema, H. (2012). Fostering team creativity: Perspective taking as key to unlocking diversity's potential. *Journal of Applied Psychology, 97*, 982–996.

Hofstede, G. (2001). *Culture's consequences* (2nd ed.). Sage.

hooks, b., & West, C. (1991). *Breaking bread: Insurgent Black intellectual life.* South End Press.

Hough, L. (1992). The "big five" personality variables-construct confusion: Description versus prediction. *Human Performance, 5*(1–2), 139–155.

Hughes, R., Curphy, G., & Ginnett, R. (2012). *Leadership: Enhancing the lessons of experience* (7th ed.). McGraw-Hill Irwin.

Ilies, R., Fulmer, I., Spitzmuller, M., & Nickson, M. (2009). Personality and citizenship behavior: The mediating role of job satisfaction. *Journal of Applied Psychology, 94*(4), 945–959.

Ilies, R., Scott, B., & Judge, T. (2006). The interactive effects of personal traits and experienced states on intraindividual patterns of citizenship behavior. *Academy of Management Journal, 49*, 561–575.

Irvine, J. (1978). A case of double jeopardy: The Black woman in higher educational administration. *Emergent Leadership, 2*(2), 61–66.

Isen, A., & Baron, R. (1991). Positive affect as a factor in organizational behavior. In L. L. Cummings & B. Staw (Eds.), *Research in organizational behavior* (pp. 1–53). JAI Press.

Jackson, J. (2002). Retention of African American administrators at predominantly White institutions: Using professional growth factors to inform the discussion. *College and University, 78*(2), 11–16.

Jackson, J. (2006). The nature of academic deans' work: Moving toward an academic executive behavioral model in higher education. *Journal of the Professoriate, 1*(1), 7–22.

Jackson, S., & Joshi, A. (2011). Work team diversity. In S. Zedeck (Ed.), *APA handbook of industrial and organizational psychology* (Vol. 1, pp. 651–686). American Psychological Association.

Jacobsen, C., & House, R. (2001). Dynamics of charismatic leadership: A process theory, simulation model, and tests. *The Leadership Quarterly, 12*(1), 75–112.

Jain, A., Giga, S., & Cooper, C. (2013). Stress, health and well-being: The mediating role of employee and organizational commitment. *International Journal of Environmental Research and Public Health, 10*(10), 4907–4924.

Jehn, K., Northcraft, G., & Neale, M. (1999). Why differences make a difference: A field study of diversity, conflict, and performance in workgroups. *Administrative Science Quarterly, 44*, 741–763.

Jones, G., & George, J. (1998). The experience and evolution of trust: Implications for cooperation and teamwork. *The Academy of Management Review, 23*(3), 531–546.

Jones, W., Hutchens, N., Hulbert, A., Lewis, W., & Brown, D. (2017). Shared governance among the new majority: Non-tenure track faculty eligibility for election to university faculty senates. *Innovative Higher Education, 42*(5), 505–519.

Joshi, A., & Roh, H. (2009). The role of context in work team diversity research: A metanalytic review. *Academy of Management Journal, 52*, 599–627.

Kanter, R. (1977). *Men and women of the corporation*. Basic Books.

Katz, D. (1964). The motivational basis of organizational behavior. *Behavioral Science, 9*(2), 131–146.

Katzenbach, J., & Smith, D. (1993). *The wisdom of teams: Creating the high-performance organization*. Harvard Business School Press.

Kayser, T. (1990). *Mining group gold: How to cash in on the collaborative power of a group*. Serif.

Keller, G. (1983). *Academic strategy: The management revolution in American higher education*. Johns Hopkins University Press.

Kellerman, B. (2008). *Followership: How followers are creating change and changing leaders*. Harvard Business Press.

Kelley, R. E. (1988). In praise of followers. *Harvard Business Review, 66*(6), 141–148.

Kelly, J., & Spoor, J. (2007). Naive theories about the effects of mood in groups: A preliminary investigation. *Group Processes and Intergroup Relations, 10*(2), 203–222.

Kerr, N., & Tindale, R. (2004). Group performance and decision making. *Annual Review of Psychology, 55*, 623–655.

Kezar, A. (2003). Foreword. In D. Gayle, B. Tewarie, & A. White (Eds.), *Governance in the twenty-first-century university: Approaches to effective leadership and strategic management* (pp. ix–xii). Jossey-Bass.

Kezar, A., & Eckel, P. (2004). Meeting today's governance challenges. *Journal of Higher Education, 75*(4), 371–399.

Kezar, A., & Sam, C. (2010). *Understanding the new majority of non-tenure-track faculty in higher education: Demographics, experiences, and plans of action*. Jossey-Bass.

Kidwell, R., Jr., Mossholder, K., & Bennett, N. (1997). Cohesiveness and organizational citizenship behavior: A multilevel analysis using work groups and individuals. *Journal of Management, 23*, 775–793.

Kimble, C. (2011). Building effective virtual teams: How to overcome the problems of trust and identity in virtual teams. *Global Business and Organizational Excellence, 30*(2), 6–15. https://doi.org/10.1002/joe.20364

Kirchmeyer, C. (1996). Gender roles and decision-making in demographically diverse groups: A case for reviving androgyny. *Sex Roles, 34*(9), 649–663.

Kloppenborg, T., & Petrick, J. (1999). Meeting management and group character development. *Journal of Managerial Issues, 11*(2), 166–179.

Knight, R. (2016). Refocusing a meeting after someone interrupts. In *Harvard Business Review* (Ed.), *HBR guide to making every meeting matter* (pp. 77–86). Harvard Business Review Press.

Kocolowski, M. (2010). Shared leadership: Is it time for a change? *Emerging Leadership Journeys, 3*(1), 22–32.

Konovsky, M., & Organ, D. (1996). Dispositional and contextual determinants of organizational citizenship behavior. *Journal of Organizational Behavior, 17*(3), 253–266.

Kotter, J. (1995). Leading change: Why transformational efforts fail. *Harvard Business Review, 73*(2), 59–67.

Kozlowski, S., & Bell, B. (2003). Work groups and teams in organizations. In W. Borman, D. Ilgen, & R. Klimoski (Eds.), *Comprehensive handbook of psychology* (pp. 333–375). Wiley.

Kozlowski, S., & Ilgen, D. (2006). Enhancing the effectiveness of work groups and teams. *Psychological Science in the Public Interest, 7*, 77–124.

Kramer, R. (1991). Intergroup relations and organizational dilemmas: The role of categorization processes. In L. Cummings & B. Staw (Eds.), *Research in organizational behavior* (Vol. 13, pp. 191–228). JAI Press.

Ku, G., Wang, C., & Galinsky, A. (2010). Perception through a perspective-taking lens: Differential effects on judgment and behavior. *Journal of Experimental Social Psychology, 46*(5), 792–798.

Ku, G., Wang, C., & Galinsky, A. (2015). The promise and perversity of perspective-taking in organizations. *Research in Organizational Behavior, 35*, 79–102.

Kuhn, T., & Poole, S. (2000). Do conflict management styles affect group decision making? Evidence from a longitudinal field study. *Human Communication Research, 26*(4), 558–590.

Ladson-Billings, G. (1998). Just what is critical race theory and what's it doing in a nice field like education? *International Journal of Qualitative Studies in Education, 11*(1), 7–24.

Lai, J., Lam, L., & Law, S. (2013). Organizational citizenship behavior in work groups: A team cultural perspective. *Journal of Organizational Behavior, 34*, 1039–1056.

Laitinen, K., & Maarit, V. (2018). Meanings of communication technology in virtual team meetings: Framing technology-related interaction. *International Journal of Human-Computer Studies, 111*, 12–22. https://doi.org/10.1016/j.ijhcs.2017.10.012

Lawrence, J., & Ott, M. (2013). Faculty perceptions of organizational politics. *The Review of Higher Education, 36*(2), 145–178.

Lawrence, J., Ott, M., & Bell, A. (2012). Faculty organizational commitment and citizenship. *Research in Higher Education, 53*(3), 325–352.

Lee, K., & Allen, N. (2002). Organizational citizenship behavior and workplace deviance: The role of affect and cognitions. *Journal of Applied Psychology, 87*(1), 131–142.

Lee-Davies, L., Kakabadse, N., & Kakabadse, A. (2007). Shared leadership: Leading through polylogue. *Business Strategy Series, 8*(4), 246–253.

Lencioni, P. (2004). *Death by meeting: A leadership fable . . . about solving the most painful problem in business.* Jossey-Bass.

LePine, J. A., Erez, A., & Johnson, D. E. (2002). The nature and dimensionality of organizational citizenship behavior: A critical review and meta-analysis. *Journal of Applied Psychology, 87*(1), 52–65.

LePine, J., Piccolo, R., Jackson, C., Mathieu, J., & Saul, J. (2008). A meta-analysis of teamwork processes: Tests of a multidimensional model and relationships with team effectiveness criteria. *Personnel Psychology, 61*(2), 273–307.

LePine, J., & Van Dyne, L. (2001). Voice and cooperative behavior as contrasting forms of contextual performance: Evidence of differential relationships with big five personality characteristics and cognitive ability. *Journal of Applied Psychology, 86*, 326–336.

Lester, J., & Sallee, M. (2017). Troubling gender norms and the ideal worker in academic life. In P. Eddy, K. Ward, & T. Khwaja (Eds.), *Critical approaches to women and gender in higher education* (pp. 115–138). Palgrave Macmillan.

Levi, D. (2014). *Group dynamics for teams* (4th ed.). Sage.

Levin, S., Frederico, C., Sidanius, J., & Rabinowitz, J. (2002). Social dominance orientation and intergroup bias: The legitimation of favoritism for high-status groups. *Personality and Social Psychology Bulletin, 28*(2), 144–157.

Lewin, K. (1947). Frontiers in group dynamics: Concept, method and reality in social science: Equilibrium and social change. *Human Relations, 1*(1), 5–41.

Lipman-Blumen, J., & Leavitt, H. (1999). *Hot groups: Seeding them, feeding them, and using them to ignite your organization.* Oxford University Press.

London, M., & London, M. (2007). *First-time leaders of small groups: How to create high-performing committees, task forces, clubs, and boards.* Jossey-Bass.

Lord, R., Brown, D., Harvey, J., & Hall, R. (2001). Contextual constraints on prototype generation and their multilevel consequences for leadership perceptions. *The Leadership Quarterly, 12*(3), 311–338.

Lott, A., & Lott, B. (1965). Group cohesiveness as interpersonal attraction: Antecedents of linking. *Psychological Bulletin, 64*, 359–302.

Lukas, J. (2014, October). *Project management: Getting back to basics* [Paper presentation]. PMI Global Congress, Phoenix, AZ, United States.

Maccoll, M. (1995). A model of Japanese corporate decision making. *The International Journal of Organizational Analysis, 3*(4), 375–393.

MacKenzie, S., Podsakoff, P., & Podsakoff, N. (2011). Challenge-oriented organizational citizenship behaviors and organizational effectiveness: Do challenge-oriented behaviors really have an impact on the bottom line? *Personnel Psychology, 64*(3), 559–592.

Marks, M., Mathieu, J., & Zaccaro, S. (2001). A temporally based framework and taxonomy of team processes. *The Academy of Management Review, 26*(3), 356–376.

Marshall, J. (1993). Organisational culture and women managers: Exploring the dynamics of resilience. *Applied Psychology: An International Review, 42*(4), 313–322.

Martinez, R. (1999). *Hispanic leadership in American higher education* [Commissioned paper]. Hispanic Association of Colleges and Universities.

Maslow, A. (1968). *Toward a psychological being.* Van Nostrand.

Mathieu, J., Kukenberger, M., D'innocenzo, L., Reilly, G., & Chen, G. (2015). Modeling reciprocal team cohesion–performance relationships, as impacted by shared leadership and members' competence. *Journal of Applied Psychology, 100*(3), 713–734.

Mathieu, J., & Rapp, T. (2009). Laying the foundation for successful team performance trajectories: The roles of team charters and performance strategies. *Journal of Applied Psychology, 94*(1), 90–103.

May, T., Korczynski, M., & Frenkel, S. (2002). Organizational and occupational commitment: Knowledge workers in large corporations. *Journal of Management Studies, 39*(6), 775–801.

Mayer, D., Kuenzi, M., Greenbaum, R., Bardes, M., & Salvador, R. (2009). How low does ethical leadership flow? Test of a trickle-down model. *Organizational Behavior and Human Decision Processes, 108*(1), 1–13.

McDermott, R. (1999). Learning across teams. *Knowledge Management Review, 8*(3), 32–36.

McGrath, J. (1984). *Groups: Interaction and performance.* Prentice Hall.

Meier, K., & Nigro, L. (1976). Representative bureaucracy and policy preferences: A study in the attitudes of federal executives. *Public Administration Review, 36*(4), 458–469.

Merriam-Webster. (n.d.a.). *Committee.* Retrieved July 11, 2020 from https://www.merriam-webster.com/dictionary/committee.

Merriam-Webster. (n.d.b.). *Task force.* Retrieved July 11, 2020 from https://www.merriam-webster.com/dictionary/task_force

Merriam-Webster. (n.d.b.). *Networking.* Retrieved July 11, 2020 from https://www.merriam-webster.com/dictionary/networking

Meyer, J., Stanley, D., Herscovitch, L., & Topolnytsky, L. (2002). Affective, continuance, and normative commitment to the organization: A meta-analysis of antecedents, correlates, and consequences. *Journal of Vocational Behavior, 61*(1), 20–52.

Miles, J., & Hollenbeck, J. (2014). Teams and technology. In M. Coovert & L. Thompson (Eds.), *The psychology of workplace technology* (pp. 99–117). Routledge.

Moede, W. (1927). Die Richtlinien der Leistungs-Psychologie. *IndustrieUe Psychotechnik, 4,* 193–207.

Mohrman, S., Cohen, S., & Mohrman, A. (1995). *Designing team-based organizations: New forms for knowledge work.* Jossey-Bass.

Monnier, N. (2017). "One faculty" and academic governance. *Academe, 103*(3), 25–28.

Moorman, R., Blakely, G., & Niehoff, B. (1998). Does perceived organizational support mediate the relationship between procedural justice and organizational citizenship behavior? *Academy of Management Journal, 41*(3), 351–357.

Mor Barak, M., Cherin, D., & Berkman, S. (1998). Organizational and personal dimensions in diversity climate: Ethnic and gender differences in employee perceptions. *Journal of Applied Behavioral Sciences, 34,* 82–104.

Morgan, B., Salas, E., & Glickman, A. (1993). An analysis of team evolution and maturation. *Journal of General Psychology, 120*(3), 277–291.

Morgenson, F., DeRue, D., & Karam, E. (2010). Leadership in teams: A functional approach to understanding leadership structures and processes. *Journal of Management, 36*, 5–39.

Morrison, E. (1994). Role definitions and organizational citizenship behavior: The importance of the employee's perspective. *Academy of Management Journal, 37*(6), 1543–1567.

Morrison, J. (2008). Faculty governance and nontenure-track appointments. *New Directions for Higher Education, 2008*(143), 21–27.

Mount, M., Barrick, M., & Stewart, G. (1998). Five-factor model of personality and performance in jobs involving interpersonal interactions. *Human Performance, 11*(2–3), 145–165.

Moustakas, C. (1994). *Phenomenological research methods.* Sage.

Mowday, R., Porter, L., & Steers, R. (1982). *Organizational linkages: The psychology of commitment, absenteeism, and turnover.* Academic Press.

Mueller, J. (2012). Why individuals in larger teams perform worse. *Organizational Behavior and Decision Processes, 117*, 111–124.

Nadel, M. (2006). Retargeting affirmative action: A program to serve those most harmed by past racism and avoid intractable problems triggered by per se racial preferences. *St. John's Law Review, 80*(1), 334–343.

Nahum-Shani, I., & Somech, A. (2011). Leadership, OCB and individual differences: Idiocentrism and allocentrism as moderators of the relationship between transformational and transactional leadership and OCB. *The Leadership Quarterly, 22*(2), 353–366.

Nelms, C. (2002). The prerequisite for academic leadership. In L. Jones (Ed.), *Making it on broken promises: African American male scholars confront the culture of higher education* (pp. 189–193). Stylus.

Neuman, G., & Kickul, A. (1998). Organizational citizenship behaviors: Achievement orientation and personality. *Journal of Business and Psychology, 13*(2), 263–279.

Neumann, Y., & Finaly-Neumann, E. (1990). The support-stress paradigm and faculty research publication. *Journal of Higher Education, 61*(5), 565–580.

Ng, T., & Feldman, D. (2012). The effects of organizational and community embeddedness on work-to-family and family-to-work conflict. *Journal of Applied Psychology, 97*(6), 1233–1251.

Nickson, D., Nickson, R., & Tjosvold, D. (2012). Constructive controversy: The value of intellectual opposition. In M. Deutsch & P. Coleman (Eds.), *The handbook of conflict resolution: Theory and practice (pp. 65–85).* Jossey-Bass.

Nickson, L. (1970). *A White House diary.* Holt, Rinehart, and Winston.

Nielsen, T., Bachrach, D., Sundstrom, E., & Halfhill, T. (2012). Utility of OCB. *Journal of Management, 38*(2), 668–694.

Nielsen, T., Hrivnak, G., & Shaw, M. (2009). Organizational citizenship behavior and performance: A meta-analysis of group-level research. *Small Group Research, 40*, 555–577.

Niemann, Y. (2016). The social ecology of tokenism in higher education. *Peace Review: A Journal of Social Justice, 28*(4), 451–458.

Northouse, P. (2018). *Introduction to leadership: Concepts and practice* (4th ed.). Sage.

O'Meara, K., Kuvaeva, A., Nyunt, G., Waugaman, C., & Jackson, R. (2017). Asked more often: Gender differences in faculty workload in research universities and the work interactions that shape them. *American Educational Research Journal, 54*(6), 1154–1186.

Organ, D. (1988). *Organizational citizenship behavior: The good soldier syndrome.* Lexington Books.

Organ, D. (1994). Personality and organizational citizenship behavior. *Journal of Management, 20*(2), 465–478.

Organ, D., Podsakoff, P., & MacKenzie, S. (2006). *Organizational citizenship behavior: Its nature, antecedents, and consequences.* Sage.

Organ, D., & Ryan, K. (1995). A meta-analytic review of attitudinal and dispositional predictors of organizational citizenships behavior. *Personnel Psychology, 48,* 775–802.

Parks, C. (1999). *Group performance and interaction.* Westview.

Pearce, C., Yoo, Y., & Alavi, M. (2004). Leadership, social work and virtual teams: The relative influence of vertical vs. shared leadership in the nonprofit sector. In R. E. Riggio & S. Smith-Orr (Eds.), *Improving leadership in nonprofit organizations* (pp. 180–203). Jossey-Bass.

Piccolo, R., & Colquitt, J. (2006). Transformational leadership and job behaviors: The mediating role of core job characteristics. *Academy of Management Journal, 49*(2), 327–340.

Piccolo, R., Greenbaum, R., den Hartog, D., & Folger, R. (2010). The relationship between ethical leadership and core job character. *Journal of Organizational Behavior, 31*, 259–278.

Podsakoff, N., Podsakoff, P., MacKenzie, S., Maynes, T., & Spoelma, T. (2014). Consequences of unit-level organizational citizenship behaviors: A review and recommendations for future research. *Journal of Organizational Behavior, 35,* S87–S119.

Podsakoff, N., Whiting, S., Podsakoff, P., & Blume, B. (2009). Individual- and organizational-level consequences of organizational citizenship behaviors: A meta-analysis. *Journal of Applied Psychology, 94*(1), 122–141.

Podsakoff, P., Ahearne, M., & MacKenzie, S. (1997). Organizational citizenship behavior and the quantity and quality of work group performance. *Journal of Applied Psychology, 82*, 262–270.

Podsakoff, P., & MacKenzie, S. (1997). The impact of organizational citizenship behavior on organizational performance: A review and suggestions for future research. *Human Performance, 10*, 133–151.

Podsakoff, P., MacKenzie, S., Paine, J., & Bachrach, D. (2000). Organizational citizenship behaviors: A critical review of the theoretical and empirical literature and suggestions for future research. *Journal of Management, 26*(3), 513–563.

Price, D. (1963). *Little science, big science.* Columbia University Press.

Proctor, T. (2010). *Creative problem solving for managers: Developing skills for decision making and innovation* (3rd ed.). Routledge.

Purvanova, R., & Bono, J. (2009). Transformational leadership in context: Face-to-face and virtual teams. *The Leadership Quarterly, 20*(3), 343–357. https://doi.org/10.1016/j.leaqua.2009.03.004

Purvanova, R., Bono, J., & Dzieweczynski, J. (2006). Transformational leadership, job characteristics, and organizational citizenship performance. *Human Performance, 19*(1), 1–22.

Quarless, D., & Barrett, M. (2017). Perspectives on administrative task forces in shared governance. In S. Cramer (Ed.), *Shared governance in higher education: Demands, transitions, transformations* (Vol. 1, pp. 117–148). State University of New York Press.

Ragins, B. (1995). Diversity, power, and mentoring in organizations: A cultural, structural, and behavioral perspective. In M. Chemers, M. Costanzo, & S. Oskamp (Eds.), *Diversity in organizations: New perspectives for a changing workplace* (pp. 91–132). Sage.

Richards, T., & Moger, S. (2000). Creative leadership processes in project team development: An alternative to Tuckman's stage model. *British Journal of Management, 11*(4), 273–283.

Riordan, C., & Shore, L. (1997). Demographic diversity and employee attitudes: An empirical examination of relational demography within work units. *Journal of Applied Psychology, 82*(3), 342–358.

Roberge, M., Xu, Q., & Rousseau, D. (2012). Collective personality effects on group citizenship behavior. *Small Group Research, 43*(4), 410–442.

Robinson, P. [Director]. (2012). *Meetings, bloody meetings*. [Film]. Video Arts.

Roehling, M. (2017). The important but neglected legal context of virtual teams: Research implications and opportunities. *Human Resource Management Review, 27*(4), 621–634. https://doi.org/10.1016/j.hrmr.2016.12.008

Rosser, V. (2000). Midlevel administrators: What we know. *New Directions for Higher Education, 2000*(111), 5–13.

Ruben, B., De Lisi, R., & Gigliotti, R. (2017). *A guide for leaders in higher education: Core concepts, competencies, and tools*. Stylus.

Ruiz-Palomino, P., & Martínez-Cañas, R. (2014). Ethical culture, ethical intent, and organizational citizenship behavior: The moderating and mediating role of person-organization fit. *Journal of Business Ethics, 120*(1), 95–108.

Saavedra, R., Earley, P., & Van Dyne, L. (1993). Complex interdependence in task-performing groups. *Journal of Applied Psychology, 78*, 61–72.

Sadao, K. (2003). Living in two worlds: Success and bicultural faculty of color. *Review of Higher Education, 26*, 397–418.

Salas, E., Sims, D., & Burke, C. (2005). Is there a "big five" in teamwork? *Small Group Research, 36*(5), 555–599.

Sandelands, L., & St. Clair, L. (1993). *Toward an empirical concept of the group* [Unpublished manuscript]. University of Michigan, Ann Arbor.

Sanderson, A., Phua, V., & Herda, D. (2000). *The American faculty poll*. National Opinion Research Center.

Santa Clara University. (2016a). *Shared governance resources.* https://www.scu.edu/governance/resources-/

Santa Clara University. (2016b). *Charter.* https://www.scu.edu/governance/resources-/charter/

Schloss, P., & Cragg, K. (2013). *Organization and administration in higher education.* Routledge.

Schmidtke, J., & Cummings, A. (2017). The effects of virtualness on teamwork behavioral components: The role of shared mental models. *Human Resource Management Review, 27*(4), 660–677. https://doi.org/10.1016/j.hrmr.2016.12.011

Schnake, M., & Dumler, M. (2003). Levels of measurement and analysis issues in organizational citizenship behavior research. *Journal of Occupational and Organizational Psychology, 76,* 283–301.

Schuster, J., Smith, D., Corak, K., & Yamada, M. (1994). *Strategic governance: How to make big decisions better.* Oryx Press.

Self, D., Bandow, D., & Schraeder, M. (2011). Fostering employee innovation: Leveraging your "ground level" creative capital. *Development and Learning in Organizations: An International Journal, 24*(4), 17–19.

Shamir, B. (2012). Leadership research or post-leadership research: Advancing leadership theory versus throwing out the baby with the bath water. In M. Uhl-Bien & S. Ospina (Eds.), *Advancing relational leadership research: A dialogue among perspectives* (pp. 477–500). Information Age.

Shiflett, S. (1979). Temporal changes in the prediction of group performance. *Journal of Social Psychology, 108*(2), 185–191.

Sidanius, J., Feshback, S., Levin, S., & Pratto, F. (1997). The interface between ethnic and national attachment: Ethnic pluralism or ethnic dominance? *Public Opinion Quarterly, 61,* 102–133.

Simon, H. (1957). *Models of man: Social and rational; Mathematical essays on rational human behavior in a social setting.* Wiley.

Simons, T., Pelled, L., & Smith, K. (1999). Making use of difference: Diversity, debate, and decision comprehensiveness in top management teams. *The Academy of Management Journal, 42*(6), 662–673.

Simons, T. L., & Peterson, R. S. (2000). Task conflict and relationship conflict in top management teams: The pivotal role of intragroup trust. *Journal of Applied Psychology, 85*(1), 102–111.

Slater, S., Weigand, R., & Zwirlein, T. (2008). The business case for commitment to diversity. *Business Horizons, 51*(3), 201–209.

Smith, C., Organ, D., & Near, J. (1983). Organizational citizenship behavior: Its nature and antecedents. *Journal of Applied Psychology, 68,* 653–663.

Smith, R. (2014). Collaborative bandwidth: Creating better virtual meetings. *Organization Development Journal, 32*(4), 15–35.

Smith, R. V. (2006). *Where you stand is where you sit: An academic administrator's handbook.* University of Arkansas Press.

Smith-Lovin, L., & Brody, C. (1998). Interruptions in group discussion: The effects of gender and group composition. *American Sociological Review, 54*(3), 424–435.

Snyder, M. (1987). *Public appearances/private realities: The psychology of self-monitoring.* Freeman.

Snyder, T. (2018). *Digest of education statistics 2018.* National Center for Educational Statistics.

Sohrabi, B., Gholipour, A., & Amiri, B. (2011). The influence of information technology on organizational behavior: Study of identity challenges in virtual teams. *International Journal of e-Collaboration, 7*(2), 19–34. https://doi.org/4018/jec.2011040102

Solansky, S. (2008). Leadership style and team processes in self-managed teams. *Journal of Leadership and Organizational Studies, 14*(4), 332–341.

Spoor, J., & Kelly, J. (2004). The evolutionary significance of affect in groups: Communication and group bonding. *Group Processes and Intergroup Relations, 7*(4), 398–412.

Staats, R., Milkman, K., & Fox, C. (2012). The team scaling fallacy: Underestimating the declining efficacy of larger teams. *Organizational Behavior and Human Decision Processes, 118,* 132–142.

Stanley, C. (2006a). Coloring the academic landscape: Faculty of color breaking the silence in predominantly White colleges and universities. *American Educational Research Journal, 43*(4), 701–736.

Stanley, C. (2006b). *Faculty of color: Teaching in predominantly White colleges and universities.* Anker.

Stanley, C., & Lincoln, Y. (2005). Cross-race faculty mentoring. *Change, 37*(2), 44–50.

Stefani, L., & Blessinger, P. (2017). *Inclusive leadership in higher education: International perspectives and approaches.* Routledge.

Steiner, I. (1972). *Group process and productivity.* Academic Press.

Stevens, F., Plaut, V., & Sanchez-Burks, J. (2008). Unlocking the benefits of diversity: All-inclusive multiculturalism and positive organizational change. Journal of Applied Behavioral Science, 44(1), 116–133.

Stone-Romero, E., Alvarez, K., & Thompson, L. (2009). The construct validity of conceptual and operational definitions of contextual performance and related constructs. *Human Resource Management Review, 19*(2), 104–116.

Streibel, B. J. (2007). *Plan and conduct effective meetings: 24 steps to generate meaningful results.* McGraw-Hill.

Sweeney, C., & Bothwick, F. (2016). *Inclusive leadership: The definitive guide to developing and executing an impactful diversity and inclusion strategy—locally and globally.* Pearson Education Limited.

Tajfel, H., & Turner, J. (1986). The social identity theory of intergroup behavior. *Psychology of Intergroup Relations, 5,* 7–24.

Tierney, W. (2001). Why committees don't work: Creating a structure for change. *Academe, 87*(3), 25–29.

Tierney, W. (2008). *The impact of culture on organizational decision-making: Theory and practice in higher education.* Stylus.

Tjosvold, D. (1989). *Managing conflict: The key to making your organization work.* Team Media.

Tjosvold, D. (1997). Conflict within interdependence: Its value for productivity and individuality. In C. De Dreu & E. Van de Vliert (Eds.), *Using conflict in organizations* (pp. 23–37). Sage.

Tompson, H., & Werner, J. (1997). The impact of role conflict/facilitation on core and discretionary behaviors: Testing a mediated model. *Journal of Management, 23*(4), 583–601.

Tuckman, B. (1965). Developmental sequence in small groups. *Psychological Bulletin, 63*, 384–399.

Tuckman, B., & Jensen, M. (1977). Stages of small-group development revisited. *Group and Organization Studies, 2*(4), 419–427.

Turner, C. S. V., Gonzalez, J. C., & Wong, K. (2011). Faculty women of color: The critical nexus of race and gender. *Journal of Diversity in Higher Education, 4*(4), 199–211.

Twenge, J., Campbell, W., & Gentile, B. (2012). Generational increases in agentic self-evaluations among American college students, 1966–2009. *Self and Identity, 11*(4), 409–427.

Twombly, S. (1990). Career maps and institution highways. In K. M. Moore & S. B. Twombly (Eds.), *Administrative careers and the marketplace* (pp. 5–18). New Directions for Higher Education.

Van de Ven, A., & Delbecq, A. (1971). Nominal versus interacting group process for committee decision-making effectiveness. *Academy of Management Journal, 14*(2), 203–212.

Van Der Vegt, G., & Bunderson, J. (2005). Learning and performance in multidisciplinary teams: The importance of collective team identification. *Academy of Management Journal, 48*(3), 532–547.

Van Dyne, L., Graham, J., & Dienesch, R. (1994). Organizational citizenship behavior: Construct redefinition, measurement, and validation. *The Academy of Management Journal, 37*(4), 765–802.

Van Scotter, J., & Motowidlo, S. (1996). Interpersonal facilitation and job dedication as separate facets of contextual performance. *Journal of Applied Psychology, 81*(5), 525–531.

Van Scotter, J., Motowidlo, S., & Cross, T. (2000). Effects of task performance and contextual performance on systemic rewards. *Journal of Applied Psychology, 85*(4), 526–535.

Vanderlinden, K. (2005). Learning to play the game: Professional development and mentoring. *Community College Journal of Research and Practice, 29*(9–10), 729–743.

Vischer, J. (2005). *Space meets status: Designing workplace performance.* Taylor and Francis/Routledge.

Vischer, J. (2007). The effects of the physical environment on job performance: Towards a theoretical model of workspace stress. *Stress and Health, 23*(3), 175–184.

Volkwein, J., & Parmley, K. (2000). Comparing administrative satisfaction in public and private universities. *Research in Higher Education, 41*(1), 95–116.

Wageman, R., & Baker, G. (1997). Incentives and cooperation: The joint effects of task and reward interdependence on group performance. *Journal of Organizational Behavior, 18*(2), 139–158.

Wagner, J. (1995). Studies of individualism-collectivism: Effects on cooperation in groups. *Academy of Management Journal, 38*, 152–171.

Ward, A., Duke, K., Gneezy, A., & Bos, M. (2017). Brain drain: The mere presence of one's own smartphone reduces available cognitive capacity. *Journal of the Association for Consumer Research, 2*(2), 140–154.

Warner, L. S. (1995). A study of American Indian females in higher education administration. *Initiatives, 56*(4), 11–17.

Wasson, C. (2004). Multitasking during virtual meetings. *Human Resource Planning, 27*(4), 47–60.

Watson, L. (2001). In their voices: A glimpse of African-American women administrators in higher education. *NASPA Journal, 4*(1), 7–16.

Watson, W., Kumar, K., & Michaelsen, L. (1993). Cultural diversity's impact on interaction process and performance: Comparing homogeneous and diverse task groups. *Academy of Management Journal, 38*, 590–602.

Wenger, E. (2000). Communities of practice and social learning systems. *Organization, 7*(2), 225–246.

Wenger, E., Trayner, B., & de Laat, M. (2011). *Promoting and assessing value creation in communities and networks: A conceptual framework* (Rapport 18). Ruud de Moor Centrum.

Wheelan, S. (2009). Group size, group development, and group productivity. *Small Group Research, 40*(2), 247–262.

Whiteoak, J. (2007). The relationship among group process perceptions, goal commitment and turnover intention in small committee groups. *Journal of Business and Psychology, 22*(1), 11–20.

Wolfe, B., & Dilworth, P. (2015). Transitioning normalcy: Organizational culture, African American administrators, and diversity leadership in higher education. *Review of Educational Research, 85*(4), 667–697.

Wolf-Wendel, L., & Ward, K. (2006). Academic life and motherhood: Variations by institutional type. *Higher Education, 52*(3), 487–521.

Woolley, A., Chabris, C., Pentland, A., Hashmi, N., & Malone, T. (2010). Evidence for a collective intelligence factor in the performance of human groups. *Science, 330*, 686–688.

Yamada, M. (1991). Joint big decision committees and university governance. *New Directions for Higher Education, 75*, 79–95.

Zaccaro, S., Rittman, A., & Marks, M. (2001). Team leadership. *The Leadership Quarterly, 12*(4), 451–483.

Zambrana, R. (2018). *Toxic ivory towers: The consequences of work stress on underrepresented minority faculty.* Rutgers University Press.

Zander, A. (1982). *Making groups effective.* Jossey-Bass.

ABOUT THE AUTHOR AND CONTRIBUTORS

Author

David Farris is the executive director for safety and emergency management at George Mason University. In addition to developing the university's emergency management program, he helped design and implement environmental protection, laboratory safety, occupational safety, and fire safety programs while working for the university's Department of Safety, Emergency, and Enterprise Risk Management. He has extensive experience collaborating with administrators and faculty on a variety of projects and has served on numerous committees to address topics that include but are not limited to minors on campus, space utilization and schedule, international student and faculty travel, threat assessment, emergency operations, and governance for state and national associations. He completed his PhD with a concentration in higher education administration from George Mason University's College of Humanities and Social Sciences in 2016 and is an affiliate faculty member with George Mason University's Higher Education Program. His research interests include organizational citizenship behaviors, university committees, and small group research. He also holds an MBA from George Mason University's School of Business and a bachelor of arts degree in biology from Texas A&M University. Visit https://universityadmin.com for more information about his research and work.

Contributors

Stephen (Steve) Bell is a professor of English at Liberty University. Before joining Liberty University in 2007, he was an Army officer for 4 years and taught literature at Azusa Pacific University for 5 years. Bell's research and teaching focuses on postcolonial and postmodern literature theory, film, and classic Western literature. He earned his bachelor's degree in English from Wheaton College, his master's degree in English from the University of Virginia, and his doctorate in literature and criticism from Indiana University of Pennsylvania.

Sarah Cheverton has more than 35 years of experience leading and managing education, training, and organizational change programs and initiatives in nonprofit, private, and public organizations. Cheverton has been an administrative and instructional faculty member at James Madison University for 20 years. After serving as an associate dean for several years, she moved to the Office of Vice Provost of University Programs and currently collaborates with others to strengthen institutional support for broader online and other distance learning initiatives. She teaches information systems courses for the Department of Computer Information Systems and Business Analytics in James Madison University's College of Business. She has a bachelor of arts degree in sociology-psychology and a master's degree in psychology with a concentration in organizational behavior.

Adam Crowe, at the time of our interview, was employed at Virginia Commonwealth University as the institution's director of emergency preparedness, emergency communications, and security, where he was responsible for business continuity, academic security, emergency management, and a portfolio of institutional risk management programs. In this position, Crowe interfaced with senior leadership and served on several institutional committees that were necessary to his role in coordinating the university's emergency management program and managing high-profile events. He is the author of three books related to social media and emergency management. He holds a master's degree in public administration from Jacksonville State University and a degree in biochemistry from Clemson University. He left Virginia Commonwealth University shortly after our interview to join a private company where he continues to work in emergency management and social media.

Kimberly Eby serves as associate provost for faculty affairs and development at George Mason University. In this role she is responsible for all matters pertaining to George Mason University's faculty's professional well-being and development, including assisting with faculty career development, recognizing faculty excellence, cultivating academic leadership, and implementing policies and practices that support faculty. Eby joined George Mason University in 1996 as an assistant professor. In 2002, she was awarded the George Mason University Teaching Excellence Award. She served for 9 years as the director of the Center for Teaching and Faculty Excellence and associate provost for faculty development. She earned her MA and PhD in community psychology from Michigan State University and her undergraduate degree from Indiana University at Bloomington.

Brent Ericson is the assistant dean of students and director of the Offices of Student Conduct and Academic Integrity for George Mason University. Ericson supervises student conduct functions and student case management and is a member of the institutional threat assessment team. He serves as a part-time adjunct instructor for a popular university transition course and is engaged in national conferences and symposia related to his field of expertise to include leadership roles in professional organizations and giving presentations. Prior to joining Mason, he worked for 9 years at Boston College in residential life and later served as the associate dean of students for community standards. He holds a bachelor's degree from Augustana College (Illinois), a master's degree from Indiana University, and a doctoral degree in higher education from Boston College.

Sharon Fries-Britt is a professor in the College of Education at the University of Maryland. She has served as the program coordinator for the higher education concentration and the director of the Higher Education, Student Affairs and International Education (HESI) program in the Department of Counseling, Higher Education and Special Education. She has published widely within peer-reviewed journals and served as a member of the editorial board for multiple journals. She has consulted extensively with colleges and universities, governmental agencies, and private industry on issues of race, equity, and diversity. She is the recipient of numerous awards, including the University of Maryland's Distinguished Scholar Teacher Award (2019–2020). Fries-Britt has a bachelor's degree in education from the University of Maryland, a master's degree in education from Ohio State University, and a doctorate in education from the University of Maryland.

Marleen McCabe is the Title IX coordinator for Northern Virginia Community College (NOVA). At the time of her interview for this book, she was serving as NOVA's associate director of employee relations. McCabe has also held the position of associate director of training and professional development. She has chaired or cochaired and been a member of several strategic planning committees, professional development committees, the College Senate, and NOVA's task force on Title IX and Violence Against Women Act (VAWA) compliance. She has worked closely with the Virginia Community College System's Chancellor's Office on several strategic initiatives that affect 23 community colleges in the Commonwealth of Virginia. Prior to coming to NOVA, she served as the director of human resources for the largest court in Virginia, where she facilitated professional development workshops on change management, team building, conflict resolution, and performance management. She holds a master of arts in English from Kent State and a doctorate in English from George Washington University.

Houston Miller is a professor of chemistry at George Washington University, a visiting professor in the Department of Chemical Engineering at Cambridge University, and a Bye Fellow of Robinson College, also in Cambridge, England. Miller's research uses laser diagnostics to explore combustion science, atmospheric chemistry, and biotechnology. In addition to his numerous publications, his research has yielded five patents and patent applications. He began his studies at Oberlin College and received his PhD in chemistry from the University of Virginia.

Kevin Rockmann is a professor in the School of Business at George Mason University. Rockmann's research investigates the development and the influence of various types of attachments in organizations, whether they be at the individual, team, professional, or organizational level. His research has appeared in *Academy of Management Journal, Academy of Management Review, Organizational Behavior and Human Decision Processes, Small Group Research,* and the *Research in Managing Groups and Teams* book series. He has designed and taught courses on leadership, organizational behavior, and negotiation at the MBA and executive education levels. He received his business administration bachelor's degree and doctorate from the University of Illinois at Urbana–Champaign.

Nick Swayne is the executive director of the 4-Virginia program and program coordinator at James Madison University in Virginia. As director, Swayne leads and coordinates six Virginia institutions of higher education in meeting the mission to promote collaborations that leverage the strengths of partner universities and improve the efficiency and economic impact of higher education across the commonwealth. Swayne founded the JMU X-Labs in 2015 as part of the 4-Virginia course sharing and redesign initiatives. The JMU X-Labs has gone on to achieve national acclaim as an innovative learning space. He is completing his third elected term on the Harrisonburg City school board and serves on the Governors Unmanned System's advisory board. Prior to joining James Madison University, he served 26 years in the military and retired with the rank of lieutenant colonel. He holds a bachelor of science degree in political science, holds a master of science degree in public administration, and is a doctoral candidate in postsecondary education at James Madison University's School of Strategic Leadership.

Leadership & Administration books from Stylus Publishing

The Department Chair as Transformative Diversity Leader
Building Inclusive Learning Environments in Higher Education
Edna Chun and Alvin Evans
Foreword by Walter H. Gmelch

Community Colleges as Incubators of Innovation
Unleashing Entrepreneurial Opportunities for Communities and Students
Edited by Rebecca A. Corbin and Ron Thomas
Foreword by Andy Stoll, Afterword by J. Noah Brown

Contingent Academic Labor
Evaluating Conditions to Improve Student Outcomes
Daniel B. Davis
Foreword by Adrianna Kezar

Search Committees
A Comprehensive Guide to Successful Faculty, Staff, and Administrative Searches
Christopher D. Lee
Foreword by Edna Chun

College in the Crosshairs
An Administrative Perspective on Prevention of Gun Violence
Edited by Brandi Hephner LaBanc and Brian O. Hemphill
Foreword by Kevin Kruger and Cindi Love

Building the Field of Higher Education Engagement
Foundational Ideas and Future Directions
Edited by Lorilee R. Sandmann and Diann O. Jones

Professional Development books from Stylus Publishing

Adjunct Faculty Voices
Cultivating Professional Development and Community at the Front Lines of Higher Education
Edited by Roy Fuller, Marie Kendall Brown and Kimberly Smith
Foreword by Adrianna Kezar

Authoring Your Life
Developing an INTERNAL VOICE to Navigate Life's Challenges
Marcia B. Baxter Magolda
Foreword by Sharon Daloz Parks
Illustrated by Matthew Henry Hall

The Coach's Guide for Women Professors
Who Want a Successful Career and a Well-Balanced Life
Rena Seltzer
Foreword by Frances Rosenbluth

Contingent Academic Labor
Evaluating Conditions to Improve Student Outcomes
Daniel B. Davis
Foreword by Adrianna Kezar

Shaping Your Career
A Guide for Early Career Faculty
Don Haviland, Anna M. Ortiz and Laura Henriques
Foreword by Ann E. Austin

What They Didn't Teach You in Graduate School
299 Helpful Hints for Success in Your Academic Career
Paul Gray and David E. Drew
Illustrated by Matthew Henry Hall
Foreword by Laurie Richlin and Steadman Upham

Faculty Development books from Stylus Publishing

Advancing the Culture of Teaching on Campus
How a Teaching Center Can Make a Difference
Edited by Constance Cook and Matthew Kaplan
Foreword by Lester P. Monts

Faculty Mentoring
*A Practical Manual for Mentors, Mentees, Administrators,
and Faculty Developers*
Susan L. Phillips and Susan T. Dennison
Foreword by Milton D. Cox

Faculty Retirement
Best Practices for Navigating the Transition
Edited by Claire Van Ummersen, Jean McLaughlin and
Lauren Duranleau
Foreword by Lotte Bailyn

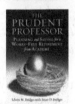

The Prudent Professor
*Planning and Saving for a Worry-Free Retirement from
Academe*
Edwin M. Bridges and Brian D. Bridges

Teaching Across Cultural Strengths
*A Guide to Balancing Integrated and Individuated Cultural
Frameworks in College Teaching*
Alicia Fedelina Chávez and Susan Diana Longerbeam
Foreword by Joseph L. White

Why Students Resist Learning
A Practical Model for Understanding and Helping Students
Edited by Anton O. Tolman and Janine Kremling
Foreword by John Tagg

Also available from Stylus

Shaping Your Career

A Guide for Early Career Faculty

Don Haviland, Anna M. Ortiz, and Laura Henriques

Foreword by Ann E. Austin

"Early faculty, please read and add some years onto your life. I wish I had this companion when I began academia. It would have saved me from multiple bouts of heartburn. This text goes over what they do not tell you as a graduate student or post-doc. It echoes great advice given to me by senior colleagues whom I respect and trust, especially in regards to tenure, promotion, grant writing and balancing work with family."—**Aaron Haines**, *Certified Wildlife Biologist, Assistant Professor of Conservation Biology, Millersville University*

"*Shaping Your Career* is full of essential tools and advice to help early career faculty members navigate many confusing processes, such as grant writing, promotion, and tenure. This book is one that can be read cover to cover or used as a quick reference guide that covers the full range of issues we confront as we begin our careers in the professoriate."—*Teachers College Record*

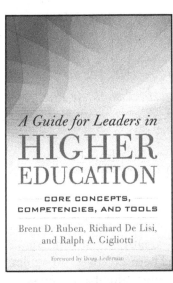

A Guide for Leaders in Higher Education

Core Concepts, Competencies, and Tools

Brent D. Ruben, Richard De Lisi, and Ralph A. Gigliotti

Foreword by Doug Lederman

"*A Guide for Leaders in Higher Education* succeeds in providing accessible and useful resources to individuals across different leadership roles. . . . As a midpoint between textbook and reference work, it is still successful at both and provides a clear and unbiased background to issues facing current leaders."—*Reflective Teaching*

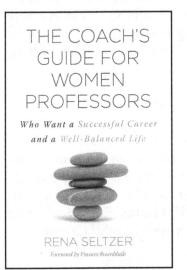

The Coach's Guide for Women Professors

Who Want a Successful Career and a Well-Balanced Life

Rena Seltzer

Foreword by Frances Rosenbluth

"I would not have gotten tenure without Rena Seltzer's skillful coaching. I am positive of that. If you can find a way to work with her as a coach, do it! But if you can't, read her book at least twice. It has all the life and career hacks every academic (male and female!) needs. Rena knows academia, in all its glories and pitfalls, and it is exhilarating to see one's world so accurately portrayed through on-point advice. I am a happier, healthier, higher impact, and more productive academic, thanks to Rena's coaching and book."—**Dolly Chugh,** *Associate Professor, New York University*

Write More, Publish More, Stress Less

Five Key Principles for a Creative and Sustainable Scholarly Practice

Dannelle D. Stevens

Foreword by Stephen D. Brookfield

"This book covers it all using a variety of innovative approaches that will appeal greatly to a wide range of readers. There are over 50 tables, charts, drawings, side-bars, and self-assessment exercises that will capture your attention. In addition, the appendices have logs and study-sheets you can fill out as you go along, helping you stay on schedule in your writing. You can dive in almost anywhere and come away with something useful to you at that very moment! Who knew that even after being an emeritus professor for 10 years I would both want and need to read this book."—**Richard Reis**, *Editor,* Tomorrow's Professor eNewsletter

"Reading Dannelle's book is like meeting with the kindest and most practical writing mentor you can imagine. Her tips and strategies are actionable and realistic, and her knowledge of the ins and outs of academic writing is unparalleled. Dannelle has been in the trenches and is generously sharing all she has learned to make our writing lives better. I highly recommend *Write More, Publish More, Stress Less* for academic writers at all levels."—**Kathryn E. Linder**, *Executive Director for Program Development, Kansas State University Global Campus*

22883 Quicksilver Drive

Sterling, VA 20166-2019   Subscribe to our e-mail alerts: www.Styluspub.com